Questionable Dismissal

Jerome Cranston

ISBN

978-1-312-79218-0

DISCLAIMER

This is a work of fiction. ALL names, characters, places and incidents are the product of the author's very active imagination or are used fictitiously and any resemblance to actual persons, living or dead, business establishments, events, or locales is entirely coincidental.

THANKS

None of my work is ever possible without the tremendous support and love shown to me by my partners in life. A deep sense of appreciation and gratitude is owed to my spouse, Janet, and my children, Kaela, Ty and Cody.

Thank you to my colleagues and friends: Kristin Kusanovich at Santa Clara University, Rod Clifton at the University of Manitoba, and Lucia Carruthers who edited various versions of this work and provided exceptionally insightful suggestions that improved it.

As always with my work, any errors and omissions are solely the responsibility of the author.

RE-DEDICATION

To my father and mother, sister and two brothers who let me tell stories and pretended to listen; at least some days.

Questionable Dismissal

FOREWARD

Deliberation is a dramatic rehearsal (in imagination) of various competing possible lines of action. . . [It] is an experiment in finding out what the various lines of possible action are really like. . .Thought runs ahead and foresees outcomes, and thereby avoids having to await the instruction of actual failure and disaster. An act overtly tried out is irrevocable, its consequences cannot be blotted out. An act tried out in imagination is not final or fatal. It is retrievable.

— John Dewey, Human Nature and Conduct

Rehearsal illuminates, opens up a situation so it is perceived in a new way. This should not be confused with the prevalent view of deliberation as a private soliloquy. For example, a woman or man pondering whether or not to commit to a lifetime relationship with another human being invariably imagines day-to-day life in and around a shared space called home. She or he should ought to consider this in relation to their careers, economic circumstances, long-term goals, and moral-social-political priorities. This is more than an armchair affair. It takes speaking thoughtfully and listening attentively. It is, after all, about decisions predicated on relationship.

An awful lot of the hard work of school leadership involves making really difficult choices. And, this is especially true when you examine the profound impact that those decisions have not only on students but also on the adults who commit to work in schools. Hiring, supervising and, even though is occurs less frequently, firing teachers is important and gut wrenching work; it really is. Yet, very little is ever presented in the current texts written about personnel management or human resource management in schools that elucidates the emotional toll of being a principled educational leader. In many instances, there is not much "personal" or "human" in them even though principals and superintendents are clearly in the "people" business. The subject of leading people is presented as if the decisions that impact the livelihoods and professional lives of teachers and support staff can be made in a clinical or objective fashion without regard for the personal costs associated with the outcomes. Almost exclusively texts on recruiting, professionally developing, retaining and terminating school staff offer technocratic approaches to school leadership that are devoid of the intricacies of the human dynamics of working in the highly socialized world of schools.

"Questionable Dismissal" is different. As is the case with the standard texts on personnel management in schools, it offers insight into the functional elements of leading schools – the policies, procedures and legal requirements of managing the people who work in schools- but it does so quite differently. The book presents how those rules when enacted impact people's careers and lives. "Questionable Dismissal," as a work of fiction, depicts what it is like to lead people in schools while negotiating the social reality of diversely minded adult educators, which is oftentimes complicated and requires us to consider how we would balance a myriad of objectives and negotiate multiple and competing causes and effects from multiple perspectives. "Questionable Dismissal" offers a picture of the world of school framed through the story of a legal deposition of a former superintendent of human resources who is forced to recount a myriad of personal realities that have to do with hiring, supervising and firing a cast of characters who range in career stage from the novice teacher eager to launch a career to that of a seasoned teacher nearing retirement, or a principal who has been there and done that and firmly believes in the school of hard knocks to the director of human resources who has never taught and is seen as not understanding the world of teaching, or a superintendent of schools who has been re-invented as the "CEO".

The universality of the characters and their stories as portrayed in "Questionable Dismissal" is written to allow readers to explore their own taken-for-granted beliefs about the "real world" of schools, and in doing so, provide them space and time to identify their tightly held and rarely challenged values. Readers are encouraged to explore the ethical frameworks that the characters operate from – such as utilitarianism, justice-oriented, rights-based, or common-good approaches to name but a few. They are challenged to try to understand and potentially empathize with viewpoints that may well be very different from their own but ones that are - all the same - "ethical".

In the context of formal schooling, given that children's educational opportunities hang in the balance, having those who lead or hope to lead schools make good ethical decisions requires a disciplined sensitivity to ethical issues and a practiced method for exploring the ethical aspects of the decisions that not only they make but also those that others make. This challenge is even truer as we encounter novel and perplexing ethical choices about how best to act in a given context.

Read, discuss and examine the novel in the context of John Dewey's[1] proposals about value of dramatic rehearsal:

- ❖ Deliberation is a dramatic rehearsal in imagination of various competing possible lines of action. Dewey uses the term drama in the sense of the unfolding of scenario, narrative, or plot.
- ❖ Our dominant interest - as we deliberate on ethical choices - are the appearances and interactions of personalities. It is the same interest which shows itself in the drama where the colourful display of incidents is, save in the melodramatic and sentimental, a display of the outworking of character. As each scenario unfolds in the novel remember that: Every object hit upon reinforces, inhibits, redirects habits already working or stirs up others which had not previously entered in.
  - ○ As you read and discuss, anticipate the responses of the characters, as well as other people who are reading the novel and, in particular, the responses of yourself to the question: How shall I act?
- ❖ Our ability both to anticipate and to evaluate the responses of others depends upon sensitiveness, emotional responses and vividness as intuitive capacities. Dewey discusses this by way of analogy to physical sensing: A keen eye and a quick ear are not in themselves guarantees of correct knowledge of physical objects.
  - ○ For Dewey, the insights arising from our sensitivity to persons and values register in our consciousness as emotions or as coloured by emotions. There must also be a delicate personal responsiveness - there must be an emotional reaction. Emotional reactions form the chief materials of our knowledge of oneself and of others.
- ❖ "Questionable Dismissal" attempts to help you learn how to draw on and improve the use of your non-quantitative, and intuitive decision making faculties. Deliberation is dramatic and active, not purely mathematical and impersonal; and hence it has the intuitive factor in it that can be sharpened.

"Questionable Dismissal" provides an opportunity for careful exploration of how personnel decisions impact others, and in the context of a graduate course or as a book study by a group of school administrators, individual understandings are aided by the insights and different perspectives of others who are committed to school leadership.

---

[1] *This is a broad interpretation of John Dewey's: How We Think (2nd ed.) (Boston: D. C. Heath and Company, 1933); Moral Principles in Education (Carbondale and Edwardsville: Southern Illinois University Press, 1975); Human Nature and Conduct (New York Modern Library, 1930).*

It allows readers to explore the basis of the ethical choices the characters make, consider alternative choices for them and what their effects might be, and hopefully help readers understand the basis of their own decisions if confronted by similar personnel challenges.

The combination of these activities with the book allows readers to begin to realize that the social reality of schooling consists of many people who are learning how to work together using a story-telling narrative. The book offers insight into the complexities of adult social life of schooling, and has been developed to be read individually but more importantly to be discussed and probed in groups with a focus on the events and the requisite functional policies of personnel management in schools and provides intellectual terrain for a subsequent analysis of how readers themselves might act if they were standing in the shoes of any one of the characters.

ONE

"Enough!" he yelled. And, he immediately caught himself, hoping that it was only him who thought he was yelling. He recalled what it looks and sounds like when composed people talk and tried to fake a rendition of that: "I can't do this right now."

Professor Bernard powered off his laptop, and dug out his cell phone that had fallen into the depths of his briefcase.

"Five minutes until class starts," he thought. Bernard hadn't planned for the impromptu student visit.

Professor Bernard kept on packing up his briefcase with the intent that his student might realize he was giving her the sign that they were done talking.

"I think I deserve an A," she continued with a smile, not the friendly kind of smile, but the winning kind. She had a surely-I-am-winning sort of smile.

"I don't want to seem rude, but I've got to teach a class in few minutes and as you know I detest starting class late," he said.

Wishing that it might seem to carry some additional weight, he added, "And, then right after class I've got to catch a flight, so I am really pressed for time."

"If you want to discuss your final grade sometime next week, send me an email and we can try to set up an appointment." Professor Bernard was a little anxious that he might forget to pack something he needed for his class or even more importantly, that he might leave behind a file he might need for the deposition that he had to attend the next day. He was also uncertain how his student might react to his uncharacteristic abruptness.

But, she looked at him as if she had just suddenly noticed he was standing in front of her in his office. It was as if she was seeing him for the first time.

Not sure what she should say next, she spat out, "I've never had a C in my whole life! I've never been given anything below a B in my entire academic career since first grade."

"I'm done having this conversation," Bernard responded.

"One of the other girls I know told me she got an A in this class last term. And, well, while I don't want to sound petty, she isn't as smart as me," she said. "I read her final paper and it wasn't that good. I think I deserve an A," she repeated assertively.

Professor Keith Bernard couldn't believe she was acting like she hadn't heard him. "Didn't you hear me?" he asked. "I'm not prepared to discuss this right now. If you feel that you've been graded unfairly, the whole appeal process is explained in the course syllabus," he said.

Then, as if to add emphasis, he added, "It's in the syllabus right below the explanation about making appointments to meet with me during office hours."

She ignored him and said, "I don't plan to beg and I can't believe you're doing this to me. It's completely unfair!" By now she was yelling.

Bernard didn't bother to reply. He gestured for her to step out of his office and as she did, awkwardly, he quickly turned off the lights and closed his office door. "Good afternoon," he said as he turned away and walked down the drab, windowless corridor toward the expansive foyer that led to the lecture halls.

As he walked, Bernard recalled how during an earlier routine conversation about the semester, curriculum, and current students, a colleague of his burst in with a frustrated comment about grade appeals and the "Entitlement Generation".

His tenured colleague was exasperated that more and more of his students were going to the university administration to complain not only about final course grades but also about insensitive professors who were out of touch with the complex challenges that contemporary students face.

"They have no sense of what is appropriate. They don't respect authority anymore. It's not like it used to be! And, their sense of entitlement is unbearable," his colleague surmised.

Bernard had responded to his esteemed associate that he thought that the increase in grade appeals might be more complex than a simple generational split. In some ways, Bernard explained, it might be indicative of a changing social order where almost every decision is appealable.

Bernard's reflective thoughts were just giving way to thoughts about his next lecture when they were suddenly interrupted.

"This will ruin my chances to get into graduate school! This is so unfair," she hurled at the back of Bernard's head. "I hope you know that this C is a career limiting move."

As Bernard kept walking in silence and entered the foyer, the last thing he thought he faintly heard from down the hall was, "My aunt is a lawyer, you know!"

6

TWO

Despite going to bed early at the hotel they had arranged for him to stay in, when the bright light of the sun hit his eyes from between the open curtains Dr. Keith Bernard woke up feeling tired. He hadn't really slept well for days. And as he rolled out from under the covers, he was reminded of the time when his brother was terribly ill and his mother kept waking him up during the night with her crying—a period of his life punctuated by sleepless nights and the constant anticipation of losing someone.

After a quick shower, Bernard skipped the free hotel breakfast because he just felt like he was going to be late, and took what turned out to be an incredibly short subway ride to the offices of Harper and Fowler, Barristers and Solicitors. He promptly checked in at the front desk and settled into a leather reception chair, realizing how early he really was. Considering the grave and combative business that likely took place behind their doors, the law office reception area was remarkably serene with tastefully chosen artwork on the walls and lush plants—ficus, variegated ivy and pothos—the kind his mother couldn't resist taking cuttings from whenever she was in an upscale office. "There was no harm in taking a small piece of the plant," she would whisper just before she ripped off an end, placed it into a wet, folded tissue and slid it carefully into her purse. It wasn't like she was stealing. "And anyway," she would add after they had left the office, "the doctor could certainly afford to buy a new plant if it died."

"They are ready for you now," the receptionist alerted Bernard after some time. "Just down the hall into the small meeting room on your right." He suddenly felt very hungry and regretted his decision to pass on the free food earlier.

The letter that had come by registered mail seemed fairly straightforward. Bernard had been asked to appear at the law office in his former city of residence to respond to some preliminary questions in a matter before a provincial labour relations arbitration board related to a claim of wrongful termination of a former employee of Arcadia School District Number 66. The letter stated:

> *Examination for discovery is a fact-finding procedure that is wide-ranging and in the nature of a cross-examination. The "Rules of Court" deal with the scope of examination for discovery, providing that: unless the court otherwise orders, a person being examined for discovery shall answer*

any question within his or her means of knowledge regarding any matter, not privileged, relating to the matter in question in the action.

And, the letter said it might take up to two days for the interview to be completed, but he "needn't worry," it said, because he would be reimbursed for any loss of salary.

Bernard had called the telephone number on the letter and was told by a polite woman at the other end that this was a somewhat informal affair at this stage. Yes, while a board-appointed stenographer would record his words, it would be a relaxed conversation rather than a formal deposition. She said the arbitration board wanted to determine if Bernard had any material information that should be considered in this case. And she added that if he did, they might call him back to testify at a later date. He had heard her say the words "subpoena if needed" but didn't ask for clarification at the time. The notion that some legal entanglement might obligate him beyond these two days suddenly disturbed him greatly. Now passing her desk, his, "thanks," sounded rather strong.

After entering the small conference room, it didn't take long for the process to take shape. "Good morning Dr. Bernard. I'm Wilson Lee, a Junior Associate here at Harper and Fowler. I will be conducting this discovery deposition. Thanks for coming in."

Bernard thought that Mr. Lee had an animated way of saying, "Junior."

"This," Lee added, indicating the middle-aged lady sitting at the other end of the small, rectangular table, "is the arbitration-board-appointed stenographer who will keep a record of this deposition. Obviously you received the letter and have some idea what this is all about. Don't you?" This was obviously meant as a rhetorical question because before Bernard could reply Lee quickly added, "Can I get you anything before we begin? Water? Tea? Maybe coffee?"

Bernard graciously accepted a cup of coffee. After calling down to the receptionist's desk, Lee asked, "Do you have any questions before we begin?"

Bernard gently shook his head from side-to-side. The stenographer indicated something about resituating the power cords to her laptop. As Lee and the stenographer ducked under the table and dragged chairs, Bernard had the amusing thought that this might be an elaborate ploy to have him fess up for his mother's horticultural crimes of years' past.

A young woman dropped off a pot of coffee, and Lee began. "If at any time I ask a question that you don't understand, will you please be sure to tell me so that I can rephrase it?"

Bernard nodded up and down and suddenly found himself gauging just how difficult the questions might prove to be, especially since he was already less apprised of the whole situation than everyone assumed him to be. He knew there was a lawsuit, and he knew it had to do with someone terminated during his tenure in Arcadia School District.

After Lee swore Bernard in under oath, he read from a script in front of him, "You are providing the arbitration panel with evidence that may or may not be used to assist the arbitrators in determining the circumstances under which the plaintiff was terminated from employment with Arcadia Consolidated School District Number 66. For the record can you please state your name, age and current address?"

Bernard tensed up as this seemed to be much more formal than he had expected and as it was unclear whether they presumed that he knew who the plaintiff in question was. As he answered the identification questions, Bernard felt a drop of sweat trickle down his side and was thankful that he had worn a blazer that concealed his shirt and his anxiety.

The confidential work product document later issued by Harper and Fowler stated the following:

> *Dr. Keith Bernard, age 50, resides at 94 Springbank West in York Landing. Bernard has been employed at National Capital University as a Senior Lecturer of public-sector administration since September 2010. Bernard has a Bachelor of Commerce degree, a Bachelor of Education degree, a Master's degree in Public Administration and a Doctorate in Labour Relations.*

Lee continued the examination. "Immediately prior to September 1, 2010, when you began working at National Capital University, can you please indicate where you had worked, what your position title was and how long you worked in that capacity?"

> *Prior to September 1, 2010, Bernard had been employed by Arcadia School District as Superintendent of Human Resources and Business Operations, for one and a half years. Before that he was the Director of Human Resources for another school district for approximately five years. Preceding that, he had been a school principal for about 10 years and also a teacher of business education for another five years.*

"As part of the deposition, we would like to have some background information about your tenure with Arcadia School District," Lee continued. "Can you please provide us with some information about your employment experience with the district, starting at the beginning? This next part is much less formal. Hopefully it's much more conversational and relaxed."

Bernard tried to arrange his thoughts in a way that might make sense to someone else. Lee had indeed presented him with a problem: How would he explain the depth of absurdity that he had endured without sounding both bitter and incoherent to a person who was really only interested in the facts?

Uncertain of what to say, Bernard fumbled, "Do you really want me to start at the beginning? How informal can I be, Mr. Lee?"

"Please," replied the unsuspecting Junior Associate, "start at the beginning and don't worry about the formality."

With that, Bernard began to tell his story.

It was not what I expected Frank Cottingly to leave behind. It wasn't really a transition file, or the kind of succession plan I had read about in management texts. There was neither an outline of what I should attend to in the short term nor any kind of strategic plan left by my predecessor showing his intended moves in the not-too-distant future. No crib notes for success. Instead, the red file folder contained random information that Frank, the previous Superintendent of Human Resources, the man I replaced, thought I needed to know.

The first page contained detailed information about the old Motorola cell phone I inherited as part of the job. Frank had carefully written the cell number on a piece of paper and stapled to it a copy of the soon-to-expire wireless contract. Below the cell number, he had written that, as the contract was about to expire, I should really consider an upgrade to a better hand-held device, and he even left me a few suggestions of what brands and models he thought might be best suited for such an important senior management position in a well-financed school district. His notes detailed the upfront costs associated with each model of cell phone and the associated hidden contract fees, plus his recommendations on how to proceed based on an analysis of the free incentives associated with the contracts. What a thoughtful fellow to do this, I thought to myself. He cared about me!

Bernard wondered if this level of detail might be inappropriate, and half expected to look at Lee and find a 'get to the point" expression or gesture. Instead, when he looked up, he saw a very composed young man who seemed to be listening intently.

"Is this okay?" Bernard asked, fairly certain he might be off topic. "Is this what you want?"

Lee smiled, poured another cup of coffee and encouraged Bernard to continue.

In the last few weeks before Frank retired—a retirement he postponed by six months so that I could finish my previous employment contract—he had found the time to leave behind a wealth of detailed, practical advice that he thought would help me be an on-the-job success and personally profit while doing so.

On the next two pages, he wrote the dates, times and locations of some upcoming work-related social commitments I needed to be aware of, noting which ones I should consider attending and others that he thought were less important. Frank even filled me in on which key players I might encounter at these events. And he went so far as to list if these events were "FREE" or if I needed to "EXPENSE ACCOUNT" them. The list included:

- ✓ BBQ with the teachers' union on April 15th - dinner FREE but bring money for the cash bar. (EXPENSE ACCOUNT)
- ✓ Dinner at the Continental Hotel for recently retired support staff, and be prepared to say a few words on behalf of the superintendent. Dinner and drinks are covered for you and your spouse, so you can take her out for dinner for free, but make sure to purchase a few (3–4) bottles of wine for the retirees' tables. (EXPENSE ACCOUNT)
- ✓ May 30th, Mayor's roundtable luncheon at city hall. Park at the Legion Hall next door, it's free. Arrive early, as they usually run out of food, and sit with the trustees but not near Bruce Sloan because he never stops talking. (FREE)
- ✓ Annual Conference for the Assembly of Superintendents and Directors of Education, usually early February, location usually somewhere in western part of province, always bad weather. (EXPENSE ACCOUNT)

He certainly seemed concerned about me; especially about me not spending my own money on any work-related events.

Finally in the file, typed at the very bottom of the second page of events and dates, was a table of four rows and two columns labeled "Staffing Hotspots." It was simply a list of names and beside each name was the name of a school.

Staffing Hotspots	
Easton McCoy	*Beaumont School*
Tony Daniel	*Festubert Elementary School*
Noelle Chabanel	*Salient Technology Academy*
Bathos Lukno	*Ridge High School*

In the margin area below the chart were two of Frank's handwritten comments in different coloured inks. The first read, "When you have time, feel free to call each of the specific principals to get more detailed information about any of the above individuals." The second, which was situated on an angle in the bottom right corner, like you might sign a crowded, office-generated greeting card, in tall and narrow cursive that resembled a seismograph reading, he had scrawled, "Good luck with everything Keith!"

I kept going back to that word "any." I was instructed to get detailed information about "any" of the individuals listed. Did he mean I could pick and choose? Did he mean one person would be so difficult that it might take me a lot of time before I could pick another? Did it mean he wasn't comfortable demanding my follow-through? Had he found a way to let me off some hook that I was ill-prepared to be hung on anyway?

To be honest, I had reservations about taking that job for months before my official start date, and long before moving my family almost halfway across the country for it. I couldn't put my finger on it, but something just didn't feel right. In hindsight, the whole hiring process was odd, but I convinced myself that it was professional enough; after all, their search had yielded me as the best candidate.

It had started one spring morning with an unexpected phone call from Chuck Stihl, Chief Superintendent of Schools for Arcadia School District. His voicemail message said he wanted to speak with me right away about an important personnel matter.

Given that it was the hiring season for schools, I just figured he was doing a reference or background check on someone I knew, so I didn't rush to return his call. When I did finally call him back that afternoon, I was surprised to find myself invited to attend an interview the next day for a job that I knew nothing about. After an early morning flight followed by a quick in-and-out interview process, I was offered the job, mulled it over, spoke to my family who were all pretty excited about the city we would be in and accepted it all within a matter of about twelve hours. Suddenly, I was in the midst of planning a move and starting a new phase of my professional career. Though there should have been something suspect about the rushed quality of it - it did seem desperately sudden - so many of the most popular management books had put change and adaptability up as concepts for success. I dutifully repeated their mantra to myself: Change is good.

Bernard noticed that Lee looked a little more relaxed now and had removed his sports coat. Lee seemed to be listening with animated interest. But, Bernard couldn't help wonder whether it was his story or the third cup of coffee that was really stimulating the young man.

Lee signaled the stenographer to stop recording with a funny flicking movement of his fingers. "I've heard about that kind of thing happening, but have never met someone who was just given a job without reference to any competition," he said. It seemed clear that Lee would probably like that to happen to himself. "Wow, please continue."

Bernard wondered if he could also signal the stenographer to discontinue note-taking at some point, but withheld testing out the gesture and continued.

My unease grew as my wife and I packed, moved our family 2000 miles to a new home, unpacked and got our children settled into mid-year placements in their respective schools. My state of mind bordered on dread, particularly because of the sudden lack of communication from the Chief Superintendent who had been so eager to hire me back in May.

Knowing that my start date was early January, I had emailed Chuck Stihl twice to ask if there was anything I should be aware of or could read to help provide me with some context or background for this new job. In my emails I expressed my preference for a proactive approach, without demanding a commitment on his part to expend a great deal of time and energy to prepare me for this position for which I had been hand-picked. I was pushing for a productive transition with no surprises.

Chuck's belated response to my second email lacked any content related to the position. Its casual tone, meant to convey warmth, had the reverse effect. In it he reassured me that all was fine with the school district and that I needn't worry about knowing anything about the position or the school district before I got there. I could, he suggested, just pick up from where the extremely competent and capable Frank Cottingly had left off. All was good, he wrote. There were no major issues for me to worry about, and he closed his email by stating that I should just enjoy the fall colours and my much-deserved Christmas break. And, he added, that while he would not be in the office on the fifth when I arrived, as he would still be on his holidays, he had arranged that someone would be available to orient me so I could get started "right away."

When I arrived on my first morning, I was met by the warm smile of the building's custodian, Maggie Antioch, who seemed a little surprised to see me standing in the district office doorway holding a stack of weighty boxes.

"Hi," I began, placing the boxes on my left leg in case a handshake was in order. "I'm Keith Bernard, the new Superintendent of Human Resources. I guess I'm the new Frank around here." I immediately regretted this lame attempt at humour and my slight overemphasis on the word Frank, which probably seemed entirely too casual considering I didn't know Frank personally.

Attempting to recover, I added in a more straightforward tone, "Glad to meet you. And who are you?"

"Hi, I'm Maggie," she replied smartly, lifting the top box off my stack. Though the tools of her trade, the spray bottles, rags and vacuum she toted, or even just the uniform, could have betrayed her profession, without these indications, Bernard considered that he could have easily mistaken her for the manager of the building. He made a mental note of her cordial and professional demeanour, and wondered if she was really in the best position she could be in at this new institution, which he knew little about. "Nobody told me you were starting work today," she said with a wide, diplomatic smile. "Other than me, there's nobody here. They're all still on holidays and won't be back until after the weekend. I guess they forgot to tell you that, huh?" I noticed that her tone implied that this was not surprising to her and she had strong feelings about people not following through with responsibilities.

14

Maggie set to work helping me get the boxes into my new office using her master key and immediately took out the trash and recycling bins that were half-full while we continued our conversation.

"Mr. Stihl had told me someone would be here to orient me and show me where to find things. Maybe I misunderstood him?" I knew there had been no misunderstanding, at least on my part, but just couldn't say that to Maggie on day one. "I had hoped to meet some of the staff and fill out the payroll and insurance forms. Is there no one here from payroll?" I knew my question was futile; there were no lights on and no signs of life through any of the windows.

"Uhmm, no. It's just me," she smiled. "I guess I am the welcome wagon then. Well, welcome Keith. Just let me know if there is anything you need!" I caught myself thinking that, so far, Maggie's interpersonal skills and professionalism might easily outshine those of the people whose offices she cleaned.

I thanked Maggie and closed my office door. For the first time, I noticed the red folder on the impressive cherry-wood desk. After taking a seat, I read the folder's contents. Stunned, a bit, by the brief, scattershot approach to this senior management transition so far, and knowing that all of the schools were still closed for holidays until tomorrow, I decided it would be best to simply phone and leave messages on the district's school principals' answering machines to introduce myself. When I came to the four principals on my predecessor's list of "Staffing Hotspots," I added a sentence or two about them getting back to me right away to discuss a personnel issue. After these calls were done, I removed my books and placed them one by one on the empty bookshelves. A few of my literary favourites tended to travel with me to any position, including my volume of Dante, with the abstract painting of the chaos of the inferno on the cover. That illustration suddenly seemed foreboding, so I tucked it between Human Resources as Possibility, Promise and Peril and Rabelais' "Gargantua and Pantagruel". Hearing Maggie working out in the hall, I regretted again my rather flippant "I'm the new Frank," especially as I would come to understand my predecessor, Frank Cottingly, as a person with whom I had little in common.

Arcadia Consolidated School District No. 66 was made up of 25 schools, most of which were located in the urban centre of Orchard Hills. A small number of its schools were scattered throughout the surrounding communities. Before I moved there, I knew the area was famous for its orchards, vineyards, skiing, golf and everything in between. I thought this would be a great place for my family to live and for me to pursue my career.

Frank Cottingly had been the sole Superintendent of Human Resources working under a Chief Superintendent since the creation of the district but had ten years before been the Chief Superintendent of one of the small school districts that was forced into consolidation. After the merger, Frank was offered what was clearly a demotion, and maybe suggesting it was "an offer" was not quite how he saw it. It is more likely that Frank was given an ultimatum, according to the accounts of some of his colleagues, to take a lower position in a now bigger district that now reported to the Chief Superintendent.

It was mentioned that he might have been presented with another option, some sort of a buy-out of sixty or seventy thousand dollars in his bank account that would have allowed him to leave without looking back.

Perhaps he was not quite ready to be unemployed at the age of 55, but also not quite ready to dismiss that image of having come across some sudden cash. So Frank accepted the position and set to work to make his time with Arcadia feel as rich as possible, even if in rather miniscule ways.

During his tenure, Frank had artfully crafted an image of a generous, humble, formerly powerful leader who was lending his wisdom gracefully to his small, manageable department. He spoke about the pressure of tight budgets and how most leaders allow too much wastefulness in their organizations. In the midst of this benevolence, Frank had a knack for finding deals for himself that were hard to find real fault with. He'd order flower bouquets for the district's office staff on Secretary's Day from a shop called "Bloomin' Things" that had a "buy five arrangements and get your sixth one free" special, even though other shops had passable arrangements at much lower prices if he divided his order into five. He worked it out so his wife would have a beautiful arrangement each February in her favourite vase—opaque milk glass—and she was always ready to brag to her friends the day after Valentine's Day, and even the day before, in anticipation of his consistent thoughtfulness.

Frank also found ways to get the little two- or three-percent kick-backs from big-box stores where he bought super-sized lots of office supplies. Never mind that his staff had to find space to store 1,000 plastic spoons and cases of binder clips or soft drinks that regularly appeared. He used these outings to catch up on some personal shopping too.

Frank used to say that he hated wasting gas, so it only made sense to shop for his home needs at the same time and, really, it didn't take much longer. He would wave his long, personal receipt in one hand while handing the business receipt to the accounts payable clerk, all the while shaking his head at how much he had spent of his own money, on his own things. In this way, he projected an image of importance—someone with a real budget—and took on the hip cache of seeming to be environmentally responsible in his monthly, integrated shopping sprees.

Provided it was minimally above-board, and if there were other immediate perks that came along with making the deal, Frank's tactics for finding a few free breakfasts a week for morning meetings or ending up with an extra set of tires for his family car long after his job ended were not questioned by anyone. He made it clear he was all about bottom-line minimization of costs and that he was not above the mundane task of stockpiling the supplies for central office. Apparently, you could easily find yourself treated to a free latte during a meeting with Frank, purchased using the leftover balances remaining on former employees' coffee gift cards that he seemed to be somehow in possession of. Everyone seemed content to have Frank talk about fiscal responsibility, eat and drink well during meetings, and do the unglamorous grunt work of buying large amounts of ketchup.

Lee seemed surprised by Bernard's candour. "Are you suggesting that there might have been some impropriety in Mr. Cottingly's dealings?"

"Well, no, not exactly," and with that Bernard realized that his comments might have sounded overly condemning and that he had strayed quite a distance from just giving the facts.

He apologized, "Are you sure this is okay?"

Lee shrugged his shoulders and nodded for Bernard to continue and added, "Keep it flowing."

Bernard reminded himself that he was being deposed and that he had no idea which former employee of Arcadia School District was suing the district for wrongful termination.

Arcadia School District had about 10,000 students and around 900 employees. One of the things I learned early on was that no one knew exactly how many employees the district had. It seemed to be taken for granted that this precise number was, somehow, incalculable.

The Human Resources Department, which was really just my executive assistant and I, had on record that 895 people were employed based on the active personnel files. But, my executive assistant also said that we really weren't sure how many people were employed at any moment since the records weren't up-to-date. She reassured me that while we might not have accurate files, it wasn't an important concern because everyone who was hired had to be fulfilling a legitimately publicized position. I was dismayed when my assistant tapped the side of her temple and said, "It's basically all up here," but would later be so very thankful for that claim of hers. However, the Payroll Department, which was one person who entered the employee payroll and benefits data, seemed to think there were about 917 employees drawing salaries. He admitted that he wasn't quite sure about that number either, but that I need not worry. Everyone who worked there did such a fine job, he felt, and then he added with a nod to educational salaries in general and a touch of pride in his work, "I can personally guarantee that no one is OVER-paid here in Arcadia!

I sat down one mid-January day and asked the two amiable co-workers who I had known for about two weeks why we seemed to have about two dozen more people on the payroll than we had on record as employees. Both shuffled through their sheets and then made various sounds and gestures meant to assure me that both 895 and 917 were correct numbers indeed. Not knowing who to offend by suggesting that perhaps one or both might wrong, I asked them to sit down together and figure out how many people we really did employ and pay. It shouldn't be that hard, I thought, since both were using the same data and software. From then on, in discussions that had to do with numbers of employees this initial murkiness between what is truly unknowable and what remains unknown because of a lack of thorough investigation never ceased to be a bit awkward.

They never did get back to me with the actual number, now that I think about it. But solving the problems that plagued this division would not be as simple as reconciling two figures.

Around the same time, I discovered there were another few dozen or so, again no one could provide an accurate number, of non-unionized personnel supposedly on the payroll that were scattered throughout the district. This fact might have helped account for the discrepancy between payroll and employees but still did not make things add up.

There were reading clinicians, a district psychologist, site coordinators, assessment specialists, a couple of dozen educational program liaisons assigned to work with at-risk youth, and there was a cook.

Yes, even though all schools normally contracted cafeteria staff at their local site, there was a school cook on the central payroll, but at least I understood what that job entailed. Some others held positions whose functions remained elusive to me for months. And every time I asked why the number of positions seemed to have increased by 100 over the past ten years, or we had positions like the "Master Painter" or "Associate Athletic Liaison" at one of our high schools, someone always stepped forward to say that all of these people were important contributors to the black box of student learning.

I wondered if some of this was a real-life example of Parkinson's Law. Penned by Cyril Northcote Parkinson in a humourous essay published in "The Economist" in 1955, Parkinson's Law states that work expands so as to fill the available time for its completion.

Parkinson noted that in bureaucracies, the total number of those employed seems to be governed by this central axiom, which explains mathematically how a school district's central office could expand over time and increase in size due to two principle reasons. First, an official, such as a school superintendent, tends to want to multiply the number of his or her subordinates. Secondly, a superintendent can raise his or her profile and perceived value by supervising many employees who in turn have to supervise other employees. All of this, of course, accounts for needless growth in the end, and costs taxpayers dearly.

It did seem that the senior administrators of Arcadia had a lot of personnel to supervise. Among other things, I was surprised to find out that the cook was under the watchful eye of the district's Assistant Superintendent of Student Potential, the administrator responsible for insuring that all student programming outcomes were met at all schools. When I asked why this arrangement was so, I was given a long speech on the connection between hunger and learning capacity, then told, "I actually brought this cook in from my former school gig and she's fabulous. Everyone knows that students can't learn and reach their potential if they are hungry, silly."

By most current standards, Arcadia was a moderately-sized school district. It should have been functioning as a well-managed organization given its annual operating budget of $80 million and 895-917 or so employees. Instead it operated more like a small-town grocery store, a co-operative that most everyone had grown fond of running, well, cooperatively. Actually, the co-ops that I knew of in my former hometown were more organized. Here in Arcadia, with friends of friends being brought in randomly to create an expanding baroque mesh of decentralized personnel hiring decisions, I could think of no model to compare it to, until I recalled the surreal, disturbing image of the giant monolith of entangled plastic garbage that was discovered floating in the depths of the ocean, staying together somehow and trampling fragile ecosystems as it passed by...

"It sounds like you didn't get off to a good start in your new job" Lee offered. "Is that a fair assessment, Dr. Bernard?"

"No, it didn't start off well," Bernard replied, composing himself a bit, "but I did try to remain optimistic that things would improve once I understood the central office culture." And then, because he was in the habit of advising young adults about vocational decisions, and a little tired of being in the spotlight himself, he asked, "Mr. Lee do you think you will enjoy being a lawyer? Have you enjoyed the work so far?"

Lee didn't need much time to think and said, "I'm sure I will like being a lawyer. Being a Junior Associate is not like the real thing; it's not like being a real lawyer. At least that's what everyone tells me. I know that I have to survive this phase and learn what I can. I'm sure all of the hard work will make me a better lawyer, one day. Partner material, I hope!"

Bernard didn't say what he was thinking, which was that for many employees, the happiest two days of a job are the day you get it and the day you leave it. People get jobs that they are not well suited for all the time. In fact this phenomenon is the very basis of the Peter Principle, which states that in a hierarchy every employee tends to rise to his or her own level of incompetence.

Formulated by Dr. Laurence J. Peter and Raymond Hill in their 1969 book "The Peter Principle," it explains how in hierarchical organizations, members are promoted so long as they can demonstrate competence—sometimes just minimally so—in their current positions. Sooner or later, they are promoted to a position in which they are no longer competent, and there they remain, unable to earn any further promotions. However, Bernard knew that not every case of advancement was an example of the "Peter Principle." And anyway, the pain of being stuck in a bad job isn't just about a poor job-fit on the part of an employee. An excellent person-job fit could be definitely soured by the problems in management.

There's no shortage of advice explaining how to take a bad job situation and transform it into a positive and profitable one, and usually some folk-wisdom about making lemons into lemonade can be found in these prescriptions for cultivating "stick-to-it-iveness." Certainly it is true that having the patience and fortitude to do such work can be admirable, but the attempt to make lemonade out of sub-par lemons doesn't guarantee that the concoction you end up will be particularly palatable.

"Ok, what do you think, Dr. Bernard, about the idea of working through the tough times and dealing with the job adversity?" Lee asked.

"Trying to work through it is one approach, but there is another," Bernard said. "Should you ever find yourself with a difficult boss or toxic workplace, do whatever you need to do to free yourself from the trap as expediently as possible."

Lee was surprised by Bernard's candour.

"In truth, only rarely will you see a coyote that chews off its own leg to escape from a steel-jaw trap," Bernard continued. "Similarly, it could be argued that these leg-hold jobs paralyze people, leaving them to suffer a slow agony, all the while giving employees plenty of time to ponder their plight as they blissfully try to fix a dysfunctional organizational culture"

Bernard took a deep breath, "Each day you show up to work and you wonder, 'why was I so stupid to put my foot into that trap? What was I thinking? But, here I am, so I might as well be content, endure the excruciating pain, and make the most of it.' I guess you could choose to stay trapped and wait to see what happens with the attitude that things will get better. Or alternatively, you could gnaw off your leg and get out of the trap of an unreservedly miserable job and hobble off like a three-legged animal, maimed, but still alive licking your wounds."

Lee, the junior lawyer, sat in stunned silence.

"There is nothing noble and worthy about staying in a bad job. So-called experts and friends alike are lying when they tell you that you can muddle through the putrid muck of misery called work even if it seems unbearable at the time and you will become stronger from it. That's rubbish, utter rubbish and akin to the sentimental notion that what doesn't kill you will make you stronger. No, what doesn't immediately destroy you can still kill you eventually."

Lee jumped in, "Is that a reference to the Kanye West song 'Stronger'?"

Bernard smiled and admitted he didn't know much about anyone named Kanye, adding that his comment was a reference to existentialist Friedrich Nietzsche who had proposed this as a maxim about work. "When it comes to abusive behaviour, that which does not kill you immediately will not necessarily make you stronger but may actually slowly eat away at your emotional, mental and physical health and steal away your vitality,"

Bernard explained. "While it is true that you are, at the very least, when gainfully but painfully employed, earning a pay check, it is equally true that non-toxic work environments do exist and should be sought out. After you've met your family's basic needs, beware if on some level you are selling off part of your spirit simply to buy your children iPods."

Unsure of whether to subject Lee to any more off-topic insights, Bernard's mind jumped to the next equally nauseating workplace lie.

It's often stated that you should make every effort to build a great working relationship with your boss even if he is a jerk, and if you are unable to do this, you are supposed to exit gracefully without burning any bridges. This is not about simply respecting your boss or manager; this is about the importance of recognizing that the person is indeed a jerk in how he conducts public business and handles himself and understanding that a jerk can't help himself or I suppose herself from being a jerk anymore than a tree can help being a tree. So, you can accept him or her, as is, a full-blown jerk, doing what comes naturally to a jerk, and live with it. Or, if you can't stand to work with an ass, you can update your résumé and look for meaningful work elsewhere.

The fact is, Bernard's experience had shown him that working for a jerk doesn't always have a bright side. It will not help you vet future employment opportunities more carefully. People won't be more likely to reward you with job opportunities or promotions because of your dogged perseverance under a bully tyrant. That's a load of malarkey. Consider the cyclical history of dysfunctional personal relationships that many people are drawn into. They are attracted, almost magnetically, to misery, playing a pivotal role by staying in a difficult situation, knowing it's bad, but hoping for change and accepting the toxic person's behaviour without consequences. This teaches toxic people that they can get away with it—and they do. So, whether there's a toxic boss or a cancerous corporate culture or an orgy of dysfunction with colleagues, you need to decide to either get with their program and become one of them or get out.

And if you do choose to get out, then what? Conventional wisdom states: that you should take the high road and resign gracefully. What you say about your ordeal could always come back to haunt you, right? Not necessarily. Saying something that clarifies your personal and professional standards and explains the necessity of your leave-taking can send the clear message that you won't be treated as a punching bag. Your former boss or co-worker might become cognizant of the high cost of their behaviour, and could seek to improve their interactions with other people in the future. Isn't that what we tell kids about schoolyard bullies? Tell the bully to stop bullying you and then tell her that if she doesn't stop, you will tell someone in authority about what has happened, and don't hang around where bullying is happening. It is possible to say what you need to say respectfully and without theatrics. If management doesn't offer an exit interview, it's probably best to quit and hold your words until you can tell a sympathetic friend about your ordeal or, even better, write a best-selling book detailing your horrible experiences. But, if you can swing it, nothing beats the bittersweet taste of a lingering exit interview that lets them know what you really think.

Bernard didn't say any of this either. Instead he looked at Lee sympathetically and just added, "I guess it helps if you really love the work you're doing."

Lee smiled at Bernard, leaned back into his chair and asked Bernard, "Could you give us a sense of how you would describe the typical approach to human resources management in most school systems?"

Bernard paused only a second before jumping in: "Human resource management is often presented as a strategic approach to the management of an organization's most valued assets—the people working there. Dr. Michael Fullan has suggested that system-wide school improvement can only occur if you have the right people working in the rights jobs at the right times. And I will add the following caveat; the public expectation is that system-wide school improvement ought to be achievable with a minimal public investment."

The recipe for success is quite simple, Mr Lee.

First, assemble a talented and dedicated staff made up of teachers, teaching assistants, principals, and vice-principals. Then add a little administrative support, in other words, the ones who really run the schools, and the necessary number of loveable custodians. Lure some unsuspecting, underprepared and underpaid people to act as educational assistants, but do not tell them what 'duties as assigned' might really mean since you never know what it means yourself. Don't train your teachers to manage the educational assistants even though you expect that they will. As needed, hire some district clinicians or consultants or directors of curriculum, technology or transportation. Then layer that with some highly paid superintendent types who will certainly require a small staff of assistants too.

Insure that all of these people all possess the essential, varying levels of knowledge, skills and personal attributes that are required by regularly assessing them against somewhat vague and almost always contested performance standards. Inspire them to perform at their best with a shared focus on education so that the students can achieve the prescribed learning outcomes as set by sometimes far away ministries of education. And, do it without exceeding the public's tolerance for taxing and spending.

Lee seemed a bit stunned by the formula. He looked surprisingly like one whose ideals are in the process of being shattered.

"Of course, I mean that tongue-in-cheek, Mr. Lee. Personnel management is never really that simple, obviously," Bernard said before making a mental note that Lee still looked rather dejected.

Without waiting, Bernard went on. "When I glanced back down at the page in front of me on my very first day and mouthed the four names on the piece of paper that had been inside the red file folder: 'Easton McCoy,' 'Tony Daniel,' 'Noelle Chabanel,' and 'Bathos Lukno,' I thought, how bad can it be? With about 900 employees to be managed, and only four personnel problems, I reckoned I could handle the job. Little did I know then that there would indeed be a reckoning."

With that, Lee looked up at the clock on the wall and clearly stared at it, rather deep in thought. Bernard wondered if he had looked like that in his lecture yesterday. Lee glanced over at the stenographer and suggested, "Should we take a break now? Maybe just ten or fifteen minutes though to stretch our legs? Do you want to get some fresh air or something to eat, Dr. Bernard?"

Then almost as if he needed another excuse for the break, or maybe because Bernard seemed to not be moving very much, he added, "How about we give the stenographer a rest? Are you okay with that?"

Although it seemed like the deposition had just started, Bernard nodded, stood up and walked out the door.

THREE

When Bernard returned to the lobby from the washroom he smelled lemons, and thought maybe the receptionist's lunch or perfume could be responsible. Then he realized it was the fancy hand soap he had chosen to wash his face with, for some reason, while on break that now seemed to be clinging to his cheekbones. The receptionist told him to head back down to the meeting room. Everyone was waiting for him, she said. As Bernard entered the room, he saw that a second young man in a suit had joined Lee and the stenographer, and the first thing that came to mind when Bernard took a good look at the husky figure next to Lee was "bouncer." Unlike the self-possessed Lee, who seemed to be managing a complex deposition with a certain ease, the new gentleman appeared to have just thrown on his suit and seemed to be unable to move in it very well. It seemed to Bernard that he might have been a former athlete who had gone into law after a career-ending injury perhaps.

"I hope you don't mind, but I asked Peter Hart, to join us," explained Lee. He is also a Junior Associate and is interested in human resources management and labour law. We graduated from Law School together, and I thought he could sit in and learn something. Are you okay with that?"

Before Bernard could respond, Hart was inclining the whole right side of his body forward, possibly a function of the tight sleeves of his jacket, and reaching his hand across the table to offer a firm handshake in the same eager way a job interviewee first greets a potential new employer. Bernard looked over at Lee and nodded that Hart's presence was fine with him.

Looking down at his notes, Lee said, "As part of this discovery deposition, we would like to get some information about your professional experience with employee terminations, specifically while at Arcadia School District. Can you please tell us that?"

Bernard wondered, briefly, why they wanted to jump right into terminations. He suspected it had something to do with his reputation as a hired gun who could fire almost anyone who, by general agreement of all stakeholders, deserved it, with no visible display of emotion. He wasn't too unlike a bouncer himself, he mused, before launching in.

"Contrary to popular belief, it's not impossible to get rid of a public school teacher," Bernard began. "But it can be difficult, onerous and come at a great cost. School trustees often complain that for employee discipline and discharge, arbitrators and courts hold management to a standard that approaches perfection—and it's almost true. There is good news, though, a shimmer of hope in a sea of despair. The fact is that ridding a school of a truly problematic teacher is achievable, if true responsibility is taken. Through common sense, attention to detail and rigourous adherence to the law, it is possible to terminate a teacher's contract of employment for dereliction of duty."

Bernard recalled that he had a great PowerPoint presentation on this whole subject that never failed to rile up his graduate students. He had no such props to lean on here. Bernard looked over to see if Lee and Hart were listening and after catching a big grin from Hart, he thought "wrestler, maybe?" then continued.

"There is no doubt that the stakes are high in dismissing a teacher for gross incompetence or dereliction of duty. Unionized teachers who commit serious offenses, such as theft, assault or sabotage, have been able to keep their jobs and in some cases, avoid discipline altogether when employers have failed to follow procedural rules contained in collective agreements or codified in law, or if they failed to meet the demands of natural justice."

"But, I learned quite some time ago that I possessed two traits that helped me manage the difficult task of teacher termination effectively, and staff issues in general, which were a commitment to act with integrity, and a dogged-perseverance to not give up. By integrity, I simply mean a commitment to try and act truthfully and in a forthright manner regardless of the consequences. Sometime this meant I had to be less aggressive in my dealings with errant employees than I might be naturally inclined to do. Oftentimes, it meant taking on extra work to make sure that the rules were followed and people's employment rights weren't violated. By perseverance I mean being patient and remaining focused on both the means and the ends. These two qualities helped me deal with a number of employee terminations, involving both teachers and support staff, before I began work in Arcadia School District."

Bernard looked directly at Hart. "You're probably aware that it has been more than 30 years since the California appellate court dismissed the first lawsuit commenced by a student against a teacher for negligent breach of a duty to educate. The U.S. court held that a court was not the place to assess claims of educational malfeasance. And since then, American courts have repeatedly dismissed actions for educational malpractice, citing their reluctance to interfere with the implementation of educational programs and policies, and other considerations.

As I am sure you both know that by applying the American jurisprudence, Canadian courts have been equally vigilant in denying recovery for educational malpractice. No Canadian court has allowed an action for damages against a school board or its teachers for failure to provide an appropriate education. In other words, when there is a firing to be done, we in the schools have to do it ourselves."

Lee and Hart nodded because this was supposed to be common knowledge among lawyers, something learned and memorized in law school, of course, but then looked at each other to see if the other really had ever heard of this, but could not connect on this point in time, because Bernard was on a roll.

"All of this suggests that it is almost impossible to fire a teacher for incompetence or educational malpractice because those terminations are based in negligence law, which requires proof around the thorny question of causation. The plaintiff must demonstrate that the defendant's conduct was the proximate cause of the plaintiff's injury. So employers are faced with the seemingly insurmountable task of proving a causal link between the teacher's conduct and the student's injury, that is, the failure of the student to learn. The causation issue underscores a critical distinction between teaching and other professions. In medicine and law, for example, the professionals—not the client—are primarily responsible for the outcome of services rendered. However, it is inherent in the very nature of education that students are active participants in the process, sharing significant responsibility for the outcomes. As you both know, education is a cooperative art while law is an operative art."

"In Canada, teacher incompetence prompts so few terminations because the dismissal process is onerous. The fear of reprisal from teachers' unions is also so great that most administrators find it is not worth the effort. Instead, they approve transfers or hide struggling teachers where their deficiencies can go unnoticed—by creating jobs as consultants or directors in district offices. "Percussive sublimation," a process described by Laurence J. Peter, is a real phenomenon that involves giving problematic teachers or principals pseudo-promotions rather than dealing with them through termination procedures. The sad result is that it either keeps marginal teachers in the classroom, or from time-to-time promotes truly incompetent employees who have not succeeded in the classroom to management positions," Bernard said.

"However, you can always accelerate the termination process, or circumvent it, if you have the stomach for creating a very hard-to-refuse offer to someone you want to get rid of," Bernard explained. "It's regarded as one of the dark arts of personnel management: the ability to negotiate a buy-out of a teacher's contract by offering him enough money to not come to work and move on with his life, elsewhere. Apparently I was one of the few people who could put together these offers and still go home and sleep like a baby each night. It's an expensive and yet effective way to get rid of incompetent teachers. While it's relatively common in the for-profit companies to see generous, voluntary severance packages, most people in education become queasy at the very thought of it. Their sense of morality and stewardship over scant financial resources prohibits them from even considering that it might be worth it to pay someone to not teach."

"I'm not one of those individuals who are above buying off someone to go away. I have no problem offering someone enough money to leave quietly, forgoing the messiness of a protracted "Termination Without Cause" process. I'm not talking about letting pedophiles or criminals off the hook, because in those cases there is usually enough evidence of egregious behaviour to warrant a defensible termination. In these cases, I am talking about the mediocre teachers who were only marginal when hired and since then have regressed. And, now they just need an incentive to move on in life, and leave teaching. However, it isn't easy because in many cases they have been given 'employment permanency' through an unwarranted contract extension. Thus, getting rid of them is more of an art than a science."

The precedence for determining reasonable paid notice was established by the 1960 case "Bardal versus Globe and Mail Ltd.," which stated that, "There can be no catalogue laid down as to what is reasonable notice in particular classes of cases. The reasonableness of the notice must be decided with reference to each particular case, having regard to the character of the employment, the length of service of the servant, the age of the servant and availability of similar employment, having regard to the experience, training, and qualification of the servant."

The bottom line is that each case is decided on its own merit and facts, which determines the appropriate amount to be paid.

A key factor that is seriously considered by arbitrators and judges in wrongful termination cases is the employee's age. It's presumed to be much more difficult to find a new job for older teachers, and the impact of job loss is considered greater as people age. Also, the length of employment is important because the longer a teacher has worked for a district, the longer administrators have had to assess the person's competency, and as a result the greater the awards in these cases of wrongful termination. Arbitrators may also look at the nature of the work performed—whether it was generic or more specialized. The size and sophistication of the organization matters too. Large, lucrative organizations owe their employees greater care and attention and, presumably, can afford to pay more in a buy-out. And, some organizations may even pay for career transition counseling so that an "employee" is assisted in finding alternate employment. All of these, on an arbitrary sliding scale become guidelines for determining how much money is enough for the acceptance of a structured severance agreement."

"Of course, if you don't have the necessary documents for evidence to warrant a termination, you probably will not have enough money to cushion a teacher's fall from grace. And if those documents are about a complete stranger, there could be subjective elements to them that read as factual to an outsider. Finding a way to do the right thing becomes paramount. Even though they never appeared on the list of qualifications for the job of Superintendent of Human Resources, integrity, perseverance, and a willingness to straddle the ambiguous margins between right and wrong allowed me to be very effective in that position."

Lee, who looked like he had been waiting to say something for a few minutes, finally interrupted and asked, "Actually Dr. Bernard I wasn't so much interested in the legal precedence of firing an employee as much as I wanted to know what concrete experience you have had in dealing with them, terminations that is. Can you tell us about the first time you had to terminate someone who was employed by the school district?"

Lee's emphasis on the word "terminate" made Bernard feel like he was being asked to explain the mechanics of a hit man's latest assassination. The tone was faintly admiring.

Bernard apologized and continued.

As the person in charge of district personnel, it was obvious from the get-go that my success in solving personnel-related problems and occasional need to conduct a termination procedure would be largely influenced by my ability to tap into my Executive Assistant's vast mental database of employee profiles and district protocols. Desiree Giroux had a keen knack for understanding which of the district's written procedures were frequently followed and which were not. But more importantly, when asked, and sometimes when not asked, she could efficiently paint a portrait, in the most fair-minded manner, of any of the hundreds of school district employees, including their strengths and weaknesses.

Her descriptions were sumptuous and insightful: "condescending to all but a genius in curriculum development," or "late for every meeting and falls down in committee work, but the south side's best science teacher." Or my favourite: "chaotic introvert." In the case of Frank, my predecessor, she let slip: "If it's good for the district, it's good for him, and vice versa."

I didn't ask for these "bon mots" from Desiree; they usually came as I was walking back into my office, just before my door closed, giving me the chance not to acknowledge hearing them if I thought that showed more propriety.

Desiree had no formal training in psychology, but she was great at reading people. I especially appreciated her ability to give me a succinct historical rundown of the few district employees who would generate the greatest number of personnel challenges.

Even her own name she insisted on shortening for those of us in the office, "For efficiency's sake please call me Desi. It doesn't sound so old and fussy," she would say."

And so, within the first few weeks of my job, Desi became a valuable partner. She could condense a yearlong scenario into a three-minute synopsis. And she relied entirely on the facts, when she knew them, or pointed out that she was withholding parts when she was not aware of the circumstances. To her great credit, she did all of this without suggesting she thought any one of our employees was a total mess.

Desi was, in large part, my main strategy for tackling Arcadia School District's own manifestation of the "Pareto Principle" head on. The "Pareto Principle" — also known as the "80/20" rule and the "Law of the Vital Few" — states that a few key players, 20 percent, the folks like Desi, contribute greatly to the success of an organization, more than their numbers justify, and that at least 80 percent of the personnel nightmares are created by another 20 percent of the employees. I knew I needed Desi to point out the desperate few who comprised that troublesome 20 percent, the creators of 80 percent of the administrative and management nightmares that would inevitably suck away the greater part of my energy and time.

Charles Garnier was the first principal who actually telephoned me in response to the message I had left on his voice mail a couple of days into the job, when I had told him that I had found the name, Easton McCoy, written on a note in a red file-folder on my desk indicating that there might be some kind of personnel issue. I figured Easton McCoy was probably in that 20% group making 80% of the management waves at Garnier's school, but waited to hear the full story.

In his gentlemanly east-coast intonation, Garnier began, "Well Keith we haven't met yet but I'm told that you're here, that you have been brought in here, to help me fix this problem, to help me clean up this mess. I mean it isn't the only reason that you were brought in. You come highly recommended by Frank, you know?" Months later, Garnier would confess over a turkey sandwich on rye that he never much trusted Frank's word on anything, including his initial words about me.

"Listen Keith I have this teacher, Easton McCoy, and well Keith, he just has to go. That's it. It's just that simple. He just has to go. Okay?" I waited a little while for more details to come, but nothing came.

Finally, I responded, "Charles you will have to help me out a little more here. What's the problem with Mr. McCoy? And, what do you mean that he just has to go?"

Garnier began with an odd nervous laugh, "Keith, he just has so many teaching deficiencies, just so many, which are problematic enough by themselves, but now he has the whole school community screaming they want him fired. In the past four months, I don't think there was a week when I didn't get a call from an outraged parent. Keith, I've tried to work with him, but I just don't think we can afford to keep him any longer. It's hurting us, we're losing students because of him and we're going to lose more if something doesn't change. So, what's your plan?"

"Well, seeing as I have no idea what you are talking about Charles, I need a day or two to take a look at his personnel file and then can I get back to you?" The actual problem around Mr. McCoy's teaching was not revealed in this conversation, just all the understandably reactionary expressions from people stuck with a problem they don't know how to attend to. I really needed to get my hands on his file and see how he had been handled in the past.

"That's fine Keith, take a look at his file, but you need to know that we need to move quickly on this. Parents are calling me and threatening to pull their kids out of the school if nothing is done about him soon. They mean it, you know. They will pull their kids out, and then what are we supposed to do? I know I was hired to run this school and make improvements, but I can't do it all by myself. I didn't create this problem."

"Okay Charles, just give me a day or so to read over the file and then I'll let you know what I think we can do."

Garnier seemed a little calmer, or at least he pretended to be, when he finally responded, "Sounds fine Keith, but I need to hear from you soon." Then there was a pause and he added, almost as if it were an afterthought, "By the way Keith, you may not have his complete file; his complete personnel file, if you know what I mean."

I knew right away that he was referring to an unfortunate but all-too-common practice in which administrators keep unofficial files on staff. They know they shouldn't do it, but they do. They think that the walls of a personnel file are bound by some kind of a semi-permeable membrane that allows hand-scribbled notes to suddenly appear "officially" in an individual's personnel file. Somehow almost magically, the detailed hand-written scraps of paper transfer across the ether from there to the fireproof filing cabinet that houses all of the official personnel files. They are usually trying to problem-solve when they begin this parallel assessment game. They are usually trying to help.

"Charles, are you saying that there is his personnel file, which I have here in my office, and then a second file about Mr. McCoy over there, which we both know shouldn't exist?"

There was an awkward pause and then Garnier spoke. "Hum, now I'm not sure what I am saying but some of his issues may be, well they may be kind of undocumented or they may be documented but in an unofficial way."

My stomach sank as I probed further, "Charles, when can I come out to see you? When are you free for an hour or two in the next two days? And, do you know we may have a really big problem here? By the way, can you send me a copy of whatever you have in that other file right away? Can you do it personally as soon as I hang up and not pass it on to your secretary to do?"

Garnier seemed a little embarrassed and irritated by my insistence, "You bet Keith, right away. I'll have it faxed, no I'll fax it myself, as soon as I hang up. I'm so glad you are here to help us out. Frank has said many good things about you."

I hung up and wandered into the reception area by the fax machine about a half dozen times over the next few hours before anything arrived. As I wandered back and forth between my office and the fax machine, and sometimes just hovered in between, I wondered, "How could this all be so messed up? What the heck has Frank been doing for the past 10 years while he was in charge of human resources? And how come Garnier, a veteran principal with extensive experience seems oblivious to basic management protocols regarding employee personnel files?"

I dreaded the thought that with hundreds of teachers and more than two dozen principals in the district that there may be a whole lot of pages in dozens of unofficial personnel files floating around out there, giving principals solace that all professional indiscretions and rare instances of malpractice had been duly documented.

As Bernard was speaking his mind was running through what he thought should have been basic practice and known to anyone who takes on the responsibility for staff supervision.

The management of personnel files is a straightforward matter. Legally, there is only one official personnel file for each employee. And, this official file is the only file used in decisions respecting any, and all, terms and conditions of employment. While it is possible that copies of some or all of the material in the personnel file might also be kept in some form of confidential files of a school administrator, there should never be anything in that duplicate file that does not exist in the official personnel file. Ideally, each item should be numbered and listed on an inventory sheet, which should record each item in the file, its number, title, a brief description of its nature, the number of pages or parts in it, the person who added the item, and the date it was added to the file. The personnel file should only contain material that really pertains to the employment of the individual.

Often the personnel file will include, a person's curriculum vitae, university transcripts, letter of application, references, salary and work history, evaluations, disciplinary material, decisions and recommendations together with the reasons arising from personnel decisions, and copies of material reflecting professional development and achievement. Any material that has not been added to the personnel file should not be used in any process to the employee's disadvantage. Employees have the right, during normal business hours and upon reasonable notice, to examine the entire contents of their personnel files. And, the examination may be carried out in the presence of a person designated by the superintendent. Employees may not remove the personnel file or any of its contents from the office. It was all so obvious; that employee terminations could not rest on the scribbling's found on differently coloured post-it notes in the multiple desk drawers of incensed school personnel.

Nevertheless, Bernard knew that what often gets labeled as "common-sense," may in fact not be very common, and he knew that Garnier's aside meant a great deal of potential trouble. Maybe Garnier would prove to be in the 20% troublemakers group too.

Bernard looked at Lee and said, "I decided I had better write all of my thoughts up about personnel file management in a memo and have it put on the agenda for the next principals' meeting. I had a feeling that what I thought should be common sense among the principals might be instead rather uncommon.

Garnier and I had decided to meet early the next week since neither of us had enough time between scheduled meetings to have a proper discussion. But in the meantime, I began to read what he had faxed me from his unofficial "Easton McCoy" non-personnel, personal file. It amounted to about a dozen pages of hand-written notes documenting parental complaints about McCoy and his behaviour toward students, parents, and his colleagues in and out of school. There were also one-sided recollections of what Garnier had discussed with McCoy about these complaints, and there were a few pages of hand-written student testimonies about McCoy's unacceptable behaviour in classes, duly signed by students.

Here is what I could glean from the official McCoy personnel file and by talking to Desi: A previous school principal, Richard Hehr, had hired Easton McCoy. Richard Hehr, I would later surmise, was a less than stellar educational leader who happened to occupy an office down the hall from me and who had been handpicked by Chuck to be the district's Assistant Superintendent of Organizational Compliance.

Chuck publicly asserted, whenever he felt it was warranted, that it was Richard's outstanding record in all matters to do with school budgeting and staff selection that rendered him an asset. "By gosh," Chuck would bellow, "this district was so very fortunate to have a man of Richard's calibre in a leadership position." Not only had Richard been a successful school principal, but he had also expanded his expertise by taking a leave of absence from education to work as a horse identifier—someone who verifies horses at racetracks—and he had, for a short time, owned a llama farm, which unfortunately went bankrupt after the public lost its appetite for free-range llama meat in the early 1990s. Obviously, a man of many skills, Chuck would say Richard Hehr's "down to earth" qualities could only be an asset to a complex organization such as Arcadia.

After listening to Chuck go on, I made a mental note to remember that Richard would be the best person to consult if the district encountered any llama-related challenges or if I was thinking about gambling at the race track.

But as I read through the pages that Garnier had sent, it was obvious that this was not a clear-cut case. It would not be easy to fire McCoy. I just had to see what I could do to help out Garnier and his school community.

It seems that Richard as principal had hired Easton McCoy specifically to launch the school's innovative "Water-Ski Academy." Beaumont School was a relatively small kindergarten to grade 12 school of about 350 kids located in an affluent community, and the water-ski academy was developed as an initiative by Richard to stave off the annual enrolment losses they were experiencing.

Nearby, a newly built private high school offered numerous elective programs and Richard accused "them" of deliberately poaching Beaumont's most gifted students. The water-ski academy idea was borrowed from similar initiatives launched in other small schools that had been faced with declining enrolments. In some cases these academies had worked; hockey schools or baseball academies sprung up and so did student enrolments. In other cases the initiatives did nothing to stop the losses and were declared, typically, after a short time, failures.

However, Richard was certain that the unique niche of having a bona-fide water-ski academy was different and a sure thing. About two years after launching the academy, Richard was transferred to another school in the district, 150 miles away from Beaumont School, before being abruptly promoted by Chuck to a central-office position.

While Richard was moving forward in his career at central office, the water-ski academy began to languish and was eliminated due to continually insufficient enrolment in its programs and the resulting excessively large budget overruns.

One winter day on a return flight home from a meeting at the Ministry of Education office, I broached the subject of the Beaumont Water-Ski Academy with Richard. He was adamant that if he had still been principal of the school, the academy would have not only have been viable but would have flourished. It would not have failed. "Not on his watch!" he declared emphatically, and not without some anger.

Moreover, Richard claimed, Chuck needed him to go to Amiens Collegiate to get the staff on track. There were simply, "too many slackers teaching there," he said. "The Amiens community needed someone with my kind of backbone. Someone to force the teachers to get moving and teach well," he went on. "I would have stayed at Amiens, but Chuck needed me at central office to help turn the ship around."

It made me wonder if, rather than recruiting a highly qualified cohort for central office duty, Chuck was unknowingly employing a form of "Negative Selection," which occurs in rigid hierarchies when the person at the top, wishing to remain in power, chooses his or her associates with the prime criterion of incompetence to eliminate any possibility of an overthrow. The associates do the same, and over time the organization becomes rife with incompetent leaders. I pulled myself away from that thought and just figured there must be more to Richard than meets the eye.

I listened a little bit longer as Richard explained that his promotion to a central-office position, his six-figure salary and the district credit card to use for entertaining were all just part of his selfless response to serve the school district's best interests. It was, he insisted, part of the heavy burden he bore in his tireless efforts of servant-leadership.

Richard ended his soliloquy with a sigh, adding how he was looking forward to getting some much needed sleep on the flight as he had been putting in far too many late nights at the office trying to get everything fixed. He was, by his own accounts, fighting the good fight, but simply exhausted from all of the hard work.

As he stopped talking and we boarded the plane, all I could think was that perhaps he and I had become officers at the helm of our own Exxon Valdez, a metaphor that seemed hauntingly relevant and absurdly jarring. While the March 1989 Exxon Valdez crisis was not the largest oil spill in history, it was, and still is, considered to be one of the most devastating human-caused environmental disasters. During the trial proceedings, we learned that the ship ran aground on the Bligh Reef, spilling 10.9 million gallons of oil into Alaska's pristine coastal waters in part because of simple sleep deprivation. The officers' exhaustion-induced psychosis led to grievous errors in judgment.

Like it or not, I would be taking a ride on this organizational ship with Chuck steering and Richard by his side. And I knew there would be trouble ahead. As the plane lifted off, I hoped Richard got some much-needed sleep that morning, and also hoped the ship I had found myself on wasn't headed for disaster because of a little hubris by one of its highly-paid helmsmen.

The result of the Water-Ski Academy debacle, while not a large-scale environmental catastrophe, led to chronic issues of over-staffing and a large deficit in Beaumont's budget, one that the school had no ability to address and repay, and one that drained the school district's small operating surplus. Unrealistic community expectations added to the pressure to spend lavishly with the hope of building a more viable school. The concept of cutting your losses had not occurred to anyone with the means to affect the only real solution.

The interim principal who followed Richard, Damien Molokai, had decided that Easton McCoy should be kept on staff rather than declared redundant and terminated as the water-ski program closed down operations.

When I asked Molokai why he had kept McCoy even when he didn't need him anymore, he said it was because McCoy filled a void, met a need. And after all, McCoy lived in the area, and it would be a shame for him to sell his house and move, even if the school didn't really need him. Plus, Molokai added, he had always heard Richard, his leadership-mentor, say that the district had plenty of money hidden away in central office and could afford an extra teacher at Beaumont.

I had to ask, "Did Richard Hehr really say that?" Molokai looked like he was trying very hard to remain both silent and still in a non-responsive manner, but as I stared at him and waited, he finally exhaled and nodded affirmatively.

Looking into McCoy's employment history, I learned that when he had applied for his initial teaching job, he had not been a particularly strong applicant based on his subject-knowledge or pedagogical skills— or even on successful classroom experience.

Richard admitted as much to me.

But, I also found out from Richard that McCoy had lots of experience working the water-ski circuit as a champion trick skier. And really, this is what the program had needed, Richard stated. "Someone with credibility." The school had a load of effective teachers, Richard proclaimed, as if that fact somehow appropriately offset the number of employees who couldn't teach well. And Richard generally had kept a tight rein on his staff, he said.

But, McCoy, Richard argued, was special because he had been a champion, a proven winner and he had provided newspaper clippings with his résumé showing him standing in a Speedo while holding up his trophies. This was, of course, all near the front of his official personnel file and had been the primary reason Richard offered him the job.

And, while I couldn't find any documentation to suggest that McCoy was a poor teacher based on performance evaluations - because Richard had only ever conducted one evaluation - I did find loads of newspaper clippings with pictures of McCoy in a very small bathing suit.

As for that one performance evaluation, Richard had indicated that McCoy should be recommended for a permanent teaching certification. The evaluation, which carried Richard's signature, was based on a single classroom observation done in a physical education class on June 17th, two years after McCoy was first hired. Apparently that was the only documented classroom observation ever conducted on McCoy.

From that assessment, someone deemed him a competent enough teacher to receive a continuous teaching contract with the district.

As I was finishing up my phone call to Richard to confirm the existence of this one and only measly performance report, I signaled to Desi with our agreed upon sign for: "Do you have any Tylenol?" It was a one-handed T made over the forehead, kind of like a windshield wiping gesture over your brain. She laughed at me from her desk and grabbed her perennially messy gym-bag-size purse from which she surely would drum one up.

As I read the notes that Garnier had faxed over, it was clear that among his concerns was the fact that McCoy had serious anger-management issues. He frequently lost his temper in class and would regularly shout at students. McCoy often used heavily sarcastic tones to address and discipline students, and referred to them in class as "lazy," "unmotivated," and "spoiled brats." This seemed to be a common theme in the notes, which had been scribbled down from Garnier's conversations with parents. Garnier indicated that he had made McCoy aware of most of these complaints, but that each time they met in Garnier's office, McCoy just shrugged off the complaints as the whining of parents who pandered to their child's whims.

Garnier's notes also included student allegations of McCoy's physical aggression directed towards them. In one case, a few kids reported that McCoy threw a basketball, hard, at a student when he lost his temper in physical education class. Garnier had interviewed numerous students who said they witnessed it. Their singular recollections corroborated each other's stories, making the facts pretty clear. One student clarified the incident further, "It looked like Mr. McCoy tried to throw the ball at Desmond's privates."

According to McCoy's statements, which were found on the next page of his "unofficial" file, the ball simply slipped out of his hands, and in some aberration that defied the scientific principles of gravity, it flew horizontally across the gym and hit poor Desmond in the mid-section.

McCoy admitted that to some, it might have looked like he threw the ball. And maybe it seemed as though he had lost his temper, but neither was true. He was holding a ball and projecting in an authoritative teacher's voice when the ball suddenly slipped out of his hands and hit Desmond who, at that exact time, was facing him with his pelvis pushed forward.

"It was just one of those freak accidents," McCoy added.

The tendency to shirk the burden of responsibility permeates family rooms, boardrooms, staff rooms, and beyond. We live in a time when taking responsibility for one's actions is like a contagion that can be avoided with enough hand sanitizer. It's a syndrome that can be epitomized in the words of Kenneth Lay, former chairman of Enron Corporation, the energy giant that claimed revenues of nearly $101 billion prior to its 2001 collapse. Lay's public statements after the debacle and collapse included, "Of anything and everything that I could imagine might happen to me in my lifetime, the one thing I would have never even remotely speculated about was that someday I would become entangled in our country's criminal justice system."

Lay insisted that the responsibility for Enron's collapse—which swelled the U.S. unemployment ranks by more than 20, 000 and cast a cloud over the future of hundreds of thousands of pensioners—emanated from somewhere else other than from his actions.

Continuing with my investigation, I found two unusual letters in the official McCoy file. The first was a letter from McCoy to a law firm asking them to disclose any and all information they may have relating to allegations of criminal misconduct that may have occurred while he was a teacher in another jurisdiction. Confused, I stopped and re-read the letter because, while it is customary for teachers to undergo a criminal records check as part of the screening process, this letter was quite different from the standard form.

By the time I finished reading the second letter, I was dazed and confused for sure. Addressed to Frank from a law firm, the letter stated that less than one year prior to his hire, Mr. Easton McCoy had been granted an "absolute discharge" by the trial judge in relation to his "plea to one count of uttering a threat to cause bodily harm."

"What the hell?" I thought as I read on.

"This means that as a result, there is, in essence, no penalty imposed upon you and that you have no criminal record."

I promptly popped the Tylenol Desi had left silently on my desk while I read.

"Let this further serve to confirm that, in addition, the judge has placed you on a Peace Bond for a period of 12 months on the conditions that you have no contact, directly or indirectly, with the victim, Ms. Doe, and that you keep the peace and be of good behaviour."

The letter went on to read:

"Obviously, if you were ever charged in the future, the police and the Prosecution would have a record of the discharge and could produce that for Court purposes."

With both official and unofficial file contents colliding in my head, the next morning I called up the secretary at Beaumont and told her that I would be driving out the one and a half hours to meet with Garnier. She should kindly let him know to clear his appointments for the day. I tried not to think too much about it as I drove and attempted to just enjoy the rolling valleys of the wine country. However, neither beautiful scenery nor the two Tylenols I had taken did anything to help. My head pounded the whole way.

Shortly after I arrived at Beaumont School, I sat down with Garnier in his office to discuss the matter. It began with Garnier speaking, "I'm not sure if you knew that McCoy had been previously married? Did you know that Keith? I didn't know that when I started here. I just found out. You know we never get told the whole story, do we?"

"You know what Charles, I don't really know much of anything about Mr. McCoy, so how about I just listen. There really isn't much in his personnel file, and some of it I can't discuss with you. But, I did read what you sent over via fax. How about you just fill me in on what you think I need to know?"

"Well, I guess he was married before and then divorced and is now remarried."

I wasn't sure what any of this had to do with his teaching, but I knew enough to let him continue.

"It has been alleged, by some very reputable parents no-less, that maybe he is involved with the unattached parent of one of our current students. Just between the two of us, I think he's sleeping with her."

I wanted to wait, as I knew Garnier would fill in the ever expanding void of my ignorance, but asked. "Where did you hear this from?" I knew I shouldn't ask him, but I did.

"Apparently he had a vocal falling out with the woman at one of the local bars here that's a very popular place. Have you ever been to Whiskey Alfredo's? It's sort of a country bar and its really pretty good. You should try it."

"Nope, never been. Please continue." I said.

"It's small town Keith; people talk." Garnier looked at me sympathetically as if he were teaching a remedial class about small-town life, with a focus on the small pond of human companionship and affection available, the inevitability of infidelity and the all-too-common bad choices one might make about dating a student's parent.

"He's been in quite a few relationships with local women. I mean a whole lot. I guess he is a young man. You know what it's like." Garnier realized what he might say next and stopped.

"Well at some point, it became known that Easton had been charged, although I hear the charges were dismissed, with getting physical with one of his former girlfriends. I think he has anger issues and probably issues with women in general."

I looked at Garnier blankly, still unsure of the story's relevance.

Unable to elicit any commiseration from me, he seemed to take the conversation sideways. "Yeah, it seems that your colleague at central office, Richard Hehr, found out about all of this right after he hired McCoy, but decided that he couldn't really do anything about it since the charges had been dismissed. So, here we are now," he sighed.

"You know Keith, if I had been the principal back then, I certainly would have done something. Things would not have been allowed to escalate to this."

I'm not an overly cynical person by nature, but I have heard that line so many times that it has lost meaning for me and makes me wary of anyone who utters it: "If I had been in charge, all of this would never have happened. There would be no bad hires, incompetents would be fired, and there would be peace in the Middle East."

"Charles," I said, taking a pause, "you need to tell me what you are dealing with now. What is happening at the school with McCoy? And what does any of this have to do with his ability to teach?"

Garnier indicated that parents were contacting the school - "almost daily" - and threatening to pull their children out of the school if something wasn't done right away to get rid of McCoy because he had developed a reputation for being a womanizer and for being verbally abusive.

Garnier admitted that Beaumont was already losing some students for a variety of reasons, but he was particularly concerned that families would walk away at the end of the year if there was any chance one their children might have McCoy as a teacher.

As far as Garnier was concerned, parents were losing confidence in the school, and in him as principal, because they had lost all confidence in McCoy's abilities as a role model and teacher. Before I could even formulate the thought about a principal's need to save face, he had totally turned it over to me.

"What are you going to do about it Keith?" he asked.

When I pushed Garnier to get to the point, to give some evidence that this had an impact on McCoy's teaching effectiveness, he bluntly avoided the question.

I didn't say it, but I sure thought it: McCoy, who had been charged, and who had pleaded guilty to uttering threats to cause bodily harm to someone he presumably loved, had now surprisingly, developed a sudden problem managing his anger and controlling his verbal outbursts. And, we seemed surprised by this? A teacher who had been observed for evaluative purposes only once, and only in a single Physical Education class, near the end of June when most of the curriculum has been covered, had been found to be less than competent but was still offered a tenured position with the school district? Could anyone claim that his inability to carry out the professional duties and role modeling required of the education professions had not been predicted?

Yet Garnier—and everyone else I encountered while working through this case—seemed to be genuinely surprised when I asked why someone didn't intervene sooner.

The response was the same each time: they would put their hands up in the air, shake their heads from side to side, and try to look as innocent as possible while saying, always the same five words: "Who could have predicted this?"

And, I concluded, "A blind donkey with three legs could have seen this coming!"

As I have done many times, I kept my thought to myself. While refusing to hire McCoy based on the dismissed charges would have been illegal, to suggest that one couldn't predict that he might have anger management issues was absurd. This letter from the lawyer was all the more reason why someone should have kept McCoy under a watchful eye and documented any teaching deficiencies appropriately, consistently and early on.

I began meeting with Garnier regularly and trained him in formally documenting any concerns he had about McCoy's teaching proficiency or his professional interactions with students, parents and colleagues. Every time he wrote down something that seemed to be substantial, Garnier would call me, and I would advise him to have a professional conversation with McCoy about what Garnier perceived was going on and, more importantly, what was going wrong.

I told Garnier to give McCoy a copy of everything that would be formally entered into his personnel file and to let McCoy know that he was entitled to union representation in any meeting that was disciplinary in nature. Garnier followed my advice and suddenly McCoy's personnel file began to accumulate official, documented concerns that identified teacher deficiencies and substantial performance problems. In this way we opened communications with McCoy showing him the respect due to a staff member who was accused of wrongdoing, and at the same time, began to legitimately build a case against him.

The two junior lawyers in the small meeting room let out a few deep breaths and moved a little from side to side in their chairs the moment Bernard signaled that some sort of formal documentation process had begun for McCoy. Just the thought of not having something on paper was probably nightmarish for them, given their training. Bernard noticed the time.

"There are three more termination scenarios that I should probably apprise you of. Should I switch to another scenario for a bit given that we are going a little over here?" he asked.

Peter Hart just blurted out, "Oh, yes Dr. Bernard," and then looked at Wilson Lee, realizing that he probably should have deferred to him, but adding "if it is ok, of course, with Mr. Lee?"

Lee again showed now qualms about looking hard at the clock and then nodded for Bernard to continue.

The little light on my phone was flashing red to indicate that I had voicemail. A Mr. Tony Daniel had me a left message to call him back as soon as possible. Daniel's message had that friendly singsong melody that people sometimes use when they are actually quite desperate, but wish not to appear so.

"Hi, this is Tony Daniel from over at Festubert Elementary School. We haven't met, but I am pretty sure you may have heard about me. If not, you will. Frank, the last guy who did your job, may have told you that I'm the teacher who is always calling and looking for a transfer to another school. Don't get me wrong, I like this school and there isn't any issue. I get along with the principal and all the staff. I just want a change. I just need a change. I know the transfers aren't handled for another four months, but I was hoping that maybe we could talk and I could explain all of this to you. Can you give me a call back? Oh, and have a great day."

I called over to Desi's office and asked if she could explain why Tony Daniel was leaving me a message now, two weeks into January about wanting a transfer. Desi said she would come by later and explain, but in the meantime she would email a copy of the online "Teacher Transfer Form" and the Arcadia Administrative Procedure.

I began with the online form and found that it was pretty straightforward. It read:

"In order to facilitate staffing for the next school year, teachers who have a continuous contract and who are interested in pursuing the possibility of a transfer to another school in the District must complete this form. This transfer form will be shared with principals in the District. Completion of this form does not guarantee that a teacher will receive a transfer. Teachers are encouraged to promote their career aspirations with the principals of the schools to which they would consider transferring to."

After I stopped thinking about what the phrase "career aspirations" meant in practical terms for teachers seeking a transfer, I took a look at the copy of the administrative procedure about the assignment and transfer of teachers. The procedure identified the timelines and the processes for handling teacher transfers. In the preamble to the procedures, it stated:

"The appropriate placement of teachers is a major consideration in delivering a quality education program."

The procedure then went on to state:

"1. The superintendent of human resources is responsible for coordinating teaching staff assignments and transfers as follows:

1.1. Opportunities for transfers within the district will be advertised in the schools and will identify any special interests or skills that are necessary to meet student and program needs.

1.2. Staff members wishing to be considered for a transfer shall advise the superintendent of human resources in writing of such intensions on or before March 1st."

Well it was six weeks before the March 1st deadline, and I wondered if this was the beginning, middle or end of what already seemed like a frustrating process for Daniel, based on his need for immediate assistance.

Later after Desi finished the district mailing, I found out that Daniel was a seven-year teaching veteran who had been asking for a transfer out of Festubert Elementary for the past three years but had been denied that transfer by Frank each of the years he requested it. No reasons were ever documented for the denial, but, according to Desi, the word among principals was that Daniel was not a terrific teacher, maybe not very good at all, and no one wanted to take him. Seems they were all content with the fact that Festubert Elementary was stuck with a lemon named Tony Daniel.

Desi even divulged, matter of factly, that many of the principals suggested that Daniel was a whiner who could never be satisfied. A number felt that no matter where he went to teach, he would not be happy unless he were allowed to run the school. Daniel had been at another school before his current assignment and had requested the transfer to Festubert.

I wasn't sure if the whole "Daniel Affair," as I thought of it, was a reverse case of "The Dance of the Lemons," also called "Passing the Trash" or "The Turkey Trot." This form of teacher transfer seems endemic in education and stems from the belief, more grounded in myth than in reality in Canada, that it is impossible to get rid of incompetent teachers, especially after they have received a continuing contract. It is true that one of the main reasons for this enduring myth is the strength of teachers' unions who are legally required to protect teachers by negotiating strong collective agreements and ensuring that they are not fired without cause. They do go to bat for every terminated teacher, including teachers terminated for some very good reasons, and it is also true that all teachers are owed legal representation. But my own experiences with the teachers' unions, the ones I once belonged to and the ones I would, in this new job, be positioned somewhat as adversary to, was that they no more wanted students to be subjected to incompetent teachers than I did.

Bernard pushed back from the table and took a good look at the two young lawyers watching him. That last comment about teachers' unions seemed to have drawn them in with just a bit more fervour than he had seen the entire meeting.

What happens is that out of a fear of having to do the intense and time-consuming work of documenting teaching deficiencies and then providing support for improvement or initiating termination procedures, school districts instead take these disappointing, foolish, untrustworthy, inept or the like teachers and transfer them repeatedly or, depending on the school culture, just leave them be, therefore essentially ignoring the problem. Inherent in these multiple, purposeless transfers of poorly performing teachers is the unfounded belief that a new context will beget absolutely new behaviours, attitudes and skills. Such is not the case, however.

"It's the lemon thing again," Lee interjected, gaining a quizzical look from Hart either because of the fact that it was out of procedure for Lee to interject anything, or maybe just because the comment did sound a bit strange. Realizing he had their attention, Bernard continued. "Yes. In this case, based on what Desi intimated about some shared sentiment among the principals, they were just following the locally prevailing custom, which was to just leave the lemon where it was so as not spread its acidic juice."

"I called Daniel and explained that I would keep his transfer request in mind and promised him that I would review the file during the upcoming transfer request period in March. He reluctantly thanked me and ended the conversation by saying that was exactly what Mr. Cottingly had assured him, each year, for the past three years."

"As I hung up the phone, I had a hard time deciding whether his resigned tone was just sad or actually threatening. I realized that being compared to Frank in this way did not sit well with me, even if it was procedurally correct on both of our parts to have handled this teacher request, initially, in this manner."

"Not too long after dealing with Daniel I had a telephone conversation with John Lalande, the principal at Salient Technology Academy and the site of my third staffing "hotspot." It was a pleasant conversation and the first time a dialogue over one of the personnel problems started off on a good footing. A little shudder went up my spine as I contrasted this brief and straightforward conversation to the rough start with McCoy's case earlier that month."

"Hello, Keith," Lalande began in a rather business-like manner. "Welcome to Arcadia District. I certainly hope you and your family managed to get settled in over Christmas. It's John Lalande from Salient Technology Academy. I'm just returning the very interesting voice mail message you left me."

I thanked him for his prompt reply and for showing such hospitality and then explained how I had found the name of Noelle Chabanel written on a page left by Frank, along with a note that I should contact Lalande for more information about the matter.

"Well," he said in a puzzled tone, "I have no idea what that is all about. There is no problem with Mrs. Chabanel as far as I am concerned. I wonder why Frank did that? I mean she may have some issues, perhaps, but I certainly don't have any with her. I get along with pretty much everybody," he added. "I certainly do have high standards for teachers, and I don't apologize for that. But, no I don't have any issues with Mrs. Chabanel."

I asked Lalande again, hoping to give him an opportunity to recount if there really might be something, anything that might have led Frank to put down Noelle Chabanel's name.

"No," Lalande responded with an air of certainty. "I have no issues with Mrs. Chabanel. We're all absolutely fine over here with her."

As soon as he said that, I got the feeling that he wanted me to go away, to never call about this again, to cross her name off the paper and get on with my busy job. And I could have. I had it from the principal's mouth that there was no problem. But, I had an instinct that either he was clueless and missing something or he was covering something up. The former could likely be the case, as he had seemed so authentically congenial.

However, as the British philosopher Bertrand Russell wisely stated, "The problem with the world is that the stupid are cocksure and the intelligent are full of doubt." I, of course, would never suggest Lalande was stupid, but maybe a little clueless.

I thanked Lalande for his time and for returning my phone call and told him I looked forward to meeting him very soon. As I hung up the phone, I rolled my ergonomic chair backwards a few inches to see if Desi had returned from lunch. By now, she and I had a good understanding of my job transition. All I needed to say was "Noelle Chabanel," and something more helpful than Lalande's comments would be presented to me for reckoning. She wasn't back yet.

Next on my list of staffing hotspots was Bathos Lukno. Before I received a phone call back about Lukno, which came nearly two weeks after my initial phone message, I had already read his personnel file, his real file. In his cover letter Lukno wrote that he hailed from a pretty well known carnival-touring group that travelled from state fair to state fair throughout the upper Midwest U.S. and sometime central Canada. He was fairly articulate about how his professional background could be easily applied to the teaching profession, and also proud of the fact that he held dual citizenship in the U.S. and Canada. During the colder months he wrote that he did dinner theatre "gigs" at resort restaurants and also made money as a painter and set designer in community theatres. When the politically incorrect "Carnie" profession started falling into disfavour, Lukno turned his attention to legitimate theatre in high school auditoriums. It seems that he had gone through an "Alternative Certification" process to acquire his teaching credentials.

He had been hired ten years earlier on a probationary teaching contract, a full-time position, as a theatre generalist teacher that was to be a split between Daele Middle School and Ridge Comprehensive High School. Although separate buildings, Daele and Ridge were physically attached by an atrium that doubled as a library and they shared an auditorium space needed for performances, which included the adjacent scene shop where Lukno had been working.

At the end of Lukno's first year, Senan Welsh, formerly the principal of Daele but who had since been transferred to Valenciennes Elementary, completed a summative performance evaluation, which was in Lukno's personnel file. The evaluation could be described as mediocre at best. Of the 11 teacher performance areas listed in the template, Lukno was only given a rating of "Excellent" in two, was listed as "Satisfactory" in six, and was marked down as "Needing improvement" in the remaining three.

One of these areas on the "Needing improvement" list was in his relationships with teacher colleagues and school administrators. But even so, Welsh's evaluation of Lukno recommended he be given a continuing contract. And so, in August of that year, on behalf of Arcadia School District, Frank sent a letter to Lukno offering him a continuing teaching contract with the district. No other written evaluation was ever done. The only other pages in the file were copies of two letters

Lukno sent to third parties—unusual additions to a personnel file, I thought.

The first letter was about three years old. It began:

Dear Mr. Wells, We have been engaged in a facility review now for over six months.

Lukno went on with some patronizing introductory comments about the progress that had been made since the facility review had begun. These didn't seem that important to me, but then I was drawn to one of Lukno's sentences in the next paragraph.

There are a number of concerns I have about duty-of-care issues with students and have been unable to have any of them resolved to date.

What was Lukno talking about when he wrote about "duty-of-care issues," I wondered? And, who was Wells? I scanned back at the address and did a quick "Google Search," and concluded that Wells was a consultant who must have been hired to undertake a facility review of Ridge Comprehensive High School's theatre facility, the "Metal Box Theatre."

In the letter, Lukno had referred to an email he had received from the principal of Ridge:

Mr. Wells will be in town next week for his final visit. I look forward to going over his recommendations with you in order to see what we need to do to complete this year and then get on with life as normal next year.

Something about the phrase "getting on with life as normal" gave me a strange feeling in my stomach.

The letter to Wells went on:

As Clayton Hamilton in "Theory of the Theatre," says, "Applause begets applause in theatre, as laughter begets laughter and tears beget tears." Together, I am confident we can restore the deep joy I have for serving in the theatre program at Daele Middle School. I have had time to reflect upon the circumstances leading up to the accident that precipitated this facility review, and have...

I stopped on the word "accident" and remembered a story about a community theatre version of a "Passion Play" done in Iowa where an inexperienced actor playing a guard was late to the theatre and failed to go through the proper safety check-ins. Before his scene he grabbed a real spear instead of the fake weapon and hurt the guy playing Jesus so much that he had to be hospitalized but he ended up doing fine.

Lukno continued quoting a conversation I assumed he had with Wells during an on-site visit:

> *As you have indicated, theatre is the most stressful of all teaching assignments, and it is not possible for me to provide a safe environment without the full support of the school's administration.*

The letter listed all of Lukno's concerns, such as: class size; class composition; restrictions to keep known drug users, alcohol abusers, and students with recent histories of defiance or abusive behaviour out of "his" theatre production classes, perhaps, he added, they could be directed to his acting classes which were sometimes a little under-enrolled; the need for a few instructional aides to help him keep an eye on the deviants; and his need for a rock-solid commitment that the administration would remove any undesirables from his classes for any reason Lukno saw fit to raise.

Lukno had capitalized the word "ANY" in his letter right before he wrote the word "reason." But in the letter there was nothing specific about the accident. I finished the letter and then went back and re-read it and was caught by something near the end.

Lukno had written the following to Wells, which should have provided some warning to me. Had I only known at the time that, like the Greeks who had consulted the Delphic oracle on everything from important matters of public policy to personal affairs in order to read its pronouncements correctly, I too was really looking into my own oracle in the form of a chaotically composed letter from a ranting teacher and seeing a shadowy premonition of my future, I might have chosen to stop right then and there, put away this file, and take Frank's "any" from the transition file more literally, as in, ignoring whichever hotspots I felt like ignoring. Lukno continued:

> *As I see it, there are a few options left for me without having the aforementioned concerns addressed. I can presumably do battle with the system and school administration and try to work my way up the chain of command, creating enemies all the way along and adding to an already stressful situation. I can get a doctor's note and leave this position I love and seek another assignment in the district. Or, I guess I could leave the school district altogether and look for another job with another district and see if they are willing to accept my conditions as terms of employment.*

But, there are some important personal reasons why I would like to remain in Arcadia. I have a great deal to offer any school in the district. I have an extraordinary rapport with all students, intellectuals as well as those who are struggling with disabilities and horrid home circumstances. I bring creativity, a powerful moral undertone to all my teaching. I am a gifted teacher who can reach students other teachers have difficulty reaching.

I am either truly an asset worth keeping and am not delusional about my abilities, in which case the district should accept my recommendations and implement them. The other option is I am delusional, which I can assure you I certainly am not.

Sincerely yours,

Bathos Lukno, B.Ed. T.A.D.

I found that I did not know what to make of Lukno's complaints, but I did make note that he was the only person I have ever encountered who used his "B.Ed." as part of his signature. And, I also had to use Google to learn that the "T.A.D." stood for a "Theatre Arts Degree."

Somewhere in my subconscious, I registered the sense that Lukno's propositional statement to Wells of either being delusional, or not, would give this case greater complexity than usual, no matter what the details of the unknown accident actually turned out to be.

The second letter was not really a letter but a printed copy of an email message sent from Lukno to a Mr. Jackson, a different contract safety consultant. In it Lukno repeated many of the same thoughts he had expressed in his letter to Wells. Although this time Lukno rambled on a little bit more with details about the inadequacies of provincial funding for the arts in schools, his interpretation of what "in loco parentis," meant and references to the very important nature of this email as he was taking time to compose it on his Sabbath morning. Lukno wrote something about an accident that had occurred in the theatre shop in September. He was careful to note in bold that this was the first accident that has ever happened in one of his classes over the course of his entire career. And this accident, he emphasized again, was not at all his fault, not at all.

We have to look at all of the flawed decisions outside of my theatre program that led to this accident.

About half way through reading the email, I was left with a sense that Lukno was propagating his own grassy knoll conspiracy, suggesting that a secret society of school administrators was re-engineering a future that did not include him teaching theatre classes, but might include drugs, loud music and kids running wild with power tools.

Lukno clearly saw himself as a defender of all that is morally good in the world and took it as his personal mission to save not only his students' but also all of our souls. He went on to list his recommendations for what was required for the theatre program to provide a safe learning environment, which were the same items in the letter he had sent to Wells.

But his email ended differently:

> In closing I would like to suggest that just because things have been done a certain way in the past does not mean that it is proper to continue to do them today.

He went on to explain how the regulations requiring seat belts and the mandatory use of motorcycle helmets didn't exist years ago.

> But, by implementing these safety devices, countless tragedies have been averted. The circumstances of schools have changed. In the past if a student didn't comply with the expectations and rules of the school, well that individual either quit or was expelled. Nevertheless, as this is no longer the case, we now have a group of people enrolled in schools who years ago would not have been allowed to remain.
>
> Unfortunately, there are many young people who hear that the government is considering the decriminalization of marijuana and then assume marijuana is safe, and some even think it is safer than alcohol. I have no love for how our current governments are destroying future generations.
>
> I sincerely hope that you are able to convince the "powers that be" to seriously consider the aforementioned suggestions, so that I can continue my career managing the theatre program. And, as my idol Edwin Forrest said, "A passion for the dramatic art is inherent in the nature of man."
>
> Sincerely yours,
> Bathos Lukno, B.Ed. T.A.D.

If I had taken it correctly from my reading of Lukno's personnel file, he genuinely believed there might well be an organized conspiracy to pollute the moral fabric of society by decreasing the legal drinking age to 18 years and by considering the decriminalization of simple possession of marijuana.

And, while Lukno might be correct that each of us, not him, but us, had contributed to the decay in social mores, it did seem odd that this consultant to whom he was writing might be able to convince "the powers that be" to fix these social ills.

Nearing the end of January, I finally received a telephone call back from the principal of Ridge Comprehensive High School where Lukno once worked. Somewhat relieved, I found out that Lukno was actually not working there, or anywhere in the district, any longer. He was on a "Long Term Disability Leave, something related to stress, I think." The principal said. And I shouldn't worry, he added because Lukno had been off work for about two years.

The principal, Luca Anselm, seemed a little puzzled about why Lukno's name might be on Frank's list of personnel problems. I asked Anselm about the incident in the theatre and was told that a student had crushed his foot in a terrible accident three years ago.

The principal explained in painstaking detail how the lighting instrument, falling from the heights of the catwalks, had landed on his foot like an anvil, leaving it completely crushed, "a bloody mess" he said, and the damage to the foot so extensive that after the boy arrived at the hospital the doctor's weren't sure he'd ever fully recover use of it. Certainly, he'd have a deformed foot that would disable him for the rest of his life. I was thankful my own kids were into sports. I found myself picturing a teenage boy in great pain, draped in a tattered costume, being carted away through the school halls to an ambulance, a Jesus-like character with a backpack and a crushed foot.

According to Anselm, right after the incident, Chuck demanded to know how this happened. He wanted to know who was to blame. Anselm said Chuck was insistent that someone be held responsible.

Anselm said it was Chuck's idea to launch the facility review. He said it was being dealt with confidentially, but it involved some safety consultant Chuck had brought in, the district's insurance company and a lawyer - as there was a lawsuit that had been launched by the boy's family against the teacher, the school, and the district seeking redress for negligence. He said only Chuck and Frank knew what was really going on in the case.

I pressed Anselm about how Lukno ever got a job at Daele and Ridge Comprehensive schools, and why, if Senan Welsh had truly felt that Lukno was "mediocre at his best" would he in his right mind recommend Lukno for a continuing contract?

Anselm said it was a matter of having no one better to choose from given the very limited pool of talent who applied for the job. "It's hard to find a really good high school drama teacher who isn't a flake," he insisted. The only applicant, and therefore the best candidate for the schools' combined drama program, was Bathos Lukno. He admitted that he and the Daele Middle principal had figured they could recommend Lukno for a continuing teaching contract with the hope and prayer that with enough coaching, Lukno might improve to be "good enough." Or, he added, perhaps Frank might be able to read between the lines and not offer a continuing contract to Lukno based on a lukewarm assessment.

I paused and felt my stomach turn. I was hearing a principal admit to accepting "two feet and a heart beat" for a job opening, and hoping, mistakenly, in the power of positive thinking to transform the barely mediocre into a "good enough" teacher.

Let's bring the behind-the-closed-door story about hiring in a lazy or haphazard manner into the light. Somehow we have bought the myth that good principals might be able to, like Alchemists, transform worthless scrap into gold.

Clearly, Anselm believed that it was possible to take a mediocre teacher and create a great one. And in the end, Lukno was awarded a continuing contract for being, well, mediocre, but with the hope that with some teaching experience and coaching by a principal or two he could be redeemed.

Funny thing though, like an Easton McCoy déjà-vu, Lukno almost saw the end of his teaching career with the district after Daele Middle had eliminated its "Introduction to Stage," classes in a time of radical budget cuts. But, because Ridge Comprehensive High School continued to offer a high school theatre program, instead of finding a better teacher with the appropriate skills to be effective by conducting a thorough and earnest job search, Lukno was transferred and was, therefore, still teaching.

Even though Anselm didn't think Lukno was very good and could have deemed him redundant when Daele stopped its theatre program, Lukno had endeared himself to the two schools by becoming a jack-of-all-trades and filling voids as they appeared. Lukno took on supervision of the school yearbook club and became the regular repairperson for the school mascot costume after it took a beating at the homecoming football game. He coached the prom king and queen on proper deportment when riding in the convertible limousine, and offered help with the lighting for the band, orchestra and choir concerts. In doing all of this, Lukno broadened his teachable areas, or rather, those teacher-service areas that people are glad to not have to cover themselves, and made himself indispensible. And now that there was no theatre program at Daele, he had become Anselm's problem.

Anselm told me that the word among principals was that Lukno was highly intelligent and very articulate, but emotionally unstable, and by unstable, Anselm said he did not mean just ordinarily odd, if I got what he meant.

By the end of the month, after I visited the Middle school to meet with the school's administrative team, I found out that the principal and vice-principals Lukno had worked with during his tenure at Daele could recall times when Lukno had made what some, the so-called "sensitive-types," might construe as racially derisive comments, and from time-to-time cracked a few homophobic jokes. They said they faintly remembered some staff suggesting that Lukno may have made profane or lewd remarks about women in general. But, none of it was meant to be taken seriously, they assured me.

I asked if anything, anything at all, had ever been done about these allegations of gross professional misconduct?

"We talked to Lukno about it and told him to clean up his act," said one of the vice-principals, a former college volleyball star who liked to come to work in his European-styled tracksuit with a whistle around his neck in place of a tie.

"You told him to clean up his act?" I responded hoping desperately for more. "What did you mean by clean up his act? And, then after you told him, then what happened?"

He never responded to my first question.

"Well we didn't hear anything from anybody again so we figured it had worked," the principal replied.

"You didn't hear anything? Did you ask anyone if anything had changed? Did you document any of your conversation or follow up on your stern warning?" I was trying not to sound overly condemning.

There was no reply, just some awkward grinning faces looking back at me. They looked like a pack of teenage boys who were just caught looking at dirty magazines. I half expected them to start snorting in nervous laughter. They made no such noises, thankfully!

I left Daele School exasperated, and a few days later I decided to find out where Lukno was and what he was up to in relation to his long-term disability leave. I was told that his medical leave was most certainly a "stress leave" that had begun in October two years before my arrival, about a year after the accident. Lukno had maintained very little direct communication with the district's central office from the January after the year his leave began.

In fact, the Benefits Coordinator, Paula Miki, told me she thought he might have moved out of province and married a doctor, a homeopath. Paula explained that Lukno had been married, divorced and was now, she thought, remarried. Maybe it wasn't a homeopath but rather a chiropractor, she thought before she said she wasn't sure.

However, from what she told me it sounded like Lukno had been embroiled in a very ugly divorce that included a messy custody battle. Paula told me that during some early period of the divorce, it was rumoured that Lukno had been living at the Ridge School for a few months. She said people were saying that he had slept in the teachers' lounge, showered in the locker room and made his meals in the Home Economics classroom.

I later asked those same three grinning administrators about the story. They said they had heard the same rumours and thought some of it might be true, but decided not to pursue it. They were busy running the school, offering programs to kids, keeping them safe.

"Anyway," as Mr. Tracksuit explained life to me, "It didn't seem to really be our business if some poor teacher came up against some hard luck for a few months. It could happen to anyone. Whose wife hasn't sent him packing for a few nights? What's the big deal with a teacher sleeping a few nights at the school anyway?"

This time I didn't bother to respond. I couldn't think of a decent word to utter.

It was clear that Lukno was a problem; potentially a terribly big nightmare. But, he was also a nightmare who was on a long-term disability leave and not teaching or living anywhere near the school district. However, like most of my nightmares, which I try to forget about as soon as I wake up, I gave Lukno little thought right after that late January period because I thought I had more serious personnel issues to deal with.

After a month on the job, I felt content about what I had accomplished in a relatively short period. Blissful and ignorant, I convinced myself that I had an idea of what each of these four staffing hotspots might be about and began to think through various personnel approaches and strategies that I might employ that were consistent with the organizational requirements of efficiency and effectiveness. I tried to think very scientifically about how I might solve these problems, which had names like Easton, Tony, Noelle and Bathos.

Hart slid his iPhone into Lee's view and nodded towards Lee with wide-open eyes as if to make sure he caught Lee's attention. Recognizing the well-rehearsed signal, Lee said, "This seems a natural point in time to take a break. How about we all just take ten-minutes?"

Bernard walked down the wide hallway decorated with pictures of people like Nelson Mandela and Mahatma Gandhi, until he reached the reception area. Without much purposeful thought, he sat down in one of the large leather chairs, the one between the ficus and the coat rack in the corner. As he stared at the plant's waxy, stiff leaves, and glanced down at the few dried leaves crumpled on the soil in the pot, his thoughts drifted away from the deposition and surprisingly, he found that he was thinking about his older brother, Jimmie.

When he went to him at the funeral home he expected to see Jimmie as he last had seen him when he was still alive, face drawn, cheeks sunken, and skin slightly greyish. But, when he walked up to Jimmie's casket he saw his brother as he had looked every day before he got sick. His cheeks weren't sunken, his skin had colour, and he looked pretty good. He looked like he was sleeping and at any moment would sit up, look around, smile at the joke, and ask "what the hell am I doing in a casket Keith, you big jerk!"

Bernard remembered just staring at Jimmie's face. When he got home later that evening his mom asked him what Jimmie was wearing, she said she couldn't deal with an open casket, but he found he couldn't tell her. His mother wanted to know if Jimmie was wearing the striped, mauve tie or the dotted, red one. She really liked the mauve one she had given Jimmie when he graduated from college.

He never really looked at his clothes, and couldn't remember what Jimmie had on. Bernard was angry that he couldn't remember what Jimmie was wearing. He told his mom it was the mauve one, and she smiled and replied in a smooth, calm and dazed voice that that made her happy, very happy.

His heart sank when he realized he was still – twenty-four years later – grieving his loss. As far as Bernard was concerned, Jimmie was taken far too soon. Jimmie barely had a chance to live. Who dies at 27? He was cheated out of living by a monster called AIDS. It got into his body and in six months killed him. Bernard had always prided himself on the fact that he had a fairly good knack for learning lessons from life's twists, turns and slaps in the face. He had just spent several hours sharing much of what he had culled, distilled and salvaged from the mishaps of his experience in the education profession. But the loss of a brother in this way left him with no handy principles, propositions or bon mots to share about life. Compared to such a life-changing loss, everything else was a walk through the park, even the tales that comprised his deposition.

Bernard heard the nearby elevator doors open and sighed a heavy breath. He took a quick look at his watch, stood up and walked back to the meeting room, brushing his hand through the lime green leaves of the potted tree.

FOUR

After the short break, Bernard, Lee, Hart and the stenographer sat down in the conference room again. Wilson Lee asked Dr. Bernard if he had had a chance to get something to eat during the brief break, and apologized for the fact that the deposition was really - in some ways - quite intrusive.

"If you don't mind," Lee said, "I would like to ask you a little more about your relationship with the Chief Superintendent of Schools, Mr. Chuck Stihl. It was Mr. Stihl who hired you for your position in the District after all, correct?"

Nodding his head in the affirmative, Bernard looked down at his lap for a moment and found himself seeing an image of Chuck Stihl barreling down the highway in a blue Subaru with snow flying out from under all four of his high-end all-season tires, which would have caused him to laugh if he had been at home in his living room with his kids and not in this grey room with the brown table and now six law people. He waited for the next question.

Lee began, "Can you please provide some background to the working relationship you had with Mr. Chuck Stihl, the Chief Superintendent of Schools at Arcadia Consolidated School District Number 66? Can you describe how the two of you interacted and worked together?"

Bernard paused for a moment, wondering where to begin. He settled on the absolute middle and opened his mouth to speak.

I wasn't quite sure why Chuck insisted we drive the five hours straight west to attend the annual conference for the Assembly of Superintendents and Directors of Education rather than fly to the event. He had made it very clear that this was a "must attend" meeting for both of us, and I also came to realize that each of us driving there separately, in the middle of winter, seemed to be a given for him.

I generally don't mind driving, but thought that if I explained to Chuck, very rationally the logic—from a cost-benefit point of view—of flying, and included the argument that flying decreased the risk of being involved in a traffic accident, he might think my hesitation to drive was based on some empirical knowledge rather than on my wimpy inclination to avoid winter road hazards.

"While I appreciate your thinking on this matter, Keith," he said, "if it's all the same to you, I'm going to drive myself. I have a long day planned and just don't see being able to get out of the office until well into the night. I'll do what I always do, and just pack up my stuff, drive a few hours until I get tired and then find a hotel along the highway to stop at. I'll grab a quick breakfast early Friday, and drive the rest of the way and arrive fresh and ready for business. This works better for me than catching a five a.m. flight on Friday," he added with a smirk. "But, if you want to get up that early and fly, go right ahead. I plan to drive myself, like I always do."

It was funny that there was no mention of carpooling, which would have been truly cost-efficient. Completely confused, but not wanting to seem confrontational, I simply let Chuck know that I would meet up with him on Friday morning at the opening session titled: "Strengthening Public Trust."

I did notice that the receipt for Chuck's extra hotel stay was included in the pile of reimbursable employee expenditures a few days after his return.

There is a great deal of interest in the topic of public trust and educational leadership, illustrated by a proliferation of books, articles, and workshops devoted to the moral dimension of leadership. This topic is nothing new, as John Dewey—the influential early 20th century American philosopher, psychologist, and educational reformer—pointed out decades ago when he framed our understanding of education as a deliberatively moral endeavour.

While some of the work of school administrators involves choosing between competing goods, there are times when the work really involves deciding between two evils, and choosing the lesser of the two: simple things, like costing out two different travel methods for a trip taken on the public's money often had this feeling for me, and complex things, like being able to retain only one of two fantastic and equally valuable teachers. Resources of time, money, materials, and personnel are finite, and choices—really difficult choices—have to be made about how best to deploy them. Educational leadership done well entails deliberate and thoughtful wrestling with the moral dimensions inherent in choosing a particular course of action that is in children's best interests. But, it's hard to fathom how this is ever done outside the context of our own personal values - values that we usually take for granted but that deeply inform our choices - especially in stressful situations.

Christopher Hodgkinson—who wrote about the intersection of values and ethics and educational administration—was correct in concluding that there is an inescapable role that values play in administrative decision-making. These underlying values of decision-makers do not just tell us something about the ends and the means that go into making decisions, but they also reveal something more important—and potentially troubling—about the person making them.

When I arrived at central office on the Monday morning after the conference, I promptly headed upstairs to the accounting office to get someone to help me learn how to properly fill in my first expense claim.

As I sat down and produced all of my receipts and boarding passes, the accounting clerk said, "Oh, I see, you flew to the conference."

Noting her somewhat concerned tone, I replied, "Yeah, I did. Is that a problem? Did I do something wrong?"

"Nope, you didn't do anything wrong," she said. "But none of them ever fly," she added. "They always drive."

"I checked with Chuck and explained that it would actually cost less if I flew," I said, feeling the need to justify myself. "And, I got a decent deal on the ticket. I'm pretty sure it cost less than a mileage claim would have been."

"I am sure it did … cost less," she replied with a smile as she took the receipts and boarding passes from me and pulled out the expense claim form from her filing cabinet drawer. That smile had a few different shadings to it.

"Are you sure I didn't do anything wrong?" I added again, feeling rather uneasy about not understanding the sublime humour of the moment.

She stapled the papers together, wrote my name and the date on the form, and then just began to talk. "Chuck says the optics of flying doesn't look good. He cares a lot about looks and says it might look like central office staff are jet-setting around the province on the public purse."

"But, it cost less," I tried to say before she cut me off.

"Of course it doesn't really have anything to do with public perception," she continued. "I process all of their expense claims, and they all drive because then they can claim car mileage on top of the car allowance on top of the per diems. I guarantee they are making money this way. It all adds up to quite a bit, and I am sure covers the cost of their leased cars. Plus it keeps them out of the office and their homes a little longer, and who knows what's going on in their families. And, if they don't eat at expensive places, then they can hang on to some of the meal money. It's a pretty good deal if you ask me, and no one ever sees you step foot on a plane. I guess it looks good, but from where I'm sitting, it stinks!"

"You didn't do anything wrong, Keith. But, I think you are different from them, and I get the feeling that you have a lot to learn about central office administration." She stood up and filed away my expense claim.

I smiled an awkward, forced smile of thanks but was not sure how to respond to her comments. I just turned and walked out of her office.

It has been said that ethics philosopher and 1950 Nobel Laureate Bertrand Russell was once questioned by Harvard University's Board of Governors about having an extramarital affair with a student.

When faced with the hypocrisy of being an Ethics professor engaged in immoral conduct, Russell argued his private affairs had nothing to do with his professional duties.

"But you are a Professor of Ethics!" maintained one of the board members.

"I was also a Professor of Geometry at Cambridge," Russell rejoined, but "they never asked me why I was not a triangle."

Lecturing on ethics was a job for Russell; it didn't mean he had to live an ethical life! Was speaking about moral imperatives just the "job" of Chuck Stihl? Was it unnecessary that he should have some too?

I headed back down the staircase to my office and pulled the conference binder, with its large decoratively printed front cover, "Ethical Leadership for a Sustainable Future," out of my briefcase and placed it on the bookshelf next to the one Frank had placed there from the year before titled, "Getting to the Soul of Leadership." As I looked at the binder, I wondered how different I was from the others. In learning more about how to be a central office administrator, I wondered if I would be reduced to finding little perks here and there and legally tucking away cash for car payments.

Bernard paused to catch his breath and realized that Lee, Hart and even the stenographer were looking at him and smiling. Not sure if they were amused by something he said or by him, he said rather self-consciously, "That isn't all I could say about Chuck Stihl. But that characterizes the working relationship we had and, I think, our very different approaches to the profession."

"Maybe we can leave that for now," Lee said carefully, "and get back to your background in dealing with employee relations."

Bernard wasn't offended by the fact that the much younger Lee had control of this conversation and was steering it. He admired the job Lee was doing and thought that it would probably be nice to work with Mr. Lee. "Certainly we can change topics," Bernard replied. "What was the question again?"

"How about you continue with the information about your background in dealing with employee terminations, perhaps going on with what you were saying about McCoy?"

Bernard responded, "By early February, I called up Easton McCoy and set a time when we could sit down and discuss all of the concerns that were being drawn to my attention. I suggested we do this over coffee, knowing that perhaps that would lend ease to what was potentially not an easy meeting. But in strict professional terms, I also told McCoy that he was entitled to a union representative because, while I was not certain of it, this might lead to some form of disciplinary action. McCoy declined the offer and simply said he wanted to meet with me and talk. He said he had heard good things about me, and while he didn't know me personally, he felt he could trust me enough to meet without a union representative present."

As he spoke, Bernard's mind wandered off to his lecture on David Hume, an empiricist and Scottish philosopher of the Enlightenment and one of the most important figures in the history of philosophy. As Bernard would reinforce with his students, Hume clearly illustrates one of the biggest problems with any kind of relationship centres on issues of trust. Bernard's PowerPoint slide would read:

David Hume wrote of two farmers:

"Your corn is ripe today; mine will be so tomorrow. 'Tis profitable for us both that I shou'd labour with you today, and that you shou'd aid me tomorrow. I have no kindness for you, and know that you have as little for me. I will not, therefore, take any pains on your account; and should I labour with you on my account, I know I shou'd be disappointed, and that I shou'd in vain depend upon your gratitude. Here then I leave you to labour alone: You treat me in the same manner. The seasons change; and both of us lose our harvests for want of mutual confidence and security."

Bernard would explain to his class that Hume recognized what is referred to as unequal affections that can contribute to the problems of trust because, just as we are inclined to act in a kindly way toward our nearest and dearest, we often are inclined to act less kindly toward strangers and enemies. The farmers have, he tells us, no kindness for one another, and any willingness to act justly to give the other his due must therefore be an artificial and not a natural virtue. Trust is not to be explained in terms of natural inclinations. How, then, is it to be explained?

Sociologists suggest the answer to the question of why people trust each other, even individuals they have just met, is based on the unfounded belief that efforts between people will be reciprocated. I'll do this for you today, without expecting anything tomorrow in return from you, or anyone, with the confidence that down the road you or someone else will return the favour. This trust, this act of hope and faith, is a form of generalized reciprocity that is so necessary and fundamental to civilized life that the majority of moral codes all contain some equivalent to the "Golden Rule," that says "Do unto others, as you would have them do unto you."

Trust requires that you place confidence in others not to hurt or abuse you should you, or they, make an error or mistake. Trust is what allows us to drive down an undivided highway at 100 miles an hour, music blasting, head bobbing and not become paralyzed by a crushing fear that someone on the other side has decided that today is a good day for autocide, and is simply going to swerve into your lane and create a head-on collision.

Trust fundamentally requires both hope and faith. Hope in a goodness that springs from simply being human and a willingness to take the risk that people are not inherently evil, bad or ill willed. But, trust also requires faith, a faith in the fairness of life. A faith in the "boomerang effect" that what you throw out to the world in good-will will eventually come back to you at some point unknown. Trust is the glue or cement of human relationships that allows you to need others to fulfill yourself.

Bernard caught himself and the others sitting in silence and realized that while he had been thinking, he hadn't said anything.

Smiling at the stenographer, Bernard said, "For some reason, people like McCoy, without really knowing me kept telling me they felt they could trust me. More often than not, I wished that they had not chosen to say that because I hadn't remembered signing any social contract promising that I was more deserving of trust than any other central office administrator. And, their need to say this gave me the feeling that my new situation was populated with untrustworthy sorts. Those that hired me were likely perceived as such by the majority of the workforce at Arcadia."

McCoy came into my office, his arms slightly open and palms facing me, like when an actor, having finished a monologue, cues the audience to give him applause. His gesture reminded me of a farmer giving up on his crops or a saint giving a blessing. Because of this, it was impossible to shake his hand. After he sat down, I outlined all of the concerns that had been brought to my attention and told him how important it was that he began to address them immediately. I explained it all in painstaking detail and gave him a copy of what needed to be demonstrated and by when and reassured him it was possible that he could succeed at meeting the long list of required improvements by the given deadlines. He spoke of the parallelism between the hardships of teaching and water-skiing.

McCoy thanked me for taking the time to explain it and told me how I had put him at ease. Before he could say, "I feel I can trust you Keith," again, I had offered him a cup of coffee. I guess the offer of a cup of coffee and the willingness to listen, even as I disagreed with his rendition of the facts gave him some solace. And, as he left, he raised his hand that didn't have the paper coffee cup in it and gave me a big thumbs up, and then as if trying to show respect on some level, he raised that same hand to his brow in a sort of salute, but leaning to the side as if to make it funny, which for some reason made me feel very awkward.

Two weeks later, I issued McCoy a "Notice of Intensive Supervision," which even more abruptly outlined the numerous deficiencies in his teaching and general school-related conduct and tried to make it pointedly clear what was required to retain his job: "demonstrate considerable improvement." There were so many areas for him to have to demonstrate considerable improvement in—in a timely manner—that one might suggest that I had given him an impossible task. To be frank, no pun intended, I'm not sure that I believed that McCoy could succeed at this, ever.

I had numerous school visits and meetings with Garnier over the next month where I reviewed his documentation of McCoy's lack of teaching proficiency and non-improvement and the escalating deterioration of his relationships with both students and parents.

"Is it okay if I go in a slightly different direction?" Bernard asked Lee. Hoping that everyone might see the connection he was trying to draw between two imaginary points he added, "While this was going on some of those other staffing hotspots began to boil over. Is okay if I take a detour here?"

Lee nodded affirmatively.

During all of this, I discovered that John Lalande had not been forthright about a simmering personnel issue between Noelle Chabanel and himself. Chabanel, I also discovered had for some time been suffering from Lupus and her health was in a bit of a free-fall.

Employers are required by law to reasonably accommodate the special needs of individuals where these needs stem from the kinds of group factors associated with and outlined in many human rights codes. Such things as disability, religion, and gender are privileged grounds under which individuals may seek to have a reasonable accommodation conferred upon them. Failure to make reasonable accommodations is a form of discrimination prohibited by law unless an employer can prove that the accommodation would create an undue—and undue is a critical term here—hardship for business operations. The onus is on the employer and not the employee to show that reasonable efforts at accommodation have been made before simply claiming that it creates an undue hardship. The basis of all of this is that the accommodation helps to give capable people who do not fit a particular "norm" a fair chance to succeed personally and professionally, to contribute within their profession and to contribute to society as a whole. Accommodations are intended to prevent a disability from becoming a determining factor in the assessment of a person's knowledge, skill or capability to perform a job. Accommodations are individualized, as the severity of disability varies among groups, and each person responds to and succeeds differently with a given disability. Each situation is unique and must be assessed individually.

The concept of a "duty to accommodate" refers to the obligation we have, as an employer, to take steps to facilitate the employee's ability to be a participating, productive member of the staff. It is a right conferred by the "Canadian Charter of Rights and Freedoms," which has been upheld by numerous court decisions, and since then one that has come to be accepted as a fundamental right of humanness.

Desi popped her head through the door opening about ten minutes before Chabanel showed up at my office to remind me that I had agreed to this meeting two weeks prior. I had written down Chabanel's name and the time in my agenda, but for the life of me could not remember why I had agreed to meet with her.

"Remind me, if you will Ms. Giroux, why the heck I am meeting with Noelle Chabanel?"

Desi told me that Noelle was a 10-year teaching veteran suffering from Lupus with aperiodic symptoms. According to Desi, Chabanel was considered a marginal teacher by the principals she had worked for even prior to her diagnosis, but as her health worsened she was even less effective. But, as Desi pointed out none of that mattered because there was no documentation to support any of those allegations of mediocrity. As Desi finished, she left me Chabanel's personnel file, and the only evaluative documentation was her initial summative evaluation, which noted she was a very good beginning teacher. However, her file also contained her applications for a number of professional development initiatives and projects. There was the application to become some kind of a consultant, which would be funded by a multi-national telecommunications conglomerate, and then there was another lengthy application to work with the local college's teacher preparation program as a "Knowledge Consultant," and accompanying this application was a glowing principal's recommendation attesting to just how good Chabanel was signed by none other than Senan Welsh – the same man who signed Lukno's evaluation recommending he be offered a continuing contract based on a subpar assessment.

I later found out that many of the principals in the district, with Frank's support, had appropriated the unfounded notion that if they wrote glowing recommendations for staff that they wanted to wish away, perhaps the lemons might catch on with another outfit, a partner organization, that would effectively get them out of the classroom and find them a new calling. Many of them believed this was the most appropriate way to deal with marginal teachers: write them strong letters of recommendation, which might sit in their personnel files, and tolerate the deficiencies with the faint hope that the teachers might get other offers and leave the district, or even teaching, altogether.

Just before the appointment, Desi knocked three times on my already open door and added quietly, "Oh, I probably should tell you that she thinks John Lalande, her current principal, is out to get her."

"Is he," I asked, "you know, out to get her?"

Before Desi could answer, I noticed a woman had arrived outside of her office door. The woman seemed a little anxious and was fidgety.

As Desi turned to walk away from my door, she mouthed the word "yes."

From what I knew about it, Lupus is a disability often characterized by a pattern of exacerbation and remission. The symptoms vary and range from being mild to much more severe. I knew that Lupus was one of those disabilities that many people have difficulty understanding because the symptoms are often not "observable." I also knew that it could be exacerbated by stress.

When I met Chabanel, I was most surprised by her nervous demeanour. As she took a moment to choose where to put her bag and where to sit, I wondered if her nervousness was related to her ongoing physical issues, or a reaction to me. As I watched her flutter about my office I wondered how much accommodation we had been making for her and what she might require in the future.

I remember thinking that Chabanel's behaviour reminded me of a librarian I supervised who had once been caught embezzling late book fines, but I knew that it was unfair of me to see her posture and gestures as evidence of some unknown guilt. She was reluctant to take off her coat when I offered to hang it up and seemed to keep looking over her shoulder from time to time as we spoke. It was as if she was prepared to run out of the room if things became uncomfortable.

She explained that as of the time of our meeting, she was assigned to a full-time equivalent teaching position, which in educational jargon meant she had the equivalent of a full time job but in reality her position was shared between two schools, which were located five miles apart. One half of her job was as a half-time kindergarten teacher at the Somme School, which was where she had done her student-teaching, teaching at a grade level that she had been trained for and where she loved to be. Chabanel told me how she and the school's principal, Katie Tekawitha, worked so well together and understood each other. "We're on the same page," she blissfully stated. She went on for some time about how much she loved the little kids in kindergarten and first grade.

But, her eyes sank back a little in their sockets as she explained that the other half of her job was teaching middle years at the newly constructed arts elementary school. She had been assigned, in part, to teach physical education to grades 5 and 6, and told me emphatically that it was an assignment for which she had no formal training. The principal of this school, Mr. John Lalande, she explained, hated her. She had no idea why he did, "but make no mistake," she told me, "He absolutely hates me, and there's nothing I've done to him to warrant this treatment."

She shook her head from side to side and spoke with intensity. "This just isn't good. This isn't a good situation. With my Lupus and all, I think I am being put at risk. I have never made my disability an issue, but the travelling and this assignment, well it just isn't good. Plus the stress of having to work for John is unbearable. I'm not sure what I did to deserve this assignment, but I'm hoping that next year I can have a transfer." With this, Chabanel looked me straight in the eyes, leaned forward and slid a sealed envelope across the round table.

She kept looking at it with a mildly horrified expression, the kind you have when you didn't mean to kill some bug but inadvertently find you did. "It's my formal request for a transfer to a single school and out of Salient Technology Academy. I just can't take it any more. It isn't in the letter I wrote to you, but I would really like to be assigned to The Somme School because I think I can do a better job there, and I do have a lot of friends there." Then she repeated herself, "Katie and I are on the same page, you know."

I took quite a few notes as I listened and then told Chabanel that I couldn't promise anything to her but that I would see what might work out for next year. I do remember telling her that, unfortunately, having friends at the Somme and "being on the same page," would not be factors in deciding where to assign her or anyone for that matter when it came time to deal with all of the teacher transfer requests.

Over the next few months, a pattern emerged: Chabanel would call every month, always in the first week, to ask how I was doing with the transfers. Each time, I reminded her that I would be doing nothing with the transfer requests until May, since the deadline for making requests was the end of April. And until that time, I was not prepared to deal with them one at a time.

Not long after the meeting with Chabanel, I called John Lalande to find out what was going on. I am quite sure before I called him, I relayed Chabanel's story to Desi and asked her what was up. She told me it was quite possible that John Lalande was out to get Noelle, adding, "John Lalande is a first-rate ass."

Remembering his initial response back in January to my queries about why Chabanel's name appeared on Frank's list of "Staffing Hotspots," I telephoned Lalande, the man declared by the objective Desi Giroux as an "ass." I began our conversation simply by asking him what he could tell me about Noelle Chabanel as a teacher and any issues that he may have with her teaching. I told him that I had just had a meeting with her.

"Well Keith, let me say that I don't have any personal issues with her. I get along with everybody. It is just part of my nature to get along with people. But, I have to be honest with you; she's just not very good. I won't get into it, but trust me; she just isn't a very good teacher. I have tried to make things work for her, but she is unwilling to take suggestions. You know we have a terrific staff here, and we all work well together. But, she just doesn't work well with the other teacher. Other than Noelle, we all get along!"

He seemed to be emphasizing that last comment.

He went on, "She just doesn't fit. I'm not sure why Frank assigned her here. I think maybe he just didn't know what to do with her, so he stuck her here. Don't get me wrong, I'm not angry with him, I got along with Frank exceptionally well. But I think he made someone else's problem into my problem. And I have been doing all that I can to help the district with this, but maybe there is nothing more I can do with her."

Lalande had speech mannerisms, over the phone and in person that communicated condescension and sympathy simultaneously. When he spoke, he had an air that conveyed how very wise and learned he must think he is and how lucky he felt you were to be graced with his knowledge. But, in his tone he also seemed to express sympathy for your ignorance. I kind of liked the way he spoke to me, but I could see how it may bother other people, people who actually cared if they were being patronized. Lalande also added that he wanted Chabanel to be transferred to another school, if that was her wish. But, if she were left there at his school, he could find a way to work with her or anybody else.

"Cognitive coaching," he spat out. "I suppose if the district were able to fund me to attend an advanced cognitive coaching seminar, I might be able to do more with Mrs. Chabanel." Then, I thought I heard him mutter something about the district sending him to take a professional development session in Belize, but I couldn't quite make out what he said.

I asked Lalande if he had ever done a formal evaluation of Mrs. Chabanel. He paused to think, and then said "no." Perhaps that was a bit of an oversight on his part, he explained, but only because of how busy he was with a rather demanding and politically astute parental community. Over the next six months, he never had time to do a performance review of Chabanel; just too many important needs that had to be addressed, he would say.

It was becoming painfully obvious that Chabanel was lacking in any real support from Lalande, and was having tremendous personal and professional conflict with him. He was, in her words, over the phone one day, "Out to get me!" I asked her once if she were serious about this accusation, because it was a serious claim. She responded by saying that her chronic stress and concern had been abating since she had come to see me for that earlier meeting, and maybe she didn't want to really go on record about his being 'out to get her.' Regardless, she still wanted a transfer.

By the end of February, I called her union representative, the teachers' union of which both she and Lalande were members, and discovered that the year before I arrived she had asked the union to file a formal grievance with the district on her behalf over what she believed was an issue of work-related harassment.

Chabanel alleged that Lalande had phoned her numerous evenings at home to discuss her litany of teaching inadequacies and that during the phone calls, he proceeded to rant and rail as if completely unnerved. But, she said he also asked her to meet him in some motel lounge to discuss some pedagogical matters.

She mentioned to the union representative that Lalande seemed irrational and was hard to follow in conversation, and that—off the record—she thought Lalande might have been inebriated when he made some of the calls.

According to Christina Urbain, the union representative I spoke with, the union did not file a grievance. They viewed the issue as a conflict between two professionals who could work it out. But Urbain did informally request, through a phone call to Frank, that the district make Chabanel's transfer to a single school under the supervision of another principal a priority. "Anybody but John Lalande," Urbain requested. From what she told me, Frank's response at the time was that the district might do something; but that all transfer requests are handled "in the best interests of students and learning." Plus, she said, Frank suggested that perhaps the "new guy" might be better able to get to the bottom of this and deal with it once and for all.

Urbain didn't need to tell me what that meant. It was the evasive administrative non-response and pass-the-buck ploy which, in layman's terms, meant "If I get around to it, I will think about dealing with this personnel problem, but if I'm not that interested in working hard, then I'll let it be someone else's problem, the new guy's problem."

Sadly, this was not just a festering personnel headache. It was also an ethical challenge to do the right thing in each case—a challenge that Frank had simply tried to avoid. What were left were at least two employees stuck in long-term limbo, and the creation of multiple, escalating messes for me to clean up. That Chabanel's name and not Lalande's was on the hotspot list was already a set-up, implying a preferential status for the principal, not really based on any evidence of his deserving it.

Ethicists, in very broad terms, describe two opposing approaches to such ethical personnel questions. One approach is ethical relativism, which notes that a person or an organization defines what is right. There are no absolutes, no rights or wrongs. Under ethical relativism, personnel managers can establish and follow local practices, provided they are legal, regarding the treatment of employees, even if these practices might be entirely unacceptable in other organizations. A teacher or an administrator could then define on his or her own terms, exactly what constitutes a toxic work environment or irreparable relationship, and everything would have to shift around that working definition. The opposite position is called ethical absolutism. This is the view that there is a single set of universal ethical principles, even in personnel management, which apply at all times in all circumstances in all organizations. The problem with this view is specifying what the universal principles are and developing a case for these principles being used universally. Two such universal principals, the one that says teachers should just be happy and thankful wherever they are working, and the other that says administrators are obligated to work with any teacher no matter what, were not working for either Chabanel or Lalande.

Bernard paused and asked, "Do you see what I am getting at?" Not waiting for an answer he just added, "It's all connected, the firing, the hiring, and what happens in between. It's not like they are discrete parts." Bernard suddenly smelled something good wafting in from the next room and privately hoped they might have a box lunch or something for him.

"It's been a long morning Dr. Bernard," Lee added. "We appreciate your willingness to make yourself available for this deposition. I'm sure it will be useful to the arbitration panel. How about we call it a day and reconvene back here tomorrow morning at nine o'clock? I think we might be able to finish this off by the end of the day tomorrow. I think we're moving along, doing really well."

Bernard glanced up at the clock. It was twenty-five minutes after twelve. It seemed early to "call it a day," and this certainly meant he'd have to fend for lunch. However, maybe this was partly why Lee had described the deposition as being "easy" earlier. Maybe a lawyer's day was shorter than a typical business day, Bernard thought. In either case, Bernard had started the day with a sense of dread; the whole process had dredged up some fears and memories of family and work that went deep. As hungry as he was, when he opened the extremely thick glass office door and walked into the muggy and bright day, he felt some satisfaction in getting parts of the tale of Arcadia School District #66 off of his chest. Returning to the hotel he read a little and was relieved to catch up on some much needed sleep.

FIVE

The next day, Bernard was shown to the firm's boardroom, as indicated by a gold embossed nameplate on the door: "BOARDROOM." When he entered, a professionally dressed woman about his age immediately greeted him by the doorway and introduced herself as Kimberly Marie, a Partner with Harper and Fowler.

She explained, "We had a debriefing yesterday afternoon after your initial discovery deposition with Mr. Lee. I read over the transcript. It was interesting, and you certainly covered a lot of, well let's say, terrain. Some of the other partners and I felt it might be more productive if I took the lead on today's part of the deposition." She added in a quieter voice, "It might be a little more focused. I hope you don't mind?"

Bernard shot a glance past her shoulder over to Lee, who was talking in a subdued way to a few people Bernard did not recognize. Before Bernard could respond, she added, "By the way, I have invited some of our articling students to sit in today. Hopefully you don't mind that either? You are, after all, a former educator, a teacher, correct?" Bernard wryly wondered if what professors do at universities was not called teaching, in some legal sense of the word. But then realized this was indeed all about his past, and there would be no need for her to know his current job. He could be making pizzas, for all she knew. "And I'm sure you can appreciate the value of these students learning from your experiences," she continued. "I haven't met a teacher yet who doesn't believe that experience is the best teacher."

Bernard looked around the room and noticed Wilson Lee, Peter Hart, and three other young faces looking at him. Not quite sure if it was an educational experience he was offering or a spectacle, Bernard was at least content to see the stenographer again. Bernard smiled at her and then over to Marie and as he fixed his chair to get comfortable he said he was okay with the students in the room.

"Dr. Bernard," Marie began, "do you consider yourself to be an authority in either human resources management or educational leadership?"

Bernard was caught a little off guard with the sharp question and her tone but replied, "Since it's a little arrogant to claim to be an authority, can I just say that I have a certain level of specific experience and knowledge about dealing with personnel matters in schools, and am generally seen as a reliable advisor in these areas?" His wife had often kicked him under the table at important business functions for his responses which she found to be "too self-deprecating, unnecessarily humble and probably barriers to promotion." She was probably right. But he wasn't about to fall into some trap set by Marie.

Not looking unsatisfied, Ms. Marie replied, "I suppose so." Then she added, "Based on your expertise, can you continue to explain how employee terminations were handled at Arcadia School District picking up from where you left off yesterday afternoon?"

"As I pointed out, I'm not claiming to be an expert at anything. But, if you are asking me, based on my background, to offer an opinion, to relay my story, I can do that. Is that what you want?" He felt he had triumphed on this small point, and caught a little smile from Mr. Lee for the first time that morning.

Kimberley Marie simply said, "Fine, go ahead."

By early March, it became evident that no significant improvement had been made in any of the categories laid out for Mr. McCoy, and I felt confident enough to call Easton McCoy's teachers' union representative, J. D. Brebeuf, to inform him that I would be recommending to Chuck that McCoy's teaching contract be terminated by the end of the school year. After the initial and expected procedural outrage that a union representative needs to demonstrate, Brebeuf told me he would speak to McCoy and get his side of the story. Brebeuf warned me that I was picking a fight with a powerful labour group, "tens of thousands strong," he said, who did not take kindly to vengeful central-office administrators kicking around the powerless teachers. I decided to forego mentioning the contradiction between powerful labour unions and the powerless teachers because I was convinced he wasn't the one to have that conversation with.

I was keenly aware of the long, drawn-out process that would have to be embarked on once a teacher termination case was initiated. I knew that many people had given up on the idea that bad teachers could ever be fired. But with enough firings under my belt, I felt comfortable walking that long, hard road —even if it meant going it alone. Whether my employer, past and present, saw me as courageous or foolhardy, they all seemed content to let me be a lone sheriff who was called in to clean up the town, so to speak, and rid the schools of particularly bad teachers.

"Would you like me to fax over copies of all of the materials in Easton McCoy's personnel file?" I asked Brebeuf. "It's about 45 pages of documented performance issues, all of which Mr. McCoy has been made aware of. You also need to know that in each instance when we met I advised McCoy personally and subsequently had it repeated by the school principal that he could have a union representative present with him during the meetings. In each meeting, McCoy was given a clear indication of what he needed to improve, a timeline for improvement and offers of support. I don't mind sending it all over to you. I followed up each meeting with a letter outlining our discussions, so there is a lot of paper. However, you may want to let your receptionist know that you have a lengthy fax coming."

I could hear Brebeuf grumbling on the other end of the phone, "45 pages, well fine, fax it all over. But we aren't done yet, just so you know!"

I had Desi send the fax at the very end of the business day.

In the midst of trying to deal with McCoy, I received a telephone message from a teacher named Pete Claver. He explained in his message how he was currently employed part-time with the district and that he needed to speak to me privately about a personal issue. Claver informed me how on January 31st, five years earlier, after 25 years of impeccable service in Arcadia School District, he had retired from his position as Science teacher at a high school only to be rehired on a permanent, part-time contract by the district 24 hours later to teach the same Science subjects at the same school in the same grades. One day of unemployment was all that was required to meet the legal minimum of the bona fide separation clause in the province's pension regulations, he explained. But now, Claver had an urgent and private matter that needed to be addressed right away.

Marie cut Bernard off, "Does this have anything to do with terminations?"

"Trust me, it's related," Bernard said.

Looking skeptical and uncertain of Bernard's trustworthiness, Marie replied, "Go on then, Dr. Bernard."

Later, I found out that this was an example of Frank's preferential rehiring of the recently retired teachers. This process had allowed Claver to join a select group of school district employees, known unofficially as "The Friends of Frank," who collected both their pensions and a salary, albeit a part-time salary and one without employer-paid benefit premiums. This is a practice known as "double dipping." Frank, of course, was a master of padding things out in an absolutely legal way.

The pension rules for retired teachers in many jurisdictions follow the provisions that allow retired employees to return to employment with their former employers so long as they are unemployed for at least one day and their post-retirement employment income does not exceed a set percentage established by the retirement fund's administrators and as sometimes codified by legislation.

Keep doing a fraction of the same job with an equal fraction of the salary and collect a full pension. The so-called retire-rehire shuffle is a win-win solution, if your name is Pete Claver. Curse Steven Covey, the author of "The 7 Habits of Highly Effective People," for convincing people that the perfect end to every problem can be resolved with a win-win solution; never mind that Covey never admits that some people are winning bigger than others.

Claver drew his earned pension cheque, along with a salary, and in return, the school district got an experienced teacher with no employer health benefit premiums. On the surface, it seems that both Claver and the district were winners. Of course this comfortable arrangement relied on the presumption that Claver was an effective teacher, which might have been the case but couldn't be confirmed since the only performance appraisal in his personnel file was 30 years old and had, literally, become quite yellowed with time. But, it was all I had to go on and anyway, back then the principal of the day did write that Claver: "Dressed appropriately;" "Arrived at work on time;" and "Genuinely seems to like kids."

But to me, the whole practice of double dipping reeked of favouritism and put new teachers—who are trying to gain classroom experience to launch their careers—at a disadvantage. These new teachers, who truly lack proven experience, had the potential to bring new approaches into the classroom, which is good for educational renewal. Nevertheless, the most obvious problem with the arrangement was that these "double-dippers" were Frank's friends, friends who were not only offered, but also counselled by Frank, to retire with the promise of being rehired after one day of unemployment.

Of course, when I asked Chuck about the practice, he protested that Frank had done all of this behind his back. "If I had known, I would have stopped it immediately!"

"I can't stand that Frank did that," Chuck would roar in a low growl, grinding his back teeth. "It has to stop. Don't let it go on any more. I don't want to see that crap. It's not how we do business. And see what you can do to get rid of those freeloaders, especially that Claver fellow. He's a real pain in the ass. If I had known about all of this, I would have certainly put a stop to it! We have to be moral exemplars," he continued. "Examples of ethical leadership," he spat out, "And the Claver deal stinks!"

Wanting to understand the history, the frequency of this practice and how far back the practice went before I phoned Claver, I checked Arcadia's "Monthly Board Meeting's Minutes," from the previous five years, a period pretty much dating back to the beginning of Chuck's tenure with Arcadia. I was amazed, though I probably shouldn't have been, to find out that he, not Frank, had sought and was given the Board's approval for the retiring-rehiring of eight teachers, all friends of Frank's, including Claver. It was Chuck who had drafted and presented the "Early Retirement Incentive Plan," to the Board for approval and gave Frank's friends the lovely golden parachutes to soften their retirement landing.

That afternoon, when I came over to Desi's desk and said "Eight retire-rehires?" she didn't even have to look up from her computer to offer, "Yup, the 'Friends of Frank.'" As I sat alone in my office, I smiled a pained smile and I thought maybe 'Chums of Chuck' would be a more apt description. Would these retired-for-one-day teachers add to the growing list of "staffing hot spots" in this position of mine that was feeling more and more like pages from Dante's inferno?

Finally, when I called Claver, about three weeks after he left the first message and about two weeks after he left a second and a third message, I found out that he was upset about having to pay one hundred percent of his extended health benefit premiums even though, as a retiree, he was required to pay them. In fact, he had signed a contract that clearly indicated that the employer share of premiums would not be part of his employment contract.

I guess it hadn't been an issue when he first retired, he told me. Back then he was healthy, but now, well now things were different. He was getting older and his prescription medications were getting expensive.

Claver suggested that it was a moral and ethical obligation for the district to pay for his benefit premiums just like they did for all of the non-retired teachers covered under the collective agreement. I wondered if he might want to have a tête-à-tête with Chuck about morality and ethics? I held the thought.

Normative moral relativists generally insist that there is no universal moral standard by which to judge others. In essence, they suggest that we ought to tolerate the behaviour of others even when it runs counter to our own moral standards because it's unfair to impose culturally biased norms on others. Local norms and standards—rather than broad-sweeping mores—should be the standards for right or wrong. Local context matters to them an awful lot.

Instead of asking Claver if he wanted me to schedule a time for him and Chuck to sit down, I asked if he was serious in his request. He seemed surprised by my question.

"Yes," he said, "I certainly am serious."

I told him that I didn't think it would fly with the Superintendent who seemed to have a different sense of what constituted moral and ethical behaviour. And, by the way, the request he was making would be a clear violation of the pension rules and, thus, illegal.

He waited a few seconds and then asked if I could consider making a special arrangement with him, just between him and me, to cover his health benefit premiums? "Could I, like good old Frank did, make some room for his unique case and create a special arrangement with him, a long-time, loyal and deserving employee?" He asked. There must be some pool of money available, somewhere, in an undedicated budget line that could be directed to his needs.

As I had just done a minute before, I asked him if he was serious about his request. This time he didn't respond. At that moment, he must have realized that he was a word away from having his verbal request committed to record. After a moment of silence, I heard a big exhale over the phone, I told him he should feel free to contact the teachers' union about his issues and see if they might be interested in considering this matter during the next round of collective bargaining because I had no interest in moving forward with it.

After another long pause, he responded that he had already contacted the union and that they were disinterested. Apparently the retire-rehire shuffle didn't play well with general union membership who almost unanimously felt that bringing new members into the union by virtue of recent-grad hires was a good thing. Plus since his retirement, he no longer paid union dues and was not part of the union. They wouldn't—and couldn't—take on his fight.

I told Claver to have a good day and as I hung up the telephone I smiled a little. No, I think I smiled a lot. As far as I was concerned, it was a pretty good day, if your name was Keith Bernard. It was satisfying to feel this sense of a clean and clear resolve on any of the issues facing my office. I enjoyed, for a few moments, the feeling that justice was served at Arcadia Consolidated School District No. 66.

Lee, Hart and the three students in the room, who up to this moment had been pretty quiet, felt that this was a natural time for a talking break. As if Bernard had just finished saying, "and they lived happily ever after," the students squirmed around and began chit chatting.

Marie threw them a sharp look and indicated to Bernard with a nod that it wouldn't happen again. "Dr. Bernard, can you explain how this relates to McCoy's termination?"

Feeling like someone had just pointed out that his class was off-topic, again, Bernard looked at Marie and explained that the way in which terminations are handled is very much a part of an organization's overall approach to personnel management, and very messy business. It is the fabric of how the organization deals with its people.

"None of the parts exist in isolation—none," he added.

Realizing that Marie might have taken offense at being taught in front of the students, he Bernard said, "How about I just go back to Easton McCoy?"

When I had finished talking with McCoy's union representative, J.D. Brebeuf, back in February, I knew we weren't done. By mid-March, via a phone call to Brebeuf, Easton McCoy was offered a binding, structured separation agreement, which provided four months' salary in lieu of working notice, about two week's pay for each and every year he had been employed by the district, and a letter of reference from me stating when he began his tenure with the district, what subjects he had taught in what grades, and stating that he tendered his resignation for personal reasons, if he willingly resigned his teaching position, immediately.

It took McCoy about 18 hours before he accepted the offer. I wasn't sure if he had been advised to wait before replying or if he had simply forgotten to call me back. But, when he did call, he earnestly thanked me for all the time I had devoted to this awful period in his life and all of the support I had given him. McCoy then went on a little while about how he wanted to start over, you know, have a chance to re-create himself professionally.

80

I listened and then asked if he wanted me to fax the structured separation agreement to him at school or have it sent to some other more private fax number. He told me to send it to the school, as he would go right there and stand beside the fax machine, sign it and fax it back immediately.

I said "goodbye" to McCoy and wished him well. Not wanting to give him any time to change his mind, I walked very quickly to the fax machine, placed the sheets on it and hit send.

By Friday, after almost eight years of tenure with Arcadia School District, McCoy was no longer an employee. With that, his personnel file was moved from the "Active Employees" to the "Past Employees" drawer in the large steel cabinet. Sometime later that Friday afternoon, Charles Garnier called me and thanked me for all of my help and told me, "I owe you one." At the time, I just let go of being owed anything; this was after all a part of my job.

About three months later, around the middle of May, Garnier phoned me and began the conversation with, "Keith, I think I have another problem that I need your help with." Before I could get a word in to even ask why he was calling, Garnier continued to speak. "I have this teacher …" and I knew then that I had mistaken Garnier's sentimental "being owed" for "being owned."

Looking smug Marie said, "You have made some critical statements about how things were done at Arcadia. Given your expertise, do you have any insight on how it got to be so bad?"

Not wanting to fall into what he thought was a trap, Bernard simply replied, "To be honest, I have no idea how it got to be so bad." As Marie looked triumphantly around at the students in the room, having stumped the teacher with a clever question, Bernard recalled in his mind an incident that demonstrated just how bad things had become.

After a few months on the job working with principals to refine their hiring practices, I came to expect "the look". Astonishment. Confusion. Shock. I saw it all flash across their faces as they struggled to comprehend what I was telling them.

"Did you just say that we should cut new teachers loose after just one year if we think they are no good?" asked Simon Templar, principal of Arrass Technical High School. I couldn't tell if he was painfully gritting his teeth as he spoke or flashing me a grin.

"Look," I said, scanning the room of principals and vice-principals, "if you feel—no let me change that—if you know after one full year that this newly minted teacher who was hired on a probationary contract just isn't exceptional, then cut him loose and set him free."

Advice like this always seemed to pain people. Hoping that an analogy might be insightful, I went on to explain about the time when one of my older brothers set my pet hamster free when we were kids. The damn thing took off into the household air vents and disappeared. He thought the hamster loved us enough to do the right thing and return after a short sojourn. A few weeks later, I was sure I heard my mother suck up poor Hammy with the vacuum cleaner and kill it. As she threw the vacuum bag into the trashcan, denying that the "thud" that I had heard was poor Hammy, Mom told me she was certain that Hammy was running free with some pack of wild rodents, doing what rodents do and having a grand old time. I didn't buy that story when she told it to me or believe it any more as I hauled the garbage bag to throw it into the curbside dumpster. And, I never owned a hamster again. But, my life moved forward even after that profound loss.

"After you set that marginal teacher free, which is what you should do, just move on and stop worrying whatever came of him," I explained. "If he hasn't proven to you in that first year that he is an exceptional beginning teacher, someone you just cannot do without, then why in the world would you keep him around?"

"Don't you think that is kind of harsh, Keith?" asked Templar. "I mean, come on, if it's only his first year and he is just beginning, doesn't that sound, well, just unrealistic? What if, with some coaching and support, I can get that teacher to improve and be pretty good? Then what? We all know that a teacher can get better if he is given time and support. Don't we owe these novices that at least, to be a professional and supportive colleague?"

I replied, "And, while you spend time and energy supporting the teacher, the kids in his class suffer from his lack of competency and don't learn a darn thing, or much of anything. Is that what you are willing to sacrifice in exchange for the odd chance that he will get better?"

I caught my breath and swallowed, "In reality, you don't owe him anything but a chance to show that he can be exceptional. You offered him that chance in good faith and gave him a year and a salary to prove that he was good enough to keep his job. You provided support and guidance, didn't you? If what you have seen and experienced tells you that this new teacher is not extraordinary then what is the best course of action? After a year of proving that he hasn't improved, you should thank him for the year of service and send the teacher packing. Free him from the shackles of his contract and let him go try teaching somewhere else." I knew I was losing them by the end of this, but found myself engaged in the monologue.

"You have to get past your own need to save poorly performing teachers. Okay, let me rephrase that. By all means you should support and nurture your professional colleagues, at least the ones with continuous contracts since they are, presumably, here to stay for the long haul. But the probationary teachers, the new ones, to whom we owe nothing but an opportunity, well they need to prove to you, to me and to the public that they are worth a twenty-five-year commitment that will cost taxpayers over one million dollars. Think of it like dating."

I suddenly noticed that all of the principals were listening.

"I'll presume that some of you are married, while others might be in various stages of committed relationships. And, I guess some of you might even be just alone. I guess you lonely ones can ignore me again."

No one laughed.

"But, hopefully most of you dated a variety of people for various amounts of time before you made a serious commitment and you didn't just settle for the first person who showed up at your door."

"With a bit of luck you carefully pre-screened your prospective dates, tried some out on actual dates and only then stayed with the ones you thought might be an exceptional partner in the long run."

What I didn't admit was that that wasn't exactly how I dated. I had dated anyone who said "yes," and had considered it a bonus if she offered to pay for dinner or lunch. There was no rational process involved. Nevertheless, I thought my analogy was good.

Bernard scanned the faces around the boardroom and said, "You're all pretty young, and hopefully you won't commit to be with someone for your mortal life who had the potential to be only pretty good as a life-mate. I hope you do try out different people for compatibility and then choose judiciously, kicking to the curb the people who are just not cut out for the job as your destined partner."

He looked over to Kimberley Marie and asked, "Don't you agree?"

She remained stoically silent.

Bernard continued, "I'll hope you don't commit to a long-term relationship with someone thinking: Well, our first year together was complete misery, but I'm pretty confident with enough in-servicing, professional development and coaching that I can remediate all of his deficiencies and make him a better version of himself. Hopefully, you will be content with your partner as-is and don't plan to masterfully fix him or her."

Bernard stopped for a moment and raised his glass of water for a drink and noticed the nodding faces in the room, a couple of resigned looking shoulder shrugs, but a bit of enjoyment on their faces over this analogy. With the high rate of attrition for first-year law students, Bernard thought they would be the perfect group to understand his point, except he detected that Ms. Marie seemed a little annoyed.

Bernard looked over at the stenographer who smiled back and seemed to give him a wink of the eye.

Bernard went on.

"The bottom line is that, too often, weak probationary teachers are given continuous contracts by principals who think they can save them. A great many principals need to stop doing that and get over their need to heal the broken, ineffective adults who arrive at their schools' doors wanting a permanent contract."

When I gave this recommendation to the principals and vice-principals, I was aware that it sounded harsh. I quickly added, "You're there to ensure that children are cared for, safe, and taught well. Make that your priority and mission. Otherwise, we end up with a teacher who was marginally competent, at best, at the beginning of his career and perhaps only stays hovering around the margin of competency throughout his career.

And, then one day you come to me and say: 'You know Keith, I am having a problem with Mr. Numbnuts, and I think we might need to put him under an "Intensive Supervision" evaluation cycle. He really just isn't that good.'

"Then you tell me you have tried everything you know, but after exhausting yourself and some colleagues who tried to mentor him, he just isn't getting better, or even worse, he has become, mysteriously, less competent than he was when he arrived. And I look at you, shake my head in disbelief, remind you that you—or one of your esteemed principal colleagues around this table—hired him and recommended him for a continuous contract and then ask: What in the world ever made you think Numbnuts was ever going to be any good?

"You will inevitably shrug your shoulders, try very hard not to make eye contact with me, ask me about my deaf parakeet and then after an uncomfortable silence, you will tell me that you thought Numbnuts would get better if you helped him along. After I shake my head in utter disappointment, then we—you and I—end up having to commit an inordinate amount of time and energy to getting rid of a teacher who was never that good from the outset. In frustration, I turn to you one day and say: It's like the worst kind of torture, you know, what you have done here. It's like death by a thousand cuts, and no one, not even me, deserves to die such an inhumane death."

I didn't bother to explain the reference to them. But, in the book, "Death by a Thousand Cuts," authors Timothy Goupil, Jérôme Bourgon and Gregory Blue explain that in a public square in Beijing in 1904, multiple murderer Wang Weiqin was executed before a crowd of onlookers. He was among the last to suffer the extreme punishment known as lingchi. Called by Western observers "death by a thousand cuts," or "death by slicing," this penalty was reserved for the very worst crimes in imperial China. The phrase, death by a thousand cuts, has been appropriated, some might suggest misappropriated, into the corporate world to illustrate corporate campaigns, which are organized assaults on a company's reputation to erode public and shareholder confidence by some interest group that it has offended.

Even without the reference I'm pretty sure they understood that in personnel management, "death by a thousand cuts" is understood to be the long, slow and tortuous process of getting rid of a poorly performing employee by slowly chipping away at him, thus gradually eroding his confidence in his own ability to do the job. The employer places him under pressure by heightening performance expectations carefully, just beyond his reach and capability. A schedule is set for him to demonstrate considerable improvement, which will be judged subjectively by some supervisor who knows that the goals are almost impossible to attain in the short time given. It is often called "Intensive Supervision" rather than death by a thousand cuts, because through supervision, employers can be seen as being supportive and assisting in remediating the perceived deficiencies. In reality, it is about gathering enough ammunition, sorry, it is called evidence, over a relatively short period of time so that a "Notice of Termination" can be issued. Hence, it is painful on some level for all involved.

It is a highly effective strategy to bluntly remove a poorly performing employee. But, it is also cruel, and like torture, its impact can last well beyond the immediacy of losing that job. It can have devastating unforeseen effects on a person's psyche, not only eroding any confidence he had in his ability to teach but wreaking havoc with his identity as a teacher. Yet, too often, employers use termination to resolve performance issues that were obvious at the outset of the employment relationship, instead of having the wherewithal to simply look at someone across a table and say, "Thanks for coming out for the team, but you are not good enough. I refuse to allow you to spend thirty years building your identity as a teacher only to be told you are not scoring enough points for the team and must be publicly "benched" for good. Good-bye. Best wishes and good luck in your future endeavours."

"Yes," I added before that stunned silence set in, "if a first-year teacher has not proven herself good enough in that first year, Simon, rather than having her, or me, suffer death by a thousand cuts, please recommend that we don't renew her contract."

Bernard waited for anyone to say something. But no one said a word and they seemed to look quite puzzled.

"It's all connected," Bernard said. "Terminations at one end of the employment relationship and hiring at the other end. It's never just about pulling the trigger and firing someone. That's just the ending. People often forget there was a beginning and middle to the personnel problem before it comes to the end. If school leaders take the relationship seriously, from the very beginning right through to the end, then often a terribly long and drawn out, messy ending—the traumatic kind that hurts like an ugly divorce—can be avoided."

Marie's neck and cheeks looked red, "Dr. Bernard, you seem to be pressing the point that this is highly subjective and all about personal relationships."

Bernard smiled at her and said, "That's exactly what I am saying."

SIX

"Well, Dr. Bernard since you sound like an expert on relationships, what can you tell us about your relationship with a teacher by the name of Vanessa Vayle?" asked Kimberly Marie.

"I remember her very well," replied Bernard. "But, I am not sure I would call what we had a relationship." Bernard seemed to detect a somewhat disparaging tone in Marie's voice and felt for the first time a real need to be cautious with his words: a need he swiftly forgot as the events regarding Dr. Vanessa Vayle flooded back into his mind.

"Well, that's interesting," said Marie. "What can you tell us about her?"

I had just returned to my office after a day of hefty meetings and was looking forward to sending a few documents to colleagues as follow-through, when I was startled out of my sense of solitude and determined productivity by the sing-song calling out of Desi Giroux with a melodic, "Hey Keith, Vanessa Vayle is here to see you." I looked up to confirm what I had picked up in her tone of voice, and sure enough, there it was: a faint smirk on her face, practiced as to come across as ever the professional, but clearly expressive nonetheless.

"I thought her appointment was at quarter to four? It's not even three o'clock. What is she doing here so early? School isn't even out yet," I quipped back trying not to sound too annoyed or surprised.

"I guess she couldn't wait to see you, Keith," Desi piped back still smiling. She stood with her head leaning in through my office door. Her feet and body were strategically positioned outside the door opening as if she were trying to shield herself from something that might be thrown. She enjoyed seeing me a little bent out of shape.

"Do you want me to have her take a seat and tell her she has to wait until you are ready for her in an hour?" She asked in a manner that was at once sarcastic, warm, patronizing but also pretty hard-hitting. For a moment I thought that maybe she was trying to do an imitation of me. Obviously, she already knew the answer and had left before I had a chance to figure out what to say.

When Vanessa Vayle had phoned to ask if we could set up a meeting so she could explain her "issues," I agreed, but I also remembered asking Vayle if she could give me some insight into what we were going to discuss.

"Oh," she said, "I would rather tell you in person, Dr. Bernard. I think we need some privacy, if that's okay with you? Can I meet you next Tuesday at about three forty-five? It's after school, so that works well for me. I just don't want to talk about it on the phone, so I will come to your office. You understand, don't you?"

"Okay," I said a little perplexed, "see you next week; Tuesday, just before four." And, what I did not say to her but certainly wanted to say was, "No Vanessa, I don't understand what we are meeting about."

After realizing I had few details at my immediate disposal on this person, I called out my office door for backup. "Excuse me, Ms. Giroux but can you come here for a few minutes?" As Desi closed the door behind her, I said, "It seems that I have some questions about a meeting I'm having with someone I know nothing about regarding something I know nothing about."

Desi smiled and explained to me that Vayle had been for a number of years the Science specialist at Flanders Elementary School before the modernization project. Desi was pretty sure that people said that Vayle had a "something like a Doctorate of Philosophy in Ufology", which she had earned quite a while ago. And Desi added that even though Vayle insisted she be referred to as Dr. Vayle, no one ever did since she wasn't a real doctor. Then Desi looked embarrassed as she realized, of course, that I was an unreal doctor too. Her left ear was right next to the nameplate on the door of my office: "Dr. Keith Bernard: Superintendent of Human Resources." And all she did then was move her eyes to the left and then make a little apologetic shrug and all was well.

Recovering quickly, Desi explained that Vayle had been employed with the school district for about 20 years first as a high school Science teacher for a year or two but was, now, as an elementary school teacher; maybe not the best teacher Desi said, and maybe a little flaky, but all the same, a decent educator.

"High school just wasn't her thing," Desi said. "She had trouble connecting the kids with the mysteries of the cosmos. Go figure," she added with a quirky smile.

Desi continued that Vayle had been experiencing some kind of difficulties ever since Tom Lawrence was assigned as the new principal of Flanders Elementary School. Desi thought that Vayle's problems with Lawrence went back about three years, which was when Flanders Elementary underwent a major modernization project and took on a new focus. The school was equipped with the latest in classroom technology and a significant amount of money was set aside by the school board to support an array of professional-development initiatives for teachers. Lawrence was appointed the principal, and he decided that the school should focus on marketing itself as a "technology accelerated elementary school" that embraced the latest best practices and theories of elementary education. With the support of Mr. Stihl, he advertised the school as a cutting-edge community that focused on the newest understandings of children's development and learning.

Desi said that Lawrence had been given the opportunity with the renovation to make some significant changes in staffing. A number of veteran teachers and teaching assistants were transferred out of Flanders because they did not jibe with Lawrence's new focus and marketing plan.

A mass exodus of people uncomfortable with interactive whiteboards and interactive classroom response systems was soon seen. People were transferred, either voluntary or forced based on Lawrence's recommendations and with the new vacancies to fill he hired a number of new staff. When the dust settled, there had been a visible demographic shift in the staff, to a cohort much younger than the one that had previously been there.

However, for reasons unknown to Desi, Lawrence had not been allowed to force Vayle to move, even though he had requested a transfer for her. For some reason, Frank wouldn't move Vanessa. Desi said she didn't know why, but there must have been a reason. Maybe Vayle and Frank had a special arrangement, she speculated.

As Desi explained it to me, twice a year since the completion of the Flanders' modernization project, Vayle phoned over to set up a meeting with Frank. From what Frank told her, Vayle was sure that Lawrence was trying to push her out of the school. Lawrence was trying to "out-counsel" her by suggesting she take her craft somewhere else. Somewhere she might better "fit in." At first, Frank was generally sympathetic toward her plight, Desi explained. He seemed compassionate toward the injustice of her being pushed out of a job.

For all that though, toward the end of his tenure, Frank seemed to lose patience with Vanessa. In fact he instructed Desi to let Vayle know that he was simply unavailable to meet with her anymore.

"She will be so happy to meet with you Keith," Desi gleefully stated.

"Desi," I said, literally tallying up the complex cases that were starting to cause significant trepidation, "should I be worried about this meeting?"

"You don't need to be afraid. By the way, tell me what you think of her nails," Desi requested as she walked away.

"Hello Dr. Vayle," I said as she entered the office at a high speed. "Thanks for waiting. I'm sorry I had to keep you waiting, but I had a few things to finish before I could meet with you." I didn't dare tell her that I was delving into her personnel file so that I could get a sense of who and what I was dealing with. Desi had brought the file over to my office when she first announced that Vayle was waiting to see me. There was really nothing noteworthy in the file other than yet another outdated résumé, an old teacher evaluation form from her first year of teaching, and a few congratulatory letters from a previous principal thanking her for coordinating an excellent kindergarten graduation ceremony.

"I thought our meeting was set for three forty-five, Dr. Vayle?" I asked as she sat down.

"Yes, it was, but I just decided to come a tad early. I had to see you right away. It couldn't wait any longer. And, you don't need to call me Dr. Vayle. You can just call me Vanessa, please. Is it okay if I call you Keith or do you prefer Dr. Bernard?" she asked.

"Feel free to call me Keith. Since I have no idea what this meeting is about, perhaps you could tell me: is this an open-door or closed-door meeting?" I asked out of courtesy and as a form of litmus testing for what might be coming next by way of disclosure.

An open door usually meant this was probably going to be a rather mild conversation about mundane or somewhat trivial matters. A closed-door meeting could really be about anything at all. I was really hoping for a door-opened kind of afternoon, but wasn't willing to wager on it.

"Oh. I think you should close the door," she said. Then she emphasized it, "Yes, please close the door."

As soon as I sat down, she asked, "I'm not sure if anyone told you about what is going on at Flanders Elementary School with respect to me?"

"Nobody has mentioned anything," I reassured her. "Why don't you tell me your story?"

She looked relieved by my comment.

"Oh, good," she said as she leaned in across the small round table and looked me in the eyes. "I think the principal, Tom Lawrence, is out to get me. I think he wants me fired or transferred. I think he just wants me to disappear."

I tried not to notice her fingernails but was drawn to them as soon as she placed her cupped hands on the table as she spoke. Damn it Desi, I thought, why did you have to mention the fingernails!

Although she was a woman in her 60s, and her hands betrayed to some degree, as hands always seem to do, her age; her nails were startling. They were long, exquisitely manicured and perfectly painted. Each fingernail looked like it was an original work of art adorned with flowers surrounded by studded jewels. They looked as though they had been painted by tiny fairies with even tinier brushes and then lacquered so they shone brilliantly. They perfectly coordinated with her outfit.

Everything about Vanessa Vayle, from her name, to her clothing to her nails, seemed to build a flashy illusion—the type of glitter I imagined in Las Vegas. And I wondered as she looked intently at me across the table if I was about to be drawn into what political science professor, Yehezkel Dror has labeled "fuzzy gambling."

Fuzzy gambling occurs when you find yourself in a high-stakes situation in which the very rules you thought were governing the game change as the activity progresses. Those nails were like a wild card in a game of poker and, obviously, they were part of her hand to play.

I tried to refocus as I calmly asked, "What makes you think Lawrence is out to get you?"

"Well, it's so obvious. Isn't it? I'm not one of them. I'm not one of his harem girls. I'm not young and bouncy and bubbly like all of the other women on staff. They are all so young and pretty and perky. And, it's not just the teachers, but the teacher assistants also. Haven't you noticed?" she asked, fixing intently on me. This seemed to fall into that unspoken category of "man tests" that sometimes get thrown out by some women. If I claim to have not noticed the looks of an attractive woman, I'm suddenly seen either as a liar or aloof. If I admit that I did notice, then I've noticed far too much and must be somewhat of a cad.

I hadn't really thought about it much, but now that she mentioned it, I clearly recalled the staff I had met at Flanders Elementary. I had been invited to meet with the teachers, teaching assistants and administrative assistants and I thought that everyone carried themselves quite well, and dressed a little more fashionably than the staffs at many other schools I had visited. And, yes, they did tend to be on the young side and, well, "perky" when taken together.

"He treats them like they are his groupies. Haven't you noticed how they all just hang on his every word when he speaks? They act like he is a rock-star. I don't think he likes me because I'm old and I just won't worship him like they do. I'm good at what I do, but that isn't enough for him." Then she added, "You know I'm there for the kids. To me it's all about the kids. I'm not there for him. I'm not there to flirt with him or stroke his ego." She was looking at me with a powerful gaze.

"What makes you think he is out to get you?" I asked, trying not to look down at her hands.

"I know he wants me transferred or fired. Hasn't he told you that? Hasn't he called you to say that he needs to get rid of Vanessa because she is too old, too slow, and too stuck in her ways and do not want to Skype guests in to my kindergarten classroom? Hasn't he said that I just won't change? Hasn't he told you that I'm not a team player? No, I'm not interested in playing on his team and wearing that uniform!"

The questions came fast and furious. I was having some difficulty keeping up. But I wondered if the principal might be a very conservative man who wanted the "uniform" of his teachers to be more plain than seemed to be Vayle's natural style.

"Mr. Lawrence has never called me about you," I replied. "And, if he had, I wouldn't entertain the possibility of a transfer unless he had a really good reason. Let me assure you that he hasn't spoken to me about any of this. And, if I've heard you correctly, Lawrence has no reason to want you transferred. And, as for firing you, well that isn't something I am considering."

"Oh, he wants me transferred all right. You know the other women on staff just throw themselves at him. They make fools of themselves the way they carry on with him. He loves it, you know. He loves to act like a grand sheik."

I had met Lawrence a number of times and had never thought of him as the sheik-type. But, admittedly, I had never met a sheik or a harem girl, so I had no point of reference for comparison. It seemed I was on the wrong track thinking maybe Vayle's unusually swept up and amazingly balanced hairdo, shiny clothing and nails were too much for the elementary school principal. No, that was not it.

However, now that Vayle had voiced her concerns, there was no denying that Lawrence's elementary staff was indeed all female and that they had joked and poked at him in a friendly banter throughout my visit. This behaviour, though not outlandish, may have been off-putting to staff not playing along with it. True he was the only male on a staff of

20, but that was not so unusual, the gender imbalance of elementary school teachers was a constant, but calling him a sheik with a harem, well that seemed to be a bit of a stretch.

"When we renovated the school at the end of the year, we had to load up all of our individual teaching supplies into a large semi-trailer to store for the summer," Vayle continued. "I had created a lot of Math teaching resources. I had a lot of things to box up and load. When we had to unload and unpack, well all of those other fit young women arranged to help each other out. But no one called me. No one offered to help Vanessa. They left me to unload and unpack my boxes. I had to arrange my entire classroom by myself. I have so many good resources that it took me two days—two whole days—to unload my things from the truck. Did you know that I had to sleep in that trailer overnight I was so exhausted? I just collapsed and fell asleep right there in that trailer."

I was getting tired listening to her.

"They all coordinated it through Lawrence to help each other out. They left me out. I'm not complaining mind you. I'm not one to complain, but it shows you how they're all out to get me." She then sighed a sad sigh as she fell silent.

I drew my gaze away from her fingernails to mentally summarize this conversation: Dr. Vanessa Vayle had slept in the back of a semi-trailer parked in the school parking lot, surrounded by boxes of teaching resources because the "mean girls" on staff, under the spell of Sheik Lawrence, had conspired to make her life miserable.

I was quite sure I had it correct.

"Oh my gosh Vanessa, that sounds simply horrible. I'd never let anyone run you out of a school. How did you manage to survive that ordeal? Did you say you slept in the back of a semi-trailer?" I tried to ask with a noticeable tone of compassion.

Vanessa just looked at me, shrugged her shoulders and let out another sigh. Thank goodness, I thought, she had understood my sympathetic signal.

"Only by God's good graces," she said, looking toward the heavens.

I hadn't expected such an honest reply and was a little startled. I stammered out, "If you're as good of a teacher as I have heard, then certainly you need not worry about a transfer." And I suddenly knew I meant it wholeheartedly.

She seemed soothed by my words, and might have been, but in reality I had no idea if she was a good teacher or whether or not I might need to transfer her. In reality, the only person who had told me Vayle was a really good teacher was sitting across from me with dazzling Rockette nails that flashed and danced around the table.

"It sounds like it would be unfair to the students at Flanders Elementary School to transfer you simply because you do not fit some image of what a teacher at Flanders should look like. All I care about," I added trying to sound very professional, "is a teacher's competence."

Then she sighed a little whimper, leaned across a little closer to me and whispered, "Thank you. Thank you. You don't know how much that means to me."

She scooted back in her seat. "Those kids are my heart and soul. I'm not married, never have been, I don't have any children of my own. My kids, I like to call them my kids, are my life. Everything I do is because of them. I may be getting a little older, but I still have a lot to offer them. I have an advanced degree in a very specialized branch of Physics. Did you know that? I got it about 25 years ago. I was one of the first women to get one of those. Have you ever seen my Twitter account? Here let me give you my Twitter name!"

She reached into her purse and grabbed a piece of notepaper and quickly wrote down the Twitter account's address and passed the piece of paper to me. "I was the first teacher in the district to have a Twitter account. Did you know that? Parents love it and Tweet me all the time. I've got some great Instagram pictures that I took."

The note and 10 flashing nails surged toward me. I was finding it hard to keep up with Vayle again. She seemed to have gathered a second wind.

"Oh, thank you. Dr. Bernard. God bless you," she said, and then finally she pulled back and settled into her chair looking somewhat satisfied. She flashed a partial smile, pulled her cupped hands toward her and placed them below the tabletop. Then settled back a bit further in her chair and seemed to relax. "Thank you for listening to me."

I couldn't see her fingernails anymore and thought that I wished she hadn't put them away. I had enjoyed watching those little painted scenes dancing around on the table.

When the meeting was finally over, I showed Vayle out and walked her to the exit at the front of the building.

"If you need to see me about something else that comes up, please feel free to call Desiree Giroux to set up an appointment." I knew what I was saying and couldn't believe those words were coming out of my mouth. Trapped in a moment of hospitality toward her fingernails—what a curse to suffer.

Just before leaving, she leaned in uncomfortably close and again said, "Thank you for seeing me and God bless you."

On my way back to the office, I stopped by Desi's office and found her sitting at her desk, typing and sporting a broad smile. "Well Keith, what did you think about her nails?" Desi asked without looking up from her computer screen.

"Incredible," I replied. "I have never seen anything like them. I think they matched her outfit. They are works of art. How long do you think she spends on them?" I sputtered out.

"Oh, I am sure they did take quite a long time to get just right for today. And, by the way, she will be back, you know Keith."

And, as I walked away from Desi's office still thinking about Vayle's fingernails, I called back over to Desi, "Can you get me Tom Lawrence on the phone? I need to speak to him."

"You seemed to have noticed quite a bit about her physical appearance, Dr. Bernard," Marie said. "Is that typical, your recollection of specific parts of women's bodies?'

Bernard was somewhat embarrassed by the question. "I pay attention and notice things that seem out of the ordinary," he said.

"But, you wouldn't characterize your interaction with Dr. Vayle as a relationship," asked Marie.

"A relationship?" replied Bernard. "No."

Then Marie asked, "Are there other things that stand out for you? You know from your time with Arcadia School District? Things that you seem to have a vivid recollection of like Dr. Vayle's nails?" Her tone seemed to hint that she might be looking for something scandalous.

"Well there was that time when a strange DVD arrived in the mail," Bernard said.

Seeming to be intrigued by the potential to discover something untoward, Marie asked, "Can you please tell us about this DVD?"

I had read somewhere that advertising for a job vacancy was really just a form of marketing, and since I was selling, I might as well sell it well. If I remember it correctly, the acronym was AIDA, which stood for: "Attract" them to you; get them "Interested"; have them "Desire" what you are offering; and compel them to "Act".

Maybe it's true that over time consumers become increasingly discerning, but to persuade people to do something, you still need to grab their attention, interest them in how your product or service can help them, and then persuade them to take the action you want them to take, such as applying for a job. So Arcadia crafted really intelligent job ads and made sure the distribution was as wide as we could afford and targeted really diverse populations and great teacher preparation programmes, etc. What I hadn't read about is exactly what to do when you ATWYDRW, that is: Attract Those Who You Don't Really Want.

"Did you get my résumé?" the voice asked on the other end of the telephone?

"Can you remind me who you are," I asked?

"It's Jack, Jack Cantius," the voice replied. "I sent it in for the technology coordinator position you advertised back in March. I just wanted to know if you got it?"

I didn't remember receiving a résumé from Cantius. Honestly, when he called I didn't remember much about any of the applicants, even though there were only about six. Most of them were simply unremarkable.

But, I lied. "Yes, Mr. Cantius we received it. Thanks for considering us as a potential employer, and thanks for taking the time to apply."

Few people want to admit that there are times when a lie, what is often called euphemistically a "little white lie," may actually not be such a bad thing. Think about it and try to answer—honestly answer—a question like, "Hey honey did you shrink my old high school letterman sweater or do you just think I'm starting to get fat?"

It's easier to hang onto the black-and-white thinking that all lies are bad, but contrary to popular belief, and my mother's admonitions, there are times when the rare strategic lie may make one a better person.

"Good, I'm glad it got there. I was a little worried when I sent it. But, you know I thought you might appreciate the fact that I put my whole résumé into a compressed "dvdXsoftResume" format. I sent it in Version10.0, the newest, so that you could view me, rather than simply having you read about me. Did you have to download the application? Did you get to see the avatar I made of myself helping a student upload videos to YouTube? After all, it is a technology job, and you know I actually wanted to show you what I could do for you when you hired me," he laughed a little bit, "I guess that is if you were to hire me."

Okay, right after he said that part about the DVD-whatever résumé rubbish, I knew I wasn't lying anymore. I did remember him and the disaster of Version 10.0

Thank goodness, not for the disaster but for the fact that I remembered who Jack Cantius was because I'm not sure that I really buy that line about lying making anyone a "better" person.

I remembered Mr. Cantius and the nightmare called his DVD-résumé, which had not only paralyzed my computer for three hours but also forced me to call one of our computer technicians back to central office from one of the schools to pry the disc from my computer's optical drive. In his cover letter, which was blue text on an orange background, I know because I had to look at it as it sat there unmoving and uncloseable, jamming up my computer monitor for hours, he alluded to the fact that he had held an odd assortment of jobs that required the use of computers, but then again almost every job today requires the use of computers. There was nothing on it that that showed any professional training in either computer programming, technical support or software development. Although, I think he did mention that he was committed to "life-long learning" and was "self-taught," when is came to computer applications.

Two days later I had to call another technician in to delete the annoying virus that was embedded somewhere on my hard drive. The technician told me it must have come with the application that I had downloaded in an effort to view Cantius.

"Well Mr. Cantius, to tell you the truth, there was a tremendous response to the advertisement. Really, we are somewhat overwhelmed by the volume and quality of applicants. Given that your application is being assessed against a highly competitive field, I'm just not sure what I can tell you at this point. But, thanks for applying. It was a very interesting package. We'll be touch."

Okay, I was back to believing that I was a better person for lying. But only because it saved me from saying what I really wanted to say to Mr. Cantius.

Even after I relayed to Chuck Stihl what had happened with this applicant's underwhelming cover letter and résumé, he still remained impressed or maybe in awe that a person could make a DVD of their CV, and Chuck fought hard to include him in the group of four applicants that were eventually moved forward to the interview process. I felt I was getting an accurate understanding of the warped approach to personnel administration that had been practiced in Arcadia for the past decade and a half. And, in a bizarre way, it was finally starting to make sense. I told Desi that, from that point forward, we would be more diligent and rigourous in our scouring all of the résumés we received in order to pick only the best applicants to interview.

When I finished, Desi admitted, "I always used to do a little 'sorting' for Frank. So what do you look for in an applicant's résumé?"

At first I just took in the fact that Frank, the Superintendent of Human Resources had made Desi think, apparently, that this was a part of her job. I was intrigued to find out what sorting criteria he would have asked that she apply, but held off and began to answer her. "Well, I try to go through them with a fine-toothed comb. I try to know what we're looking for and then go after trying to find those skills and personal attributes."

"That sounds nice, but what do you really mean, Keith?"

"I guess I try not to fall victim to the blasé, mind-numbing, page-turning exercises that are so enticing," I quipped. "I re-read everything in the application. I look at their writing for clarity and legibility and check their spelling. I take a good look at their university grades because the last thing we need are weak students who become dumb teachers. Don't you think? I pay attention to trends in work patterns, inexplicable interruptions or omissions. I try to pick up every bit of information that says something about an applicant's professional story so that I get a sense of the person who submitted the application."

"Ok, what else?" she pressed.

"I look to see if they meet the minimum and preferred qualifications of the job, of course. However, since language skills are important for teachers, I don't even look twice at résumés that include grossly misspelled words, bad spacing and inconsistent fonts. I just pitch them! If I think they are exaggerating their educational qualifications or padding their work history, they're pretty much out."

Unsure why she was being so persistent with her questions, I asked Desi what Frank used to do. What did he say they should be looking for in prospective employees?

"Well, when we got résumés—and sometimes we didn't get any—we would quickly look at them to make sure they had teacher certification and an appropriate degree, and then Frank would have me call some applicants into the office. If they seemed good, we hired them on the spot. Sometimes Frank said he had this feeling, a gut feeling about someone. Frank said he couldn't explain it, but with all of his on-the-job experience, he knew, intuitively if someone would be any good just by the way she or he walked into the room. If they had that teacher look about them, we just hired them. We never doubted ourselves," Desi finished with a tone of certainty.

I replied, "The person had a certain teacher walk and Frank used his gut to decide?"

Ignoring my sarcastic comment she added, "When we got applications, Frank was pretty focused on a few areas. He always wanted to know if the applicant was related to someone who worked in the district. He liked to say, "In Arcadia, we take care of our own." After that, he liked to know where they went to school."

"Really," I asked surprised by Desi's last comments. "Frank cared about the university they graduated from? Did he think some universities did a better job than others in preparing teachers?"

"No, don't be silly," Desi, replied. "He just wanted to know if they went to the same university as his own kids or if maybe they went somewhere where he knew his neighbours' kids went. He liked to have that personal connection in hiring. He said relationships were important because education is all about relationships. Frank believed it was all about relationships, relationships and relationships. Without pausing she added, "Sometimes he liked to know if they curled."

Then there was a pause, and as much as I tried, I couldn't help myself: "He cared if they curled?"

"Sure, he thought curling was the kind of activity that demonstrated real team work and social skills. Four people who acted as a single unit, focused on one goal said a lot about teamwork. Plus, he said it showed a lot about a person's patience, industriousness and character."

"Really," I replied quizzically. " I guess that explains a lot." What was I supposed to say? Suddenly, I pictured the four names on the "staffing hotspot" list out on the ice, curling away, with Frank looking disapprovingly at them from the stands. As they flailed about having thrown their curling stones nowhere near the "house" target zone right past the outlines of their own lane and onto the adjacent sheet of ice, Frank might have scribbled some note on the back of a receipt he meant to turn in soon, noting to hire them anyway, because his real criteria, which he could not even admit to himself, was that they just made it past the hog line.

SEVEN

"Thank you for the quaint anecdote. That was interesting," Marie said. Obviously there had been nothing scandalous in the DVD story, or in Bernard's relaying the consequences of imperfect screening criteria for applicants. "I'd like to get more insight into your approaches to hiring staff," Marie said. "You told us about the application process up to the invitation to interview, and of course we seem to have spent a tremendous amount of time understanding how you fire people. Sorry, I mean, how you went about terminating people. Oh that doesn't sound much better now, does it?" She added with a sly smile. "Please tell us more about how you hire people after you've done the initial screening."

Bernard knew that inevitably he would have to break the bad news about employment interviews. In most organizations, employment interviews are the most frequently used methods to assess candidates. But he had read the tome of research maligning the interview process for its lack of validity on what constitutes a "good" interview or who makes a "good" interviewer. He was aware that the process is wrought with inherent biases that interviewers hold about applicants' appearance, gender, age, and non-verbal cues. Add to this the fact that it has been demonstrated that most interviewers have poor recall of what was said during an interview and it's even harder to believe that almost all employers still rely on interviews as the most important component in hiring.

Bernard thought about what Malcolm Gladwell had recently pointed out in "What the Dog Saw"—that this blind trust in the value of the interview persists despite the fact that there is little, if any, evidence that suggests there is a transferability between a person's actions, behaviours, and attitudes in an interview context and what they are actually like as a classroom teacher. In fact, famous movement theorist and expert interpreter of human gesture, posture and stance, Rudolf Laban, observed thousands of workers and found that it took a minimum of two hours before people really became themselves in an interview. That is, people could pretend to have a certain personality and relational style for a couple of hours.

He thought about that before he decided to speak. But, Bernard said none of it.

We met early one morning as we prepared for the series of interviews scheduled to be held in that single and frenzied day. We had

24 interviews to conduct in six hours. To try and manage it, I had assembled eight interview teams, which were made up of principals, vice-principals, a few teachers of specialty subjects and me.

There were only 10 positions to fill for the coming year, none of which were long-term, but there had been over 60 applications. That was a lot of people looking for a career but applying for what amounted to part-time or limited-term positions.

I had done the pre-screening of applicants based on matching what they had written in their cover letters and résumés against the minimum and preferred qualifications lists for the positions based on accurate job profiles.

That single process of having principals commit to a description of the ideal candidate had been a tremendous amount of work. It was a step in the hiring process that most of them just weren't used to doing. The usual district practice was to place a job advertisement containing nothing more than a generic list of skills, attributes and dispositions that was so innocuous that it invited anyone to apply without stating that there were important qualifications, or skills and experiences for a specific job that merit greater consideration than others.

It took work, but I convinced the principals to change. Come to think of it, perhaps I simply wore them down by being so unrelenting in my desire to establish a more professional hiring process. In the end, at one meeting they nodded their heads in acknowledgement when I told them this was the way we were now going to do business. That level of analysis, reflection, planning that would establish clear, agreed-upon, honest job criteria was so time-consuming, I came to expect a slightly exasperated reaction as they tossed the finished documents onto the meeting room table.

But this added considerable ease to the next steps of the hiring process. No more hidden, behind-the-scenes assessments of applications using criteria that no one knew anything about. We would be upfront with the applicants about what was required to be seriously considered for an interview.

And, for the time being, I told them I would be the person who created the shortlist of candidates who would be interviewed. I told them they could advocate for a candidate if they thought I was not noticing something in the application package, but only one person got to make the call to invite applicants to interviews. Me.

It wasn't all about power; it was an attempt to move from using many arbitrary and idiosyncratic ways of assessing applicants' qualifications to, at worst, a single arbitrary and idiosyncratic process—mine. If it was unfair, at least it was equally unfair and all those who applied could be dealt with, for the first time, with a thoughtful, if imperfect, consistency.

As we sat around the boardroom table and slowly woke up our brains with coffee, I reminded them in our pre-interviewing meeting that according to human rights legislation, some interview questions are simply off-limits and just have to be avoided.

This wasn't news to them or at least it shouldn't have been.

I told them that no matter what overwhelming compulsion they had to ask a spontaneous question, they were not to do it.

Stick to the scripted interview questions. We agreed that everyone would ask the same questions in their teams and that we would use the same rating scale for all the candidates.

Back in 1966, psychology professor Edwin E. Ghiselli conceived of the idea based on the premise that past work-related behaviours are the best predictors of future on-the-job performance. Behavioural-descriptive interviews use competency-related questions that are open-ended in design and allow interviewees to draw on past experiences from their employment, education or life in general.

Get them to give you a concrete example of a time when they did something in a classroom setting that demonstrates what it is you are after. Probe the responses using the recommended probes you have been given. Try to have them situate their responses in real-life examples of things they have actually done rather than what they would do hypothetically.

"That all sounds fine Keith, but what if something comes up and I just need to probe it further and find an answer? What about that amazing question that isn't on this list you gave us? What then?" Asked Simon Templar, who liked to come across like he was a graduate of the "School of Hard Knocks."

He added, "You know I'm not new at the hiring game, and I think I'm a pretty good judge of character. I have this uncanny ability to read people. I didn't need to learn it from a textbook."

Templar looked around at the other administrators in the room to gauge their reactions to his words. He liked to see if they were looking at him and agreeing. Templar was one of those guys who liked to notice them noticing him. I had noticed he became defensive if he did not get from them just the right quality and quantity of being noticed.

He went on, "I have an ability to sense when someone is holding something back. You certainly aren't advocating that we just cave in and not ask the most insightful questions are you?" With that he stopped speaking, smirked, looked around with little knowing up-and-down nods to everyone, and waited.

"Well Simon," I replied. "Let me give you a textbook response. The employment interview is conducted to learn more about the suitability of people who are being considered for a particular job. In this case, we are interviewing for a number of teaching jobs. We have spent a lot of time trying to build profiles of what we need in our ideal candidates. We, meaning your colleagues around this table and I, developed questions and probes, which we edited and revised until we thought we had them just right. We worked on coming up with a list of "reasonable responses". You know the kind of things we need to hear in the interview to assess a candidate's response against what we think the ideal response might need to be. We were attentive to details and the limits of the law. So let me tell you what I'm hearing you say."

"You want to be able to ask a question, impromptu, that may or may not be relevant to the job being filled and ones that may or may not lead to accusations of biased or discriminatory hiring. You just want to make up questions as they come to you, unscripted and not in consultation with the group. Did I get that right?" I didn't wait for an answer and he didn't try to give one.

"Let me give you an example Simon. An applicant's marital status seldom has anything to do with her ability to teach. The interview is going well but suddenly your spider sense is telling you something is inconsistent with some of her answers, and there is a work experience gap that she hasn't explained. You pounce on it and ask her some question that leads to another and suddenly you have asked her if she has been divorced for long. She says not long but that it feels like it has been a while. At some point later in time when she didn't get the job, she files a human rights complaint because she feels that "Mr. Horny Rimmed Glasses" who interviewed her was asking her about her availability for a potential date. And, I get a call from the human rights tribunal wanting to know what is up with our circumspect hiring practices. Now you tell me, why would I give you that much rope with which to hang us both?"

"Let me be crystal clear on this point: your need to know the answer does not trump their need to be protected under human rights legislation." I sat back and surveyed the silent room that seemed a little stunned by my aggressiveness.

Templar was looking down. Sensing a small victory, I addressed the whole room,

"By the way, if you are keeping any notes about what is on the résumés or applications or things that you notice during the interview, you must not identify or differentiate candidates according to the prohibited grounds. Do not write down things like, black woman, 45-ish or South Asian man with an accent or really hot babe."

I looked over at Templar again who was scribbling out something he had written on the top résumés in his pile.

"I gave you each a list of the kind of items that are protected under human rights legislation, items such as: name changes, marital or familial status, place of birth, age, sexual orientation, national or ethnic origin, and anything to do with disability or medical history and so on. You can ask questions that are bona fide occupational requirements, but you have those listed with the position profiles."

I could see Templar now looking up and trying hard to give me what I thought might be his version of the evil eye. I added, "If you go off-script and decide to ad lib during the interview and something goes terribly wrong, I will tell our legal counsel that I advised you not to do so and that you did not take my very sound, profoundly professional advice and fancied yourself more knowledgeable than me. In other words, I'm letting you know now that you are on your own and I will not defend you or your actions should you be hauled in front of a Human Rights Tribunal."

Templar didn't say another thing to me that morning and actually didn't say all that much for the rest of the year.

Bernard looked at Lee and said, "When you are asked to apply for a job, it is customary for you to produce something like a curriculum vitae or a résumé on the assumption that it will demonstrate whether or not you are a suitable person, appropriately qualified for the position, true? It should be an honest and objective account of your career trajectory, right?"

Lee nodded at Bernard.

Bernard went on, "But that's not all that potential employers are going to want to know. They are also after the personal angle. How do you come across? Do you seem "open" to them? Is the personal chemistry going to work when you mingle with others on staff? Are you going to fit in?

In some cases, they do this with psychometric testing, or role-plays or simulation exercises outside of the formal interview. They may send you off to have lunch with a few people from the interview committee, innocently giving you a break from the formality of the interview, only to monitor your behaviour in a more casual setting. "Well, how was she socially?" they will ask your lunch companions later on.

In requesting a résumé, prospective employers are desperately looking to discover some important things about you. Yet, the scrutiny given to the vitae is not in itself sufficient in assessing whether you are suitable for the job. They want something more personal—an intuitive sense of who you are. Be very wary of anyone who says that personality does not matter, that who you are as a person has no bearing on your potential as an employee. Because the reality is, personality matters and in some cases, it matters a lot."

Lee looked a little anxious and Bernard figured Lee might be thinking back to the casual luncheon he had likely attended when he had applied to Harper and Fowler.

Lee said, "I get it," a comment that elicited a smile and knowing nod from his colleague Peter Hart.

Bernard added, "Now I should say that, even with the best plan in place and everyone supposedly on-board for it, there is still a chance it might go wrong."

"Do say how," Marie interjected, perhaps to stop what seemed like too cordial a conversation between Bernard and Lee, but not without a little hint that she was somewhat 'hooked' by the unfolding story and wanted to know how it would play out.

In reality, the interview wasn't that bad. I had probably led dozens of teacher candidate interviews prior to meeting Mr. Gene Coon and had seen plenty of candidates hobble along during the whole process. I'd even experienced a couple of interviews where it was clear from the get-go that the interview process was going to be quite difficult for the interviewee and everyone else involved. And, while there had been some awkward moments during Coon's interview, it hadn't started out that poorly. But things slowly started to unravel after he—a 20-something teacher candidate—stumbled during a response to a question about his approach to classroom management. The question, anchored in behavioural descriptive interviewing techniques, asked each candidate to provide at least one concrete example of an approach that they had successfully used to manage a difficult classroom situation involving a disruptive student. Interview tactics like these are useful to a point. But, I can't stress enough that the people actually in a position to use these tactics are usually amateurs, the kind of people commonly finding themselves in personnel management despite any formal training. Because of the blind trust that people place in the employment interview, which is one of the weakest predictors of competency and potential on-the-job success, people become overly reliant on the techniques and place much more value on them than they're worth. Heaps of research suggests that we might all be better off examining the entrails of a chicken to foretell an interviewee's potential than to let the average manager or administrator conduct an interview. Even more reckless than relying wholly on the interview is the equally dense belief that just about everyone seems to hold: that we can identify talent when we see it or hear it during an interview, or equally disturbing, that we can select prospective teachers without ever observing them really teach anything.

In Coon's case, the interview panel had met earlier in the day, before any of the interviews had begun and agreed that an appropriate response to the question would include the following elements: demonstrated capabilities in focusing on the student's behaviour rather than the student; tactics for deescalating an incident through age-appropriate interventions; a history of maintaining a calm demeanour at all times; and, a proven record of developing a follow-up plan with the student to minimize future incidents. Even Templar agreed that these were the necessary skills and dispositions needed for successful classroom management on the part of any teacher. I was beginning to be confident in Templar's ability to stay "on script."

When asked to choose a specific time when Coon had encountered a difficult student in class whose behaviour was distracting to others, and to explain, specifically, what he had done to deal with the incident, Coon looked back at us with a somewhat vacant expression.

"Well, let me think," he began, and then there was a pause of a minute or so. "To tell you the truth, I'm not sure I can ever think of a time where I had to deal with a difficult student." There was a slightly longer pause of silence, which seemed much longer than it really was during which Coon seemed to be thinking.

Then he spoke, "Nope, I'm sorry. I'm just coming up blank on that one."

"Take your time," I said. "Try to think back and pick any incident that comes to mind from any one of your three practicum rounds that you think illustrates how you handled a student discipline issue that arose in class."

After another seemingly long pause, Coon replied, "It's a really good question, but I'm sorry, I guess I just had that special kind of connection with my students. They never really caused me any problems in the classroom."

I spoke again, hoping that he would realize that no-response was worse than a weak one, "Are you sure that in all of your student teaching experiences, or experience working as a summer camp counsellor over three summers, that you can not think of any incident where you had to deal with a disciplinary issue?"

Coon looked back at me like I was completely daft, and then he spat out, "Sorry, I really just can't recall anything."

I quickly glanced over to one of the two principals who was on the interview committee and noticed her look of disbelief—pained disbelief. With Coon's non-response, I provided the perfunctionary ending to the interview by asking the interview panel if they had any further questions for the candidate. From my experience, I knew that it was typical for perhaps one or two of the panel members to seek clarification on a response at this point, or sometimes ask a supplementary question as a follow-up. But, given the sudden end to the interview, I didn't expect anyone to have a question.

Just as expected, no one said anything, as most were looking at the pages they had in their hands. Templar had put his hands together in a gesture that said, "We are through." But then Mr. Canisius, the odd fellow who had been Science Department Head for almost 20 years at Arrass High School indicated that he did indeed have a question for the candidate.

Knowing that the position was for a Grade 10 Science teacher who might also have to teach a section or two of grade 11 Physics, I expected that Mr. Canisius might have a question about the candidate's subject knowledge base and academic background. Of course, I insisted, that he go ahead and ask his question.

"Do you speak any foreign languages?" asked Mr. Canisius.

I looked over at Jenny Morales, the principal of Arrass High School and saw that she had a blank expression on her face. While I was still trying to figure out what the question had to do with teaching science,

Coon replied, "No, not really, I guess ... unless you count Klingon as a foreign language?"

I looked around and could see the other members of the interview team breaking into small smiles. But, then Canisius uttered, "nuqneH." To which, Coon responded, "nuqneH."

"MajQa'," said Canisius.

"Heghlu'meH QaQ jajvam," said Coon.

I hate to admit it, but even with considerable interview experience, I had no idea what was occurring at this point in time right in front of me. Nor did I know how to stop it and regain control of the interview process. We all sat and listened for a minute or so as the pair jabbered away in Klingon.

Then there came a point at which both men laughed out loud. I figured that their conversation must have ended with a good old-fashioned Klingon knee-slapper because then Canisius said he was done and had no more questions.

After the interview ended and Coon had left the room, I asked Canisius poignantly what that was all about.

"Well, I just thought I would provide a little levity to an obviously stressful time for Gene Coon. He seemed like such a nice guy. I can't believe you pressed him on that classroom management question. You are so cold-hearted," he said as he smiled and looked at me rather contently. "That aggressive interviewing style is annoying and makes us all look, well ... it makes us look quite mean-spirited, really. I thought I would lighten things up a bit and make the candidate feel more welcome in here. You need to stop taking yourself so damn serious. It's just an interview after all."

I sat there and said nothing, but did make a mental note to myself. "Do not ever, ever, invite Canisius to interview again. Ever!"

As soon as Bernard finished speaking, Kimberley Marie blurted out, "Time for a coffee break." And, realizing that it may have sounded dismissive, she tried to restore some civility in her tone. "I mean, this seems like a good time to take a 20-minute break. How about we come back after that and continue?"

Everyone just nodded, unsure if it was a question she was asking or an edict she was issuing.

After the recess, Bernard explained that about a week after the Coon interview experience, he had arrived at his office, sat down with a cup of coffee at his desk and settled in to listen to his voicemail messages.

"I would like to vote for Mrs. Dar Leone to be the next kindergarten teacher. Thank you." Click.

"What," he wondered "was that all about?"

He listened to the next message from a photocopier salesman inviting him to some upcoming golf tournament. "Frank attends every year," he said before he added, "It's free."

Then there was another woman's voice, "For next year, I think you should really consider hiring Dar Leone as the kindergarten teacher at Sorrel Elementary. She is really terrific and my kid loves her." Click.

Another message: "Yes, I would like to register my vote for Mrs. Leone. I think she is an excellent kindergarten teacher." And another message, and then a few more voting "yes" for Mrs. Leone.

Bernard said he was pretty sure he was beginning to understand this. Random people were phoning his work number and leaving messages with the belief that they could cast a vote for the next kindergarten teacher at Sorrel Elementary School.

Somehow the unbridled success of reality television shows like "American Idol" had convinced good people that they could use their landline telephones to register their votes for next year's kindergarten teacher. He immediately grabbed his cell phone to see if anyone had voted via a text message.

While it was a novel concept to use electronic voting as a demonstration of 21st century democracy in action, it was not one he was yet willing to entertain for staffing schools.

Bernard called Mark Lucera, the principal at Sorrel Elementary, and asked if he was either on "Candid Camera," or if there was a contest going on to pick one of next year's teachers—and he just didn't get the memo.

As soon as Lucera realized he wasn't in trouble, Bernard thought he heard him giggle a little bit. "What's with all of the phone calls about Dar Leone?" Bernard asked.

Lucera was uncharacteristically apologetic as he explained that his school secretary had been overwhelmed by parent questions about who was going to be the replacement teacher while the highly regarded kindergarten teacher was on maternity leave. He explained how prospective kindergarten parents can become antsy, quite easily, and overly involved in trying to figure out the "who" of their child's first teacher.

Lucera went on to say that his secretary told these inquisitive parents that the district office was heavily involved in making these decisions and that she did not have any information for them. Exacerbated and overwhelmed by requests for Mrs. Leone to be the replacement, she finally just gave up trying to explain the process and instead started to tell parents that they should call central office and vote for the teacher candidate of their choosing.

"Feel free to call Dr. Keith Bernard's office; I think his number is 555-1415 and tell him who you want. I'm sure he doesn't mind hearing from parents. If you get his voicemail, just leave him a message," she told them. And, like most parents are socialized to do, they followed the school secretary's advice verbatim.

Bernard explained that he then asked Lucera to thank the secretary and request of her that she stop giving out his number. He refrained from adding a comment about the need for school staff to be aware of the basic human resources practices and policies, and to not invent new ones for filling teachers jobs. But, before hanging up the phone, he told Lucera to make her promise to never do this again—or he would get even with both of them.

Bernard admitted that in the quiet privacy of his office, he was overcome by a wide smile when he realized that a parental voting procedure might certainly yield better results for selecting teachers than a formalized process that devoted a few hours to the indulgences of a pair of Klingon-speaking science geeks.

EIGHT

It was nearing mid-day of Bernard's second day in deposition, and he was both tired out and unsure of whether anything he had shared with the group had shed light on the case. Yet, even with his uncertainty he felt a sense of responsibility for answering the questions with not only as much clarity as possible, but also with enough texture so that each response was as truthful and as accurate as his memory would allow. Bernard knew that "the" truth was highly subjective.

"Can you provide us with some background as to the existing human resources policies and practices that were in place when you arrived at Arcadia School District and explain what you did or didn't do to work within the existing framework?" asked Ms. Marie. "You can, of course, do this in the form of a story, if you would like."

Then, noticing the humour in her comment, she added, "It seems to be your preferred method," as she flashed a smile of satisfaction.

Bernard returned the smile.

When I arrived at Arcadia I learned quickly that each principal, all 25 of them, held employment interviews as he or she saw fit. Each had his or her own set of exemplary interview questions which were asked of applicants in interviews that ranged from 15 minutes to more than an hour long. Some of the interviews were very formal with personnel committees, while others involved a single principal meeting an applicant at the local coffee shop for a chat.

I queried into the sources of the various interview questions used by principals and was told that several were inherited from someone else, some were created from scratch, and many others were pilfered from some Internet site. Each principal assured me that his or her questions were really good.

When I asked them how they knew the questions were good, they just looked at me with pity, a non-verbal "tsk tsk." I was used to the patronizing compassion that self-proclaimed intuitive types could wield. By my asking this question, I was proving that I was one of those who couldn't see what was plainly in front of me. They, on the other hand, were the chosen ones who—and here is the phrase that would launch a thousand bad teachers—"just knew."

I was frustrated that I didn't know what they obviously knew – or at least what they pretended they all knew. I pressed them at one of our principals' meetings to see if anyone actually had a set of anticipated correct answers to the questions. Did they have something to gauge if the interviewee was responding with some level of correctness to the question? They, all these experienced educators, seemed surprised that I expected them to develop criteria for judging the quality of a response.

"Let me see if I understand what you are doing," I said fixing my gaze on Angie Merici, the principal of Salisbury Plain School. "Each of you has a magic set of questions that will somehow help surface the evidence that the elusive, great teacher we've been searching for is in the room." I wasn't trying too hard to stifle the sarcasm.

"And, as educators, former master-teachers, you have not developed any written guidelines to assess the quality of the responses. During the interview, you just ask questions. Then you mysteriously grade the responses without any kind of grading rubric and then—poof! — decide if someone gets an A+ or an F. Is that about right?"

I could see the disapproving looks from around the table, so I tried to reign in my disparaging tone and just continue with further elucidation of the flawed personnel tactics most everyone seems to be satisfied with.

"Right now, you are using what is, at best, a traditional approach to interviewing prospective teachers where you ask a series of situational or hypothetical questions, which most of the time lead to straightforward answers.

"You might ask something like: What are your strengths and weaknesses? Or: What major challenges and problems do you foresee you might face on the job? Or: How would you handle an uncooperative or defiant student?

"And, in response, the interviewee desperately tries to provide just enough good information to satisfy you. But, even then, you may not know what 'just enough' is since you don't have any guidelines for evaluation. Without something like an answer key to measure or guide the assessment, what you are left with is a process that is highly prejudiced by momentary bias."

Wanting to provide some reassurance to the well-intentioned principals who believed that any interview question is a good interview question, I ended by suggesting, "You know, it is really the same process we typically use to establish validity and reliability in our classroom teaching assessments."

Their body language made me wonder if my assumption about how they approached classroom assessment was completely wrong. I could see Merici and a few others sitting around the table, sigh and look overwhelmed by what they must have felt was yet another change that I was forcing on them.

"Trust me, Angie," I said. "I promise I will show you how it is done. And while there is quite a shift required and practice involved in getting it right, once you learn how to use the system, there is not that much that can go wrong."

As soon as I said that, I regretted it. I knew that those quasi-prophetic statements often came back to haunt me. Let me tell you about a perfect example which Angie Merici witnessed.

There was one time when the response to a standard interview question caught me completely off guard. It's a fairly standard question that typically elicits a fairly standard response. It's kind of an abstract version of the question we had put to Mr. Gene Coon about handling a difficult incident with a student, except it asks an applicant to draw on a wider set of life experiences to answer it. A non-answer to this question would have been impossible, even for Coon, I bet. A person can evaluate the response along multiple criteria, including depth of reflection, attitude towards hardship, resiliency, ingenuity, communication skills, willingness to be or at least seem honest with one's answer, etc.

It goes like this: "Can you please tell us about a specific time in your life where you experienced a difficult or challenging event, what you did to work your way through it and how you overcame it? And, tell us what you learned about yourself from the experience?"

This particular applicant's eyes grew wide, she seemed frozen, her breathing became more rapid and her eyes immediately began to tear up. She began to ramble a little, rather incoherently, about the time her mother passed away when she was in college, and then she burst into rushing tears. She just sobbed and sobbed, and between sobs she apologized over and over again for falling apart. She tried to dab her running mascara while she explained how she had been very close to her mother and how much her mother's death, some 17 years earlier, had left an emptiness inside her that she seemed, still to this day, unable to fill.

I looked at her, a little surprised but still trying to seem composed and downright rigid, the way cold-hearted human resource professionals are supposed to be. I stood up and said, "I'll be right back," and left her sitting there in the interview room with Merici.

I came back with a box of tissues, which I slid across the table to her. As she blew her nose, she asked if she had just blown the interview.

I said "no," and then explained that the candidates usually cry after the interview when I tell them that they didn't get the job. She smiled a small smile from the corner of her mouth and slowly we continued to chat about our mothers.

I remember watching a post-game interview in 2008 with Dallas Cowboys wide receiver Terrell Owens. When a reporter asked him about Tony Roma, the team's quarterback, Owens broke down and began to cry for no apparent reason.

If it was okay for Terrell Owens—all 6 foot, 3 inches and 224 pounds of him—to weep inexplicably when asked about his teammate, then it was completely acceptable for a teacher candidate to sob uncontrollably as she thought of her mother when pushed by an insensitive clod like me.

"I thought you said there wasn't much that could go wrong," Merici said sharply after the interview was over. I shrugged my shoulders in response to Merici's statement and decided that maybe it was time to forgo many more changes to personnel practices that school year.

Bernard looked over and caught Lee smiling. He wasn't sure what Lee thought was humourous and was reluctant to ask since he hadn't said anything remotely funny.

Bernard went on to explain how some personnel issues within the district just seemed difficult to resolve, even with good policies in place; they just lingered.

"Do you remember how I mentioned yesterday that John Lalande had insisted that there was no real issue with Noelle Chabanel? Well, some personnel matters just fester and eventually become septic."

I asked John Lalande, the principal over at Salient Technology Academy, one day in early June, about the alleged phone calls to Noelle Chabanel's home over the past year. I neglected to mention Chabanel's assertions that he was inebriated during those calls, or the possible offer to meet in some poorly lit lounge.

In his defense, Lalande offered that he was just calling her in the comfort of her own home outside of business hours to make the conversations less formal and more amiable.

Lalande was astounded to hear that Chabanel found it intrusively inappropriate for him to call her at home and he laughed at the suggestion that he might have sounded agitated and aggressive during those conversations.

"Oh, no," Lalande told me, "Noelle must have just mistaken my tone. I was trying to make it less stressful for her. I was just calling her to reach out and help her, Keith. Do you think I shouldn't have done it that way? I was just trying to put her at ease, it's in my nature to try and put people at ease. I certainly didn't think it might be seen as offensive. Oh my gosh, she took it the wrong way. Honest mistake, I guess,"

Lalande used that line, "it was an honest mistake," to try and close off a few of the conversations I had with him throughout the school year.

The problem with that line is that I had been subjected to one of his "honest mistakes" in the middle of my summer holidays.

We had company from out of town and were just in the middle of barbequing dinner one late July evening when my daughter brought me the telephone.

"Hello, Keith?" the voice stammered out. "Sorry to bother you at home in the heat of summer. It's John Lalande. I was just thinking that I might need a temporary part-time teacher for September. Yes, you are correct—there is no rush on this hiring, of course. But, I know you like to get to these things right away. Yes, I guess I can put it in writing and email it tomorrow when you aren't entertaining company. It's just that, well, I never stop thinking about how to improve my school and what's best for my students. Yes, I'm aware it's 7 p.m. and it's the end of July. Yes, I remember seeing the memo that you sent out informing us that you would be taking your holidays the last two weeks of July. Okay, I can tell from your tone and the other voices I hear in the background that your company is anxious for your return. You're probably having dinner. It's just an honest mistake, Keith. How about I just email you tomorrow? Have a good evening." His voice trailed off distractedly, as if something shiny crossed his line of vision and distracted him.

I'm no expert on the matter, but it seemed that John's speech was a bit slurred. This telephone encounter reminded me of the ramblings I once endured when I found myself in an out-of-town bar, and one of the locals who desperately needed a companion just stepped up and told me his sad, drunken story.

I never got an email from Lalande that week or the next. In the end, I had to call him in late August to remind him of our July phone call and ask about the details for the job posting.

Lalande was surprised because he was quite certain that he had been very clear over the telephone about what his school needed me to do. However, he insisted that if I had not understood him or had not been able to keep up with him because I was entertaining company and maybe imbibing a little, he could email all of the details to me as a collegial favour. No worries, he said.

Desi was spot on. What an ass!

After numerous phone calls over six months to Noelle Chabanel and the two principals she was working with, and months after dealing with all of the teacher transfers, I was able to assign Chabanel to a single school with Katie Tekawitha.

I decided to assign her any place where Lalande wasn't, and thus met a very simple union request. In reality, something wicked inside me wanted to leave Chabanel at Salient Elementary with Lalande just to see him wriggle. But, I couldn't do it. After eight months with this dysfunctional district, I still maintained a shred of decency, which prevented me from using Chabanel as a way to make Lalande's life difficult.

Eventually, the district's fastest growing and most modern school got the teacher Lalande said it needed.

Katie Tekawitha, who called me incessantly because she had a vision, she said, of a certain dream team of staff members, got Chabanel. And, Chabanel and the teachers' union received the transfer she requested.

Throughout the year, Lalande continued to bumble along and persisted with finding ways to inflict pain on me. And I was frustrated by an inability to exact any form of revenge.

When Katie Tekawitha found out she was getting Chabanel, her response was, "Fine but you owe me one, Keith!"

I tried to explain that Tekawitha needed to get in line behind the other creditors who looked for some form of restitution as a result of my moral bankruptcy, but she didn't laugh.

Maybe she did think I was morally bankrupt and had acted in a cavalier fashion. After all, she was being passed a teacher who, according to Lalande, was just fine, but was also not good enough for his school.

Every time I would see or speak with Tekawitha and I would ask how Chabanel was doing, her response was a grumpy "OK."

"As a teacher, she's nothing to write home about," she would say. But if I pressed Tekawitha, I would find out, "she's not that bad either, but she's certainly not a team player." And she would end our chats by asking if somebody else could have Chabanel on their team, next year.

I responded by noting that all transfer requests were handled in the best interests of students and their learning. Plus, I reminded Tekawitha that Chabanel was there at her school because she had been booted off her previous team. And, I would ask: Doesn't everyone deserve a chance to play on someone's team?

Tekawitha found no humour in my call for compassion towards mediocre teachers, knowing my reputation for pursuing teacher termination cases in a fashion that Arcadia School District No. 66 had apparently never seen.

Wilson Lee, who had said nothing all morning and looked rather dreary, decided it was time to speak, "Did anything get better in your second year? I mean after the summer break, did things seem to improve?"

Bernard got a sense that Lee, an obvious member of "Generation Y," was concerned he might be suffering from job-hate and in some sense, professional careers weren't supposed to be this trying. Bernard smiled at Lee before he replied to the question hoping that the non-verbal gesture would shake the young man from his funk.

You know Mr. Lee, I didn't hate the work I did or the people I did the work for. I just can't stomach being around people who wield their power like a bludgeon. I read somewhere that it was Lord Acton, the 19th-century historian and moralist, who penned the poignant phrase that power tends to corrupt and absolute power corrupts absolutely. Acton held that great men are almost always bad men.

Just before the summer break, Chuck ordered 25 copies of Jim Collins best-seller "Good to Great" and assigned it to the district's leadership team - the principals and central office administrators - as our summer reading. "Good to Great" was to become, by Chuck's own admission, our blueprint for district improvement. Chuck was convinced that once read, understood and applied, the contents would transform this publicly-funded school division from one that was good into one that was great. Chuck was sure of this fact even though in "Good to Great" Collins himself admits that there is no silver bullet, no magic formula that can transform good organizations into great ones.

Chuck seemed pretty content to skip past that part of the book, and in listening to his interpretation of Collins, many other parts of the book as well. We spent a full day in September in an administrators' retreat listening to Chuck explain how good we were and how it was within our reach, if only we stretched ourselves and pushed ourselves, to become great.

It was really hard to tell if Chuck was sincere in his belief that the school district was indeed good and had the capacity to be great. Or, if that was simply some expression of the inner transference that Chuck wanted for himself, to go from good to great. The problem with much of this thinking is the fact that you first have to be good, prove yourself as good, before you should consider the possibility of being great. And Chuck seemed to assume this, about himself perhaps more than the schools, that he was good.

Have you ever heard of the Dunning-Kruger Effect, Mr. Lee? It's a cognitive bias in which people make erroneous conclusions and unfortunate choices, but their incompetence robs them of the metacognitive ability to realize what they have done.

The unskilled, therefore, suffer from illusory superiority, rating their own abilities as above average, way higher than reality. By contrast, the highly skilled underrate their abilities thus suffering from illusory inferiority.

This combination leads to a perverse result where the less competent rate their own ability considerably higher than that of their more competent co-workers.

At the September retreat, Chuck went on about how great leaders of companies, just like great leaders of school districts, who start with the question of "where?" instead ought to begin with "who?"

Chuck paraphrased Collins and said real leaders start by getting the right people on the bus, the wrong people off the bus and the right people in the right seats. And they stick with that discipline—first the people, then the direction—no matter how dire the circumstances.

But no matter, Chuck reassured us, we were all safe in his capable bus-driving hands. Even though the entire premise of this utopian transformation is founded on pruning away dead weight to let better growth happen, with Chuck, you had a leader who would accomplish it all by taking the dead branches, expired blooms, fallen leaves and rotten fruit—all of the hurt and broken-hearted teachers who were struggling—and wistfully throw them all under the wheels of the bus to create a flourishing, enviable garden.

And, he seemed convinced that he could do all of this while driving the bus, his back turned to us while watching our transformation from goodness to greatness in the handy rear-view mirror.

Narcissism, Michael Maccoby writes, in his book "The Leaders We Need," is essential for individual survival because without a dose of it, individuals wouldn't value themselves any more than anyone else. Narcissists, the gifted and productive ones, the innovators and independent thinkers, project their image of importance onto the world, thereby finding others important too, and thus improve the quality of people's lives.

Chuck saw himself as a visionary who was leading a willing, albeit ignorant, and desperate flock of disciples. But, narcissists can also be arrogant and possess bizarrely grandiose images of themselves that are unwarranted. They can be absolutely unmindful of others. They do not listen to others and have a paranoid sensitivity to others who they see as threats. This was the Chuck I experienced – a man blinded by ambition who was coercing people to follow out of fear of reprisal.

Not long after our retreat, the "Good to Great" one where Chuck told us all about the principle of getting the right people onto the bus and the wrong people off of it, a person named Bathos Lukno reappeared hanging on to the back of the moving bus, which had a jarring effect, as all things with Lukno seemed to have. His re-entry into my daily landscape was like a scene in an action adventure movie in which you think the villain has lost the trail of the good guys and gals but then appears again to the shocked, thrilled horror of the audience. Abruptly in November, I was told that Lukno had begun to send letters, yet again, but this time he was aiming high: only the newly elected school trustees were receiving his probably rambling missives.

School board elections were held at the end of October and as per usual the trustees were assigned mailboxes at central office. Suddenly, letters began to arrive and fill up their mail slots. The new trustees who didn't know what to make of Lukno's letters were advised by the Board Chair to hand over all correspondence from Lukno to the Chief Superintendent of Schools, who would deal with it appropriately.

Chuck's way of dealing with it appropriately was to bring all of the letters to me and leave them on my desk so that I could solve this problem. Chuck, who I now struggled to respect as a colleague, much less tolerate as a leader, wanted to shield the trustees from such messy personnel matters. And, he didn't think they needed to be bothered by problems, just told of solutions. Others in Chuck's position might have bothered to take some ownership, or at least worked with their Superintendent of Human Resources to strategize about solutions. My job, it turns out, according to Chuck's vision of it, seemed to be to spare not only the trustees but Chuck himself from any lost sleep by solving all of the problems that arose that had to do with personnel matters and finances in the district. Not only problems that arose, that is, that actually materialized during my tenure at Arcadia, but even problems that had been swept under the carpet or sucked up in the proverbial vacuum cleaner bag, like poor old hammy, which then got opened and dumped on my desk periodically.

The letters were all in different coloured envelopes of varying sizes, some looked like envelopes he might have had in a drawer since the 1970s, with pale daisies on them. I opened and read the first one. Some phrases, when they appear in professional correspondence, just send signals to the brain that block your normal capacity for compassion. I was surprised that my immediate reaction to Lukno's phrase "intolerable situation," which appeared so predominately in the first paragraph, was to become skeptical and worried all at once. I was not worried for the writer so much as the reader. I was definitely entering something just by delving into these intercepted letters but I had no idea of the depth.

As I continued sifting through his letter, it became clear that Lukno wanted the newly elected trustees to know of his plight and to make them aware of his perceived injuries.

His letters were all identical and began:

Dear school board member,

The purpose of this letter is to request your intervention on my behalf. I am caught in an INTOLERABLE situation.

Three years ago I was doing what I was trained to do and teaching a backstage theatre production class when a grade 12 student, who had never taken one of MY classes before, without my permission hopped onto the Cherry Picker parked under a light baton, pressed a button to go for a joyride BUT I guess he didn't see the unlocked C-clamp of the weighty Ellipsoidal Reflector Spotlight just above him. When the cab knocked into the lighting instrument it fell off the baton. Immediately, the force of it crushed his foot and broke all of the bones in his foot.

Before it happened, he had been repeatedly advised not to go on any equipment prior to receiving the detailed and specific training I needed to give. He didn't listen to me. I warned all of them of the potential dangers inherent in the theatre.

Not long after this horrible accident, which was NOT MY FAULT, the district brought in a consultant for, what I was told, a facility review. At the same time, I was directed to not talk about the incident with my colleagues. At the time,

120

the rationale seemed reasonable enough, as stories about what happened can become distorted or exaggerated through multiple retellings.

However, this had the unfortunate consequence of isolating me and left me unable to seek counsel from my colleagues. Furthermore, I found that the school administration was unwilling to talk to me about the accident.

When the consultant arrived, unannounced, I was told that it was simply a facility review and not an assessment of my teaching and classroom management skills. But, oddly, on the last visit of the on-site visits, the consultant left me with a parting comment: he said that perhaps my students were covering up something for me because they liked me. I was left wondering what the consultant had really been brought in to do?

When he submitted his report, the consultant did so directly to the school district's legal counsel. I had to press central office administration, repeatedly, to view the report, and even then I was only allowed to make notes of its contents. Being kept in the dark was the beginning of what has turned into an arduous and absurd year for me.

I was in the dark even though I was still supposed to be teaching theatre production. One afternoon, during a tour of the "Metal Box Theatre," Mr. Stihl just turned to me and said, "Lukno you have to trust the administrators." My shocked reply to him was, "Yes, but they have to trust me also." Mr. Stihl did not make any more comments to me that day.

As you may know, I began a letter-writing campaign about two years ago. I wrote letters to the school administration and central office administration because I was left feeling that my attempts to find out what was going on were being dismissed or ignored.

Not long after the accident, I had a new group of students placed in my theatre production class. I showed the class list to some of my former colleagues at Daele Middle School, and they were shocked to see the list and advised me to watch my back. According to my former colleagues who had taught most of these reprobates in Middle, these students should never have been placed together. They said this was a toxic mixture of troublemakers.

When I took my concerns to the principal of Ridge Comprehensive High School he said, "Lukno you can't handpick your students. You will be treated just like any other teacher and teach whoever we place in your class!"

I was concerned for the safety of my non-trouble making students and told them what the principal had said to me. They laughed and said, "Forget it Mr. Lukno, the principal doesn't care about us or you."

I struggled to keep the troublemakers out of the way of the other students. Nevertheless, this became increasingly stressful and eventually impossible.

To add to this, a female teaching assistant was assigned my class as an aide. She repeatedly tried to get me out on a date, made passes at me and came to school in revealing clothing. She was very aggressive, however somehow I resisted her advances. But it was uncomfortable.

Rather than document a complaint about my colleague, I took my concerns to administration trying to avoid stirring up trouble, either for the lady or myself. They seemed to laugh it off and I was surprised to see her still assigned to my class after my conversation with the administration.

Near the end of that year, I brought a letter written by a doctor who noted that my concerns should be taken seriously so that I could feel safe in my theatre classes. Or, alternatively, the doctor noted my teaching assignment should be changed as it was clearly having an adverse affect on my health.

Mr. Cottingly contacted me and told me that my doctor had no authority to determine my teaching assignment within the school or the district and that the program would continue as it was with me teaching.

By this time, I had become fully cognizant of the fact that the administration did not respect my professional judgment and doubted that they cared for me personally. It was apparent that Mr. Stihl's advice for me to "trust them" was ill advised. I had hoped the Chief Superintendent would support my quest to improve things for everyone, however he never responded to my emails.

A few months later, I began what I thought would be a short-term medical leave. About one month into it, I was informed that Mr. Cottingly wanted to schedule a meeting with me to discuss my "options." I contacted my union and was advised not to attend a meeting without representation.

My health, both physically and mentally, had deteriorated by this time and I suggested that Mr. Cottingly put into writing what he had in mind as an offer.

As with most of my requests to administration, it seemed that committing anything to writing was out of the question. I never got a written response. As far as I am concerned, the only reason not to commit ideas to paper is because you have no intention of standing behind what you propose.

Now I am at a point where my life has been put on hold. There is a "gag order" that prohibits anyone from giving me a positive professional reference. I have requested letters of reference and recommendation from some of the principals I worked for only to be told that they are not allowed to write anything. Blocking me from moving on with my life is unconscionable and is clearly obstructionist.

I believe the district's lawyers are going to use me as the scapegoat for any legal settlement that results from the druggie who mangled his own foot. I don't believe the district's lawyer is interested in what is in my best interests.

I want closure to all of this and EXPECT your support in obtaining it forthwith. Failing that, I will have no alternative but to take the issue to the Minister *of Education and/or go public. As you can well imagine, I have been placed in a situation where I have nothing to lose.*

I want the following information from the school board:

1. Who gave the directive to withhold letters of recommendation?

2. Was it Mr. Cottingly? Or was it Mr. Stihl? Or was it the lawyer?

3. What is the purpose of withholding the letters of recommendations?

4. Who represents me legally in the lawsuit that has been filed as a result of the accident?

5. I want to know who the lawyers are protecting and why the lawsuit has not been settled yet?

I feel I cannot adequately stage the spring production without top key and fill lighting because the Cherry Picker is now permanently put away in the football shed, for some reason, so audiences shouldn't expect the marvellous illusions we've been able to pull off in the past.

I am trapped in a situation that puts me at great risk, both professionally and personally. I expect the school board to do something about it. My patience is at an end. My life must go on, and I want closure to this matter, preferably amicably.

I would advise you to put together a generous severance package, letters of reference, and resolve the legal quandary immediately. Be aware that I have already lost 30 per cent of my earnings over two years, and the expensive medication I am required to take is a direct result of the poor working conditions at the school.

Truthfully yours,

Bathos Lukno, B.Ed. T.A.D.

The next day Chuck brought me another set of copies of a letter that had been mailed to each trustee. Chuck explained he had intercepted the letters and was committed to shielding our "fine and hard-working" trustees from Lukno's toxic rants. Chuck told me it was our job, our responsibility, to insure that the trustees could focus their time and energy on governance issues and not be forced to wade through Lukno's psychotic wasteland. That was our job, he said. What he really meant was that it was my job.

In each envelope was a much shorter letter in which Lukno stated he wanted to provide additional context to his earlier letter. I wasn't sure that much more context could be provided, but I read the letters anyway. In them Lukno suggested that the new trustees not speak to Chuck about the veracity of his story but instead seek outside corroboration from a former principal of Daele Middle School, who "had abruptly left the employ of Arcadia for unstated professional reasons." This principal, Lukno felt, was the least biased person and most honest he knew, and the trustees could most certainly trust him to give an accurate account of the "REAL ISSUES" that had led to the accident. In any case, Lukno wanted to make sure that the trustees knew that the long delay in resolving this issue was, "akin to torture, never knowing who to trust or why these seemingly absurd obstructions are being placed in my path."

It's funny because in reading that line, I kind of knew how Lukno felt, but I was quite certain we weren't talking about the same thing. Yet, as disturbing as his rant was, there was in it a sense of righteous indignation that didn't ring completely false.

I also knew then that the whole Lukno-affair was going to be a monumental and volatile personnel matter that would consume much of my working time and energy. This was clearly the hottest of the staffing hotspots.

"I would like to come back to the details surrounding Mr. Lukno later, please? But, right now I would like to know about the process that transpired with the selection of the district's Technology Consultant," said Marie. "I had heard that you weren't very happy with the end result of it even though you were clearly in charge of the process. I heard there was quite a bit of friction between you and Mr. Chuck; I mean Mr. Stihl."

Bernard smiled as he replied, "Now where did you hear that from?"

Marie offered no response, and after a brief pause, he began to explain.

Katie Tekawitha leaned back in a stiff conference room chair and looked like she was struggling to find a comfortable sitting position, "It's clear to me who I think should be offered the job," she said. "Bob Bellarmine may not have a commanding personality or exude charisma, but I have no doubt he will work for us."

It had taken real effort, but I had convinced Chuck to allow me to form a selection committee for appointment of the newly created district position of Literacy with Information Communication Technologies Consultant, or the LICT consultant.

Chuck debated with me about it and only conceded after what I thought was some rather clever negotiating on my part, in which I convinced him that he would be respected even more by the principals if he was seen as being as collaborative as he felt he was.

He finally agreed to allow the formation of a selection committee composed of four people—myself and three school administrators—who could review resumes, shortlist candidates, draft up interview questions, hold interviews and finally make a decision about who should be hired.

But, he made it abundantly clear that this committee was advisory only and had no authority to make a job offer. After all, he reminded me, only he was authorized on behalf of the School Board to enter into employment relationships on their behalf.

I remember the bolded section of the "Terms of Reference," which each of us had been told we must sign as part of the process.

"All committee members are to observe strict confidentiality in regard to all aspects of staff selection and may not disclose any details of applicants or discuss aspects of the selection process with any person within or external to the school district that is not on the selection committee. Any violation of this provision may lead to disciplinary action up to and including possible termination."

While Tekawitha was adamant that the LICT consultant should be reporting under the authority of the principals and not to someone in district office, the position was created by Chuck who concluded he needed to force the infusion of computer technology into classroom teaching. The use of classroom technology mediated learning wasn't happening fast enough as far as Chuck was concerned.

It was not inherently a bad idea, the creation of a position that might support teachers in their work. However, the fact that Chuck, Richard and Vixie Ashern, the Assistant Superintendent of Student Potential had decided in a late-night think tank session fuelled by Cabernet Sauvignon that the person should report to Chuck made it an idea that the principals had to oppose.

Just as irritating as the manner in which the decision was arrived at was the fact that the think tank had decided—in the best interests of students—that schools should be forced to pay for the position through the commonly used central office accounting ploy of clawing back from school-based budgets so that it looked like the costs of central administration were not being inflated and that this was a voluntary contribution to the common good and Chuck's good.

"While a principal's work is inside the four walls of the school, our work is out there," Chuck would say while pointing out of a window. "You can see the work that a principal does inside the walls of the school and thereby assess his or her impact. But nobody could ever measure the tremendous impact I have on student learning."

It was no wonder, he would suggest, that people out there questioned what we did all day and why we needed so many people working at divisional office. They couldn't begin to comprehend our work, but we, the few who could see the big picture, knew what a tremendous difference we made in our students' lives.

"True," he declared with a straight face, "we do have this state-of-the-art multimillion dollar divisional office with some comforts. But in reality, the work we do is out there. So, no one is ever here to really enjoy them."

With those words, he would lift up his large mug of steaming cappuccino and take a sip. Chuck liked to have morning cappuccino made from the very chic Italian stainless steel machine located upstairs from his office in the trustees' private conference suite.

I looked at the faces of the three people seated around the melamine-covered table in our small second-floor conference room after an interview for the LICT consultant position. They seemed not to be happy sitting there. It was the room that principals were allowed to work from when we called them in, and I noticed that the hue of their skin matched the drab beige paint of the picture-less walls. This room for working sessions of the district's leadership team was in stark contrast to the trustees' meeting room complete with high-backed leather chairs, a polished teak board table and creatively lit impressive art hanging on the walls, which these principals might never see.

As I scanned the three faces, I ventured, "What does everyone else think?"

While I waited to hear a response from them, I began to think that there was probably a theoretical basis to explain what might happen next.

Expectancy theory rests on two fundamental premises: First, that individuals make decisions about their own behaviour and commitment in organizational contexts using their abilities to think, reason and anticipate future events—simply stated: they expect. Expectancy connects people to the extent to which an individual believes that his or her hard work may well indeed lead to improved organizational performance.

Agency theory is directed at exploring the ubiquitous agency relationship in which one delegates in whole or in part some work to another—the principal delegates work to the agent. An initial agency

126

problem arises when the desires or goals of the principal and agent come into conflict or when it becomes too difficult to verify if the agent behaved properly according to the principal's wishes. A second agency problem arises when the principal and agent have different tolerances for any risk associated with a decision.

Finally, after a tortuously silent pause, Gabrielle Lalemont, the well-dressed and poised 30-something year old Vice-Principal at Flanders Elementary spoke. "I like what Bob is all about. It seems to me that he knows his way around technology and can support what we're doing at Flanders. I'm pretty conversant with computer technology, and so are most of our teachers. What we really need is someone who can work with us from a teaching perspective, a supportive perspective."

It was neither expectancy nor agency theoretical rhetoric. It was just what a person committed to improving the lives of children thought she needed.

Lalemont picked up her pace as she continued, "I can tell you what we don't need. How about that?"

I never had a chance to respond and clearly she didn't expect one from me.

"What we don't need is someone else from central office who is going to come to our school and boss us around and act like we work for him."

She looked like she was straining to stop there, but couldn't.

"One Chuck, one Richard and one Vixie are enough for me. Thank you very much! We do not need a mini-me clone coming out to our school." And with that, she stopped and took a breath.

Without trying to show a visible reaction but wondering if she had just stopped short of including me in that list, I turned to Luca Anselm and asked, "Anything else to add?"

Luca smiled his usual smile that concealed what he really was thinking and replied, "Nope, I pretty much agree with Katie and Gabrielle. As far as I am concerned Bob has the knowledge, skills and personality to work well with my staff. He has the attitude we need, a real dedication to the field and great letters of reference. I agree that he is less charismatic than Isaac and I guess that is a turn-off for some people. But we all get more than enough top-down charisma thrust upon us that I don't need one more person telling me how to do my job."

He paused and looked around the room like he thought it might have a listening device and lowered his voice. "In reality though Keith, how much say do we really have in this decision?'

Tekawitha and Lalemont adjusted their sitting positions and leaned in toward the centre of the table. They seemed interested in hearing my response and equally concerned about the room being bugged.

The question was a fair one and timely. It was just that I didn't think it was all that fair at this exact time.

The committee knew how reluctant Chuck had been to agree with my position: the decision of who to hire should be made by the people responsible not only for paying the salary but for implementing the literacy initiatives that would follow.

They knew, all too well, that Chuck had reserved "the right," as he called it, as the Chief Executive Officer—he liked to call himself that, the CEO rather than Superintendent, when he needed to fortify his own sense of worth to support his decision-making authority—to ignore the committee's recommendation and hire who he wanted, which was clearly Isaac Jogues.

Jogues was a Grade 7 teacher at the school where one of Chuck's five children attended, but had started several dot com companies before going into teaching, and impressed Chuck with his talk of earnings in the millions, even though those earnings never materialized. The two men belonged to the same exclusive tennis club and had spent many hours on the court discussing and analyzing the ways in which technology might be enhanced throughout the division while engaged in a civil pastime. Perhaps somewhere in the middle of a set one morning it had dawned on Chuck that the answer to his concerns about finding a way to force principals and teachers to make better use of technology was standing there right in front of him, dressed impeccably in his whites, preparing to hit the ball.

What the committee did not know was that Chuck had told me that as far as he was concerned, the selection committee was nothing more than a recommending body at best and that it was my responsibility to make sure that they never lost sight of that fact.

"I am not going to let my hands be tied behind my back by some committee of principals that incorrectly thinks it gets to make decisions that belong under the authority of the CEO. At the end of the day," a phrase he liked to use a lot to insure the emphasis of his point was not lost. "It's me, Chuck, who has to stand in front of the trustees—who represent the aspirations of all of the parents in this school district—and explain why I hired someone. I need to have the confidence that I hired the right person to get the job done. I need someone who can play on my team."

Again, one of those senseless references to hiring people who are team players, and I wondered if any of these poor unsuspecting prospective employees knew that they were trying out for a team of lunatics?

Chuck did not have to say it because it was so abundantly clear. As far as he was concerned, the right person to get the job done was "Isaac Jogues."

I tried not to show the creeping sensation of defeat I was experiencing and told the committee members that I would go down and let Chuck know of our recommendation that Bellarmine be offered the position.

"Are you sure you want to go that way, Keith?" Chuck responded when I told him of the committee's recommendation.

"I know Bellarmine a lot better than any of you do, as he was part of the district's leadership development cohort last winter. He worked with me, Vixie and Richard for about 10 weeks exploring what it means to be a mission-driven leader, and while we might all agree that Bellarmine is a nice fellow, none of us saw any leadership potential in him. I just don't think Bellarmine can command respect from the principals, at least not like Isaac can. I just don't think he is cut out for this hard work. No he just won't do."

While I was listening, it became evident that I did not possess the x-ray vision that my senior administrative colleagues had because I could not see through Bellarmine and detect his utter lack of leadership potential.

Chuck didn't look up from his work on his desk as he spoke to me. "Who was the committee's second choice?"

While it was true, I knew the correct answer to the question needed to be Isaac Jogues—true or not.

"Great," Chuck replied. "Isaac knows his stuff and is no pushover. You know Keith, I've had the chance to get to know Isaac fairly well over the past few years, and I like what I see in him. He has real leadership potential."

As I turned to exit Chuck's office, he added, "Remind the committee of the terms of reference and issues of confidentiality."

Then almost as an after-thought he said, "By the way, please thank them for their work on this. Their colleagues will be pleased with the results of this decision as they get to know what a terrific guy Isaac is."

As I walked into the small conference room, Luca asked, "Well Keith, what did Chuck have to say about our decision?" I looked around the bland room and noticed that they had put away their notebooks and tidied up the room a bit. They looked as if they knew it was all over before I returned.

"And, I suppose you are going to remind us now that all of this had been done under the cone of silence and that anything we discussed is not be spoken about with anyone else, right?" Tekawitha added when I announced that Chuck had taken our second choice as the recommendation he felt he could support.

"Yes," I added apologetically. "I will remind you that all personnel matters are considered confidential and ask that you refrain from discussing the decision or the deliberations with anyone else."

"This sucks," Lalemont blurted out. Without caring how it sounded, she just emphasized it by adding, "This really sucks!"

Very quietly I replied, "Yes it does seem to suck, doesn't it?"

With that, Marie politely asked if people would like to take a break, and everyone seemed rather content to have arrived at that point in the day. As they left the room, Marie reminded them that it was getting late in the day and if people wanted to get home for supper, then a short lunch was better than a long one. Then as if it had just dawned on her she said, "I'll remind all of our articling students that the details of this deposition are, of course, confidential. How about we get going again in 30 minutes?" she added.

NINE

When Bernard had ordered lunch he wanted to be cordial towards the young waitress without making it seem like he wanted more from her than a coffee refill. He made eye contact and smiled to be civil, but deliberately refrained from the kind of small talk he saw other male customers seated at the u-shaped lunch counter engaging in with her.

He wasn't sure he could take another question, even a lunch-counter question, like "do you think that rain they predicted will really hit this afternoon?" Ayn's Café was not very busy and Bernard hoped his lunch break would give him a place to escape from the intense feeling of being interrogated. But, it happened quite frequently to him, this thing where random people he had just encountered would, without any overt invitation, begin to spill out parts of their life's story, opening up to him as if he had known them for quite some time, and as if he had said, with feeling, "What's up?" He sometimes wondered if the disdain he felt for small talk, and the facial expression he adopted when hoping to avoid it, didn't have the reverse effect — somehow attracting this sharing that ranged from soulful to needy.

After Bernard replied "no" to the waitress's question about a piece of pie for dessert, she asked him what line of work he was in.

He realized the file folder and pencil just sitting there next to him were a dead give away and silently cursed himself. "I teach at a university," Bernard replied.

"I'm just waiting tables until something better comes along. I do it mostly for the tips," Sass said. Bernard didn't need to ask her name as her nametag announced it: "Your server today is: SASS".

Bernard realized that Sass had just provided him with a cue for later on when the bill would arrive and thought to himself, "there's no way I'm going to leave a bigger tip than I would have otherwise just because she said that."

Sass leaned her elbow on the counter, but turned slightly away from him and panned her head back and forth, like she was scanning the room for spies. "Before I took this job I had applied for unemployment but was denied. I don't think they had a good reason to screw me like that. I used to work in retail, high end men's accessories. That's what I did until I got fired. The manager worked our asses off, and she was pretty nasty about it. I think she figured she could get away with treating us poorly with the lousy economy and all." By now Sass was looking directly into his eyes and Bernard found himself unable to eat or drink without seeming rude, though he wanted to do both, desperately. "At the interview I was promised 30 hours a week with bonuses for sales, but not too long after the store opened my hours were cut down to like fifteen a week. My friend got fired from there after only three days. The manager complained she spent way too much time flirting with the customers.

It's bad enough that someone like me with a degree in creative writing and tons of experience in all sorts of areas was fired. But, now I can't even use the store as a reference when I apply for jobs because I know that bitch will badmouth me. If I would've sucked up more to her and played her game, maybe she would've given me a decent reference.

I had a perfect record and was never written up for any disciplinary issues, like some of the other sales clerks who texted while on the sales floor, or called in sick, more like hung-over, every single Saturday.

I'm going to go back to school to try out a few classes and maybe enroll in a certificate program at the local college. Short of house-sitting, dog-walking, or serving," and with this word she made a gesture toward his plate that was so full of disdain, it gave him the feeling the food had come from the kitchen floor, "there isn't much work out there.

You know what really pisses me off? I got fired for nothing. I let some guy use my employee discount, and she said it's against company policy. What's the big deal? It's not like I was stole something. I just think she was in a bad mood. She wasn't all that attractive. Can you get fired for that, jealousy?" On this last word she turned away from his gaze and did her room scan again.

Before Bernard could think of something to say, Sass noticed that another customer, a man in a grey business suit who was looking rather anxiously at his watch, seemed to be twisting around in his booth looking around the café for her. She smiled at the man, closed her eyes quickly and raised a finger as one does when testing the direction of the wind, all of which was to communicate that she would be right over. She reached into her server's apron and placed Bernard's bill on the table.

"It was great meeting you," she said. As she hustled away from the table, she glanced back at Bernard and said, "Have a great day."

Bernard looked at the bill and tried to figure out what kind of tip he should give her. Bernard wondered how many people, like Sass, think they are fired for no apparent reason? He figured it might be half as many of the self-proclaimed innocent convicts who are locked up behind bars for crimes they claim they did not commit. The thought occurred to him that someone should research that, and maybe he

132

could, but before he got too far with that thought he was overcome with a sort of sunken feeling in his chest when he realized it was time to return to the deposition. Bernard decided to leave Sass a five-dollar tip on the twelve-dollar bill.

"Other than the people you have described so far—Mr. Stihl, Mr. Hehr and yourself—who else from the district's senior administration worked directly in the human resources area? And, would you say that they had a similar or different approach from the one you had?" Marie asked as she read off the prepared question list in front of her.

"Well, if you look at the organizational chart, under the delegated authority of the Superintendent I was supposed to be the sole person in charge of personnel management," Bernard said, "and when it came to staffing hotspots, things gone wrong, off the hook teachers, and financial messes, you could say no one bothered me. But, as I have explained, there were other people who found their way into certain aspects of personnel management that have a sort of allure. I am not sure if it's prevalent in all professions, but in education almost anyone who wants to be involved in personnel management, specifically in the supervising and evaluating staff, is allowed to do so. It's as if no one even considers that someone could be doing it wrong. And, there is little or no sense that wisdom or aptitude might be required to do it effectively."

When I first arrived at Arcadia, I was introduced to Vixie Ashern, the Special Coordinator of Gifted Education. It was Vixie's job to oversee the educational programs for the hundreds of students in the district who had what are termed "identified special needs" and to administer a multi-million dollar budget.

No easy task, I thought. However whenever I suggested to her that I thought it was a large area of responsibility, Vixie repeatedly asserted that she had it all "under control," and didn't mind the work as she was committed to making sure these often ignored students' needs were being met. No matter how hard or long she and her team of professionals had to work, she proclaimed, it was their mission to make sure these students were afforded the educational opportunities they deserved. Her team, as she liked to call her staff, was exceptional and second to none. Moreover, she declared, she had meticulously handpicked only the very best people for her team.

I tried not to think of what trying out for Vixie's team might entail.

Less than nine months after I started at Arcadia, as a result of the realignment of the senior administration's roles and responsibilities, Vixie became the Assistant Superintendent of Student Potential. And, simultaneously she was awarded a $30,000-per-year pay hike without having to take on any new responsibilities. With no increase in workload and armed with both her new title and hefty pay raise, I'm sure that if you had asked her at this time about whether she felt any sense of discrepancy, she would have told you that her sense was that life was inherently fair, and one shouldn't question fate.

Sometime after her promotion, I found out that when the Special Coordinator's position was initially posted as a vacancy, Vixie was not Chuck's first choice to hire and was only offered the job after the first pick turned him down. Nevertheless in offering Vixie the job, Chuck had ignored the fact that she had no experience managing a school, no experience or training in personnel management or school finance, even though she would have the ultimate responsibly for a staff of almost 150 and a budget of close to $4 million dollars. Somehow Chuck overlooked these shortcomings in such a fine prospect as Vixie, the former Home Economics teacher who had finished a distant second.

Vixie's name did not ring a bell with me at first, but in my second week on the job I learned that a number of years prior I had coached her son at the community level.

"You may not remember me as we only met twice," she said as she sheepishly walked into my office when we first met. "But, I certainly remember you. You were my son's T-ball coach. What an excellent coach you were. You were his first. I used to sit in the stands and watch you at work," she sighed a little whimper before she continued. "Tito still speaks so highly of you."

Speaking in what sounded like a staged reverent tone, Vixie continued, "I'm not sure I can call you Keith. I have such respect for you that I think you'll always be Coach Keith to me." Then she smiled a girlishly coy smile that seemed very much out of place on a 50-something-year-old woman.

Bernard noticed that, moments after he said that Kimberley Marie stopped smiling and cast her eyes downward at the page in front of her.

While I could remember vaguely what Tito had looked like, partially because he stood out from the other eight-year players on the co-ed T-ball team as the only one who sported $200 Oakley sunglasses to practice, my more lucid recollection of him was more memorable because his mother had made a point to tell me at the very first practice that, "Tito was named after the most musically talented but underappreciated of the Jacksons." But, other than remembering those two facts about Tito I had no recollection of his mother.

Besides, as I sat there recalling nothing more meaningful about Mrs. Ashern who stood there grinning before me, a feeling came over me—a feeling that I was somehow about to be played. The sensation slowly washed over me as she carried on with her kind words.

"Oh yes," I smiled. "How are you Mrs. Ashern?"

"It's Ms. Ashern; I'm single now. No more husband," Vixie explained with a smile. "I got rid of him," she said, emphasizing the "I" as if to make me understand that no one would ever, in his right mind, get rid of her. Then she added, "I used to have an awesome last name. I used to be a 'Lorenz,' but decided to hang on to 'Ashern,' since it was too much work to change names again."

Over time I found out that during her years as Special Coordinator she had managed to incur annual operating deficits, hundreds of thousands of dollars worth, three years in a row. When I brought it up with her one afternoon as I poured over the district's financial statements, Vixie's response was that Matt Capernaum, the since retired Secretary-Treasurer, had never told her about the deficits and if he had, she declared in self-defense, she certainly would have fixed the problem.

After pointing out the historical problems with her budgets, I found that from-time-to-time Vixie would come to see me for financial advice. She confessed, and said she was almost embarrassed to admit it, but her "ex" had always dealt with paying the bills. Typically, her visits came immediately after I sent her a quarterly memo identifying the potential for a projected deficit in one of her budgets. She would show up to my office and declare that there must be a problem with the numbers or more likely a problem with someone calculating the numbers because she was so very careful with every penny of public money. She was, most certainly, "not spending beyond her means," she would protest.

After I pointed out that the numbers were accurate and showed her copies of the receipts for all of the various expenditures she had authorized with her signature – like the "Team meeting over Sunday brunch for 8," or the bill from "Liquor World" for the holiday celebration for "The team" she held one evening at her home - she would ask, "Can you fix it before it becomes a bigger issue?" After agreeing to resolve the issue, she would usually flash that smile again and add something like, "I'm not really that good with numbers. I'm more of a people person!"

I remember that when I told Chuck about Vixie's budget deficits, he acted shocked. But he always seemed shocked to find out that someone had not told him about an issue that—had he only known about it—he could have heroically fixed.

Following that sobering conversation, Chuck told me he was going to put Vixie on a short leash and stated that if she did not address her budgeting inadequacies, he would certainly not be afraid to use that as a cause for levying some form of disciplinary warning.

As far as I could tell, there never was a "short leash" that Chuck could use to reign in her in or even a letter of reprimand placed into her personnel file, and Vixie continued to spend as she always had. In fact, at the end of her fourth year, as the Assistant Superintendent of Student Potential, Vixie posted a record setting $400,000 annual deficit.

Once, and only once, I angrily told Chuck that it seemed as if the district's senior administrators thought their budgets were just imaginary numbers, just spending targets that were not actually grounded in the reality that taxpayers had to foot the bill. Chuck simply stared right through me as he often did and didn't respond. Maybe he wished at that moment that I was just an imaginary person, carrying on about imaginary numbers, and he could slowly close his eyes, open them, and I'd be gone.

I remember one significant conversation early on with Vixie that left a lasting impression on me about who and what I was dealing with. It was December, and my cell phone rang as I was driving to work, "Hi Keith? It's Vixie. Can I meet with you right away? I have a very serious personnel issue that's come up, and I need some advice. I need to tell you about it right away."

"Sure, Vixie," I replied as I slowed down both the car and my mind to focus my attention. "I have another meeting this morning, but I'll get Desi to postpone it since this sounds urgent."

I waited in my office for about thirty minutes before Vixie finally arrived. Looking like she had run the distance between our two offices and somewhat out of breath, she walked in with a large still-steaming latte. She apologized for being a little late and explained that she had just needed to grab her morning coffee, "You know what it's like, Keith," she insisted.

She then went on to explain how she was a little unnerved and needed to gather herself after a draining night of work. "I can't believe what a night I have had. It's all that I do these days. I get up and just work nonstop." She took a deep sigh and simultaneously sipped on her coffee, ruining the artful swirl some proud coffee barista had crafted.

With a little milk foam on her top lip she said, "I think James Fisher and Ava Pepin, one of our "Craddle2Grave" Counselors, are sleeping together. I'm not sure they are but I have my suspicions. I can tell, usually, you know. They have this look on their faces and it's just so obvious. It's one thing for Pepin to be involved in a sexual relationship with someone. She's single. But Fisher is a married man. It just isn't right. I'm not letting Pepin off the hook, but she isn't a teacher. Fisher, on the other hand, is a married man and a teacher." Vixie seemed to emphasize the word "man" in her sentence as if I might not have realized that James Fisher was biologically male.

"We have to do something about this, Keith. We have to deal with this right away. I know what Chuck would say if he found out."

I had waited until there was a chance to interrupt. "I'm not sure this is our issue to solve, Vixie. What they do away from school and who they get naked with is not really our business. It's undoubtedly not my business. And, anyway, what makes you think they're having sex?"

It wasn't stupid juvenile curiosity that drove me to ask the question, I just thought Vixie seemed a bit unglued, not just at the moment but always, and I needed to get a sense of how unglued she was. I had often thought that Vixie, a faux-brunette with penciled eyebrows, was trying really hard to look like a young Elizabeth Taylor. But because of her erratic behaviour and intense energy—like someone hopped up on a cocktail of amphetamines, anti-depressants and opiate painkillers—she more closely resembled the late, great Ms. Taylor in her declining, addiction-riddled years.

Maybe expensive coffee alone could do that to a person. I would have to watch my intake, I told myself.

"Well it might not be obvious to you but there is a way people look at each other when they are having sex," Vixie replied.

I wondered how much she enjoyed invoking this topic in a professional context, where she could mask any voyeurism under the guise of concern for "the children."

"I don't mean how they look while they're in the middle of having sex. I mean people who are having sex just have a way that they look at each other. I know that look when I see it." She seemed pleased with her recovery. "When we have meetings, they inadvertently bump hands and then smile at each other. I know what that means too. And, when they walk down the halls together, the way they walk just makes it so obvious. What are we going to do about this?" Vixie said in a panicked voice.

My first reaction was that there was so much for me to learn about human relationships, sexual intimacy and non-verbal signals. In a new way, I would start to notice people who bumped into each other while walking. My second thought was: how could I get this meeting with Vixie to end quickly?

"Well Vixie, I suppose you should just have a meeting with them—off the record, of course—and tell them that you suspect they might be sleeping together and having sex. And, mention that if they are having sex, then they should stop doing it right away. How does that sound to you?"

She didn't seem content with this suggestion and may have picked up on the derisive tone. "Well," Vixie replied. "I asked my friend Rosa Lima, the Superintendent of Deepwater School District, what she would do if she had Fisher and Pepin on staff, having sex and all, and she told me she would fire him immediately." She seemed again to emphasize her reference to Fisher - "HIM!"

I was astounded. "You told who? And, you told her what? And, she said she'd fire him?" I tried to emphasize the "him," as Vixie had but couldn't make it sound quite right.

Vixie sensed my astonishment. "Rosa and I go way back. We were just out for drinks last night, at one of the local country bars. It was "Ladies' Night," so the bar was full of men. And, well, I mentioned to her that I had this personnel issue and she offered me some collegial support. You know it's just a conversation between professionals. I trust Rosa with my life. And, anyways Keith, she says it is grounds for Fisher's immediate dismissal."

If there were ever a time when I thought my head might just spin a complete 360, this was it. "Vixie, I can't believe you spoke to anyone about this issue before you spoke to me. Do you know what you've done?"

Vixie seemed unruffled by my reaction.

"The fact that you've involved someone outside the district in a very sensitive personnel matter is just plain wrong. And, while I might appreciate Rosa's insight, even if I am not keen that you asked for it, I've got a different opinion."

I spoke slowly, "Vixie, why don't you hold off from speaking with Fisher and Pepin right away. How about you just keep an eye on things and come back to me when you've got something that we can document. Let me know when you have some concrete evidence that they have violated something in their contracts or breached the professional code of conduct."

Then I added, "By the way, I thought you said you were working last night?"

Vixie agreed, reluctantly, to my advice to say nothing to the alleged couple. However, she didn't respond to my barb about being out at the bar with Rosa, as they worked on important pedagogical matters.

As she exited my office, she said, "Does it matter that Fisher has dumped his camper trailer on the gravel parking lot across from the school and that staff claim to have seen him and Pepin coming and going from it throughout the school day?"

I caught Vixie starting to smile as the last two words left her mouth.

I breathed a heavy breath, let my shoulders and head slump towards my desk and said I would call both Fisher and Pepin and have a pointed chat with them.

The conversations were similar and were, in fact, monologues by me.

"Look, I need you to know that it has been brought to my attention that you may be involved in a romantically intimate relationship with a colleague at the school. Before you say anything, I just need to remind you of the clause in your employment contract related to the requirement that you act in accordance with the standards of behaviour expected of all of Arcadia's employees who are entrusted to act, at all times, as role models for our students. I'm not here to judge you but I will, if necessary, do my job and deal with any disciplinary actions that are required in any circumstances when the terms of the employment contract are violated."

I caught my breath and asked, "Do you understand?"

Pepin sat very calmly through my speech and when asked if she needed any clarification, she simply smiled a very gentle smile and said, "No, thanks." She picked up her coat and briefcase and walked out of my office.

Fisher reacted similarly, although just before he left the office he did add, "You know Vixie has it in for me. I'm not sure what I've done to piss that lady off but she's bent on getting me fired. She just has a hate for me!" Then he asked, "Can you get me transferred out of that school and send me anywhere that Vixie isn't?"

I didn't commit to transfer Fisher but did reply that Vixie seemed to be not particularly fond of him. Just as Fisher left my office I added, "According to Vixie, it does seem to be all your fault, and I'll see what I can do for next year."

"It sounds like you may have undermined Ms. Ashern's authority at the end, Dr. Bernard." Ms. Marie said.

"I guess it might look like that to some," Bernard replied.

"Well, Dr. Bernard it looks that way to me," Ms. Marie added. "Don't you think it might look like that to an impartial observer?"

"All I can tell you Ms. Marie is that I take no satisfaction in watching people fall on their faces. I realize that people make mistakes, some of which are egregious and other ones that have less significant implications related to their actual job performance. But, unlike some people who I have worked with I actually don't go looking to find reasons to fire people. If you think I undermined Vixie's authority, I guess that is your opinion, which you are of course entitled to; even if it's wrong."

There was a silence in the room that seemed dense and lasted much longer than the actual minute.

The next school year, near the beginning of my second year, Vixie left me a message that she needed to meet because she had a serious personnel issue with one of her "Craddle2Grave" Counselors. Not Ava this time she reassured me but another one who had "gone bad."

According to the glossy brochures that Vixie had in the waiting room outside of her office, the Craddle2Grave Counselors, or C2Gs as Vixie referred to them, offered counseling support services to students that would enable "at-risk students to find inner contentment throughout their lives, from birth, and allow for their full self-actualization, until death".

On paper they were classified as paraprofessionals who acted as resources for mostly high school students if, and when, they experienced difficulties connecting life, home and school. The Craddle2Grave Counselors were required to hold a university degree of some kind, usually in social work or psychology, but almost any degree could qualify you to be a C2Gs.

Vixie supervised them, but, in reality, the C2Gs had a tremendous amount of freedom in how they got their work done and what was considered their work. From time to time, one of them might call central office frustrated by something work-related and looking to find Vixie for a consult. But, if they couldn't find her, which happened too often for my liking, they were referred to me—a person without a clear picture about what their jobs were - but someone who was in charge of all "personnel" matters and willing to listen to them.

According to Vixie, one of them, Berni Soubirous, had been suffering from some sort of aperiodic mood disorder. Vixie explained that sometimes Soubirous was just fine and could function, while at others times, sometimes for weeks at a time, she was incapacitated and unable to work.

Vixie told me that the last time Soubirous went on sick leave things had "blown up" because in "covering for her" Vixie realized that Soubirous's case files were a mess. The files were incomplete and, in some cases, nonexistent. And then when Vixie hired a temporary replacement for Soubirous, neither Vixie nor the replacement could make sense of the case files and notes. The files, years worth of notes, were incomprehensible to anyone but Soubirous.

Vixie also said she wasn't sure Soubirous was really sick, or actually as debilitated as Soubirous claimed she was.

"Can't we do something about it, Keith?" she wondered. "Come on, the woman can't be that sick. She's just working the system!"

I tried to explain that sick leave provisions and personal days are a legitimate form of time off given to employees who must miss work due to an illness or a personal situation. Since nearly all employees need such time off from time to time, almost all businesses negotiate with their employees to establish policies regarding sick leave and personal leave days—sometimes it is entrenched in collective agreements, while at other times it's just an operating principle written into policy.

I went on to add that a sick day is fairly self-explanatory and can be used for everything from a common cold to a more serious illness that might require hospitalization. And, as an employer, we only required a doctor's note if the illness persisted beyond three consecutive days.

"If you doubt that Berni is truly ill, just ask her for a doctor's note," I added.

I saw Vixie's eyes grow wide and lighten up with the possibility of an idea. She wondered if I might consider entering into the next round of union negotiations to have the current sick leave provision re-written to say something like: "We no longer accept a doctor's medical certificate as proof of illness, because if you are able to go to the doctor then you are certainly able to come to work."

I smiled and thanked Vixie for the amusing interlude, but then quickly realized based on her expression that she hadn't meant it to be funny.

"I'd like to put Soubirous under 'Intensive Supervision,' Keith," Vixie said. "Her work isn't just subpar; it's an embarrassment to the school district. I think Soubirous's poor performance may have a negative impact on the students she has been assigned to help. It makes us all look bad. It's not just about making me look bad. I could care less about that, but we have to do something before it makes Chuck look bad."

I didn't buy what Vixie was selling, about her not caring what she looked like, but I didn't bother to respond to that comment. I paused for a moment though and wondered why she was so worried about what Chuck looked like?

I asked Vixie who had hired Soubirous, if she knew if anyone had checked to see if there was a pre-existing medical condition that might not allow Soubirous to meet the obligations of her employment contract.

Vixie grudgingly admitted she had hired Soubirous, adding, "I needed to hire someone quickly to get the work done and never had the time to complete a professional background check. I'm running on fumes! But, come on Keith," she said, "Who could've guessed?"

Although tempted to respond, I said nothing.

Over the following days, I worked with Vixie to develop an "Intensive Supervision Plan" that I thought might work in one of two ways, if it turned out that Vixie's characterizations of Soubirous' profound weaknesses were indeed accurate. The first approach was to make sure the plan was directive enough to make Soubirous realize that she was not meeting the expectations of the job and lay out for her the enormity of what was required to make satisfactory improvement to successfully complete the supervision cycle.

The end goal of this approach was to counsel Soubirous out of her job. It's an often-used strategy in intensive supervision approaches, to make it so plainly obvious to a person that the requirements of the job—as laid out in the performance expectations—are so great that resigning is a better option.

Soubirous's plan included frequent conferences during which she would meet with Vixie who would provide specific and detailed feedback to her along with concrete suggestions for implementing effective case management planning and practices, including various organizational strategies for fixing the problems now festering in the chaotic system Soubirous had created.

Failing the necessary improvement, the second goal of this plan was to make the performance expectations appear attainable to any impartial observer but to make them just beyond the grasp of any mere mortal, thereby providing us with enough leverage for terminating her employment.

Many people find this second approach to dealing with underperforming staff not just distasteful, but inhumane. Some wonder how anyone of good conscience can do this and sleep at night. That wasn't an issue for me. When it came to personnel who were detrimental to a school, I found that if I did nothing, I couldn't sleep because students' needs were simply not being met.

Whether her medical needs were exaggerated or not, it was clear that she was incompetent. Yet, I knew that Soubirous's precarious status was really not a recent development but more of a systemic illness, which to me, meant that Vixie had allowed the problem to fester to the point of rendering someone's career essentially unsalvageable.

I would have been pleased to place Vixie on the same kind of intensive evaluative tract if she was under my supervision. And, the latter goal would have certainly been the only focus of the plan.

I thought we had done a reasonable job with Soubirous's plan until Vixie told me what happened at the meeting she had scheduled with Soubirous to deliver the letter and outline the details of the plan.

Vixie sounded frustrated as she spoke, "In she walks and before I can say anything about placing her under intensive supervision, Berni just smiles at me and hands me a note; a doctor's note. I gave it to Desiree. I'm so angry I can barely speak."

Somehow she did anyway.

"The note says Soubirous must go on a medical leave for an undefined period of time. What a load of hogwash, a medical leave forever! She knew the gig was up and the hammer was about to drop. They know when I mean business. I think she's afraid of me," Vixie added with a rather inappropriate glint in her eyes.

"I suppose she just went to see some flaky doctor and got a note that said she was unfit for work. There's nothing wrong with her. She is just avoiding the fact that she isn't doing her job well. Now she wants us to pay for her to get better. I think this is an abuse of our benefits' sick-time provisions. Now what do we do?" Vixie asked.

I had to acknowledge, at least to myself, that I was a little scared of Vixie. Not in the way I might feel when facing off against a worthy and intimidating opponent. No, I was more unsettled by the unhinged qualities of the woman standing in my office, and the gut instinct that she somehow envied Soubirous's clever manipulation of the system. That's what scared me.

I explained to Vixie that we would immediately send the notification of "Intensive Supervision" via registered mail to Soubirous and that upon her return to work, and after she had received medical clearance, we would initiate the "Intensive Supervision" provisions.

Vixie was visibly upset by this delay and made it clear that she felt Soubirous was abusing the system and getting off scot-free. Vixie seemed disappointed with my response that we could only send the letter and wait for Soubirous's full recovery and return to work. On hearing this, Vixie left my office in a bit of a huff.

Soubirous never returned to work during my tenure at Arcadia and while I was there we never initiated that Intensive Supervision Plan.

Oddly enough, about three months later while Soubirous was still on her doctor-ordered medical leave, I heard that Vixie was completing a program to become a bona-fide Certified Life Coach—a program designed to help people develop balanced, self-determined behaviours so that they could manage all aspects of their lives. But, I had also noticed that her on-the-job attendance was inconsistent, at best. These weren't just sporadic absences. It was obvious to anyone who wished to notice that she had become invisible at work and was hardly ever in her office.

From what Chuck told me, one morning Vixie called him at home and sobbed over the telephone that due to immense pressures resulting from caring for her ailing cat and tremendous amounts of work-related stress that no one else in the office could possibly understand, except maybe him, that she needed some time off work—with pay—to deal with it all.

It was about three weeks before Christmas and Chuck and Vixie agreed that she could use a combination of some of her unused sick-time, some unused vacation and then receive some paid days off, at the Chief Superintendent's discretion, to carry her through—with pay—until after the Christmas break. By the New Year, Chuck was sure Vixie would be back, better than ever.

I shuddered at the thought of a better-than-ever Vixie.

I told Chuck I thought she had brought this on herself, all of the stress. And, that while I had some sympathy for her situation and her sick feline, all the same, we still had jobs to do and staff that counted on us. But, in the end realizing he was going to approve her leave, I told him that she could use all of her sick time and maybe some accrued vacation days to cover the days at no additional cost to the district.

But Chuck looked disapprovingly at me and said that we (meaning me) should show Vixie some compassion during her time of need. He said we needed to be supportive of her and her family commitment.

I wanted to, but didn't bother to ask Chuck when a cat becomes a member of the family.

Then Chuck explained that Vixie had become so sleep-deprived from working at such an intense pace, coupled with having to care for her cat that she was under an intolerable pressure. Chuck earnestly told me anyone with a heart could see that the woman needed a break.

The lights in Vixie's office remained off for a month. But, I heard that somehow she managed to pull herself together enough to have a few of her favourite staff —the team within the team, I guess - over to her place on December 23rd for a Christmas celebration.

Amazingly when she returned in January, better than ever, Vixie informed me that she hadn't needed to take any of her banked holiday time for the paid leave. She insisted that the leave, the whole month-long absence, had only required her to use five of her sick days.

As much as I protested, it turns out she was correct. Chuck had crafted a memo giving her complete latitude to work from home for the month of December. She might be absent, Chuck outlined but obviously she was working.

I put up a fight, albeit a sad, weak protest that involved some gritting of teeth and rigourous fist shaking directed toward the heavens, but Chuck just told me to forget about it. Vixie had earned it, he argued, by virtue of being such a gifted leader. "She's one of the people taking us from 'good' to 'great' Keith, I can't believe you don't see it!"

Maybe Chuck liked the fact that Vixie was a gifted follower, of Chuck. Leaders who have followers who freely choose to follow rather than follow because they are required to by structure, decree, or out of fear are the very rare individuals who are able to have respectful personal connections with others, speak and practice the language of fairness and justice, and hold themselves accountable to the same criteria and standards they hold others to.

Additionally and importantly, these real leaders are emotionally honest and have the advantage of knowing that, if nothing else, their relationship with their followers is a tenuous asset and not a hindrance, an asset that requires delicate attention and care. We know these are the traits we immediately respect and appreciate in a leader. The leadership books are rife with lists and formulae supposedly meant to articulate the best traits for leaders, but sometimes I think we could learn more by asking the question, "What are the worst traits of a leader?"

Dr. Samuel Bacharach, a professor of labour management and workplace studies at Cornell University, offers some valuable insight on his online blog into what he perceives are three failures of leadership that often come around due to subtle attitudes that tend to lead to some unintended and undesirable consequences.

Firstly, he proposes that all too often leaders have the need to make it clear that they are in charge; the boss. They constantly reinforce their authority, their status, and their expertise. Secondly, they embody hypocrisy: they say one thing, but do another. He says that this behaviour is all too rampant in so-called leadership. For leaders, this means holding others accountable to one set of criteria and standards while holding themselves accountable to another set of criteria and standards. Thirdly, they will use emotional deception: Often leaders feign enthusiasm where they have none, fake grief when they feel none, project sincerity when they do not care. Such a leader will engage in an emotional conversation and feel your pain, and two hours later, will forget that you were even in his office.

I wanted desperately to refer both Chuck and Vixie to Dr. Bacharach's website, but didn't. I knew that they just wouldn't or couldn't get it.

Marie's tone withheld interest as she said, "That's very interesting, interesting indeed. It seems like you didn't much like working with Vixie and that there was some history between you two. You seemed, maybe just to me, to be a little jealous of her relationship with Mr. Stihl."

Before Bernard could reply, Marie added, "Maybe we could just come back to your experience and background in dealing with some of Arcadia's ongoing human resources problems, if you don't mind."

Bernard thought about trying to correct Ms. Marie's interpretation, but he knew she wasn't really interested in what he might add. Feeling tired from a second long day in the law office, Bernard did not respond to Marie's comment.

Instead he just responded to her later invitation.

In December, I received a phone call from a teacher by the name of Villana DeBoti who worked at Daele Middle School. She asked if she could book an appointment to see me about a personnel matter.

I had no idea what it was about—she wasn't on Frank's list, the hotspot list—but I agreed to see her.

Within minutes of sitting down she had recounted tales to me of how she had worked with Bathos Lukno at the Middle for about three years. She described how Lukno had displayed some very bizarre behaviours. And, how he had made many profane, really terribly sexist remarks, over and over again to her.

DeBoti told me that she knew some people who had been involved in an experimental theatre troupe with Lukno and how they thought back then, almost ten years ago, that Lukno was more than just a creep. They had described him as a bit of "a stalker." She said it was commonly known that Bathos Lukno was an oddball, but wondered how, "somehow" she added, that must have been overlooked when he was hired.

DeBoti told me she had informed the school's principal and two vice-principals about it all—what Lukno was up to at the time and what she knew about his past—but as far as she knew they had done nothing about it or him.

She told me how one time Lukno had found her in the photocopy room, alone after school, and how he went on and on about how attractive she was. But she said that Lukno said he knew she was a "married woman" and was "out-of-bounds." But, then she said Lukno asked her if she had a cousin, one as sexy as she was, that perhaps he could call up one day.

She told me her jaw almost dropped off her face when he asked that question. DeBoti told Lukno he was a creep and that she would rather poke her eyes out than set him up with anyone, let alone family.

She reported it to the school's administration—as she had done before—but as before, she said, nothing was done. After that she just tried very hard to keep her distance from Lukno.

I told her I would look into her allegations but then asked her what she wished for today. It had been quite a long time since this had happened: Why come to see me now?

She didn't answer that question right away and instead went on to describe how Lukno had a soft spot for some of the Middle School's students. He seemed to gravitate to those who were disabled or marginalized in some way. DeBoti said those kids often hung around near Lukno's office and that he was a frequent champion of their various causes in staff meetings.

Before I could ask, as if she was anticipating my next question, she said there was never any sign of sexual impropriety on his part. So, everyone on staff ignored the odd relationships he had with students. But, to her everything about Lukno was rather odd and hard to ignore.

However, she said there was an incident involving one specific student that perhaps I was unaware of and needed to know about. She felt compelled to tell me about it and that's why she had come to see me.

Apparently there had been a student with some form of physical disfigurement on her neck and upper chest, a terrible burn scar that she had had since childhood. This student apparently had gravitated to Lukno and was always hanging around his office. DeBoti said the girl was the Game Master of the school's "Dungeons and Dragons Group," which Lukno supervised. And, at some point during the year the girl missed school for about a month while she underwent corrective plastic surgery.

DeBoti said that Lukno, who was a bit of an amateur artist, created a "Welcome Back" card to give to the student upon her return to school. Lukno claimed, she said, that he felt bad for the student and wanted her to feel at home when she returned.

DeBoti described the card to me. On the front of the card was a hand-drawn picture of three dogs playing poker. Each dog was holding an over-sized hand of cards with only Jokers in them. Above their pictures was the caption: "We missed joking with you." Below each dog was the signature of one of the school's administrators. Inside the card was a hand-drawn picture of the back of a semi-nude woman posed around what looked like a taxidermied scene featuring a cheetah attacking an antelope.

Misinterpreting, in part, the look of incredulity on my face DeBoti assured me the likeness inside bore no resemblance to the young woman but, rather, it bore a striking resemblance to her. I was glad to hear that but still taken aback by the rest of the card.

I wasn't sure what to make of her statement. DeBoti said that copies of the disconcerting card had been floating around the staff room, and at least once she saw a copy of the card posted to the instructors' bulletin board in the staff room. She confronted Lukno about the card and admitted to me that she had yelled at him. He shot back that she was making a mountain out of nothing, and besides, it was a private matter between him and a student and really none of her business.

To DeBoti, it was her image that Lukno had rendered in the felt tip pens as some kind of target. And after this incident, she said Lukno was more hostile toward her and increasingly she felt threatened. But then the theatre accident happened and not long after Lukno was gone.

I explained that I couldn't disclose any health information related to Lukno, his condition or his return. But did try to re-assure her that she could probably feel safe for quite some time. Near the end of our conversation, DeBoti told me she felt validated by my willingness to listen and that she was beginning to feel that she had done the right thing by coming to see me. Finally, she ended, "I think I can trust that you will do something if ever the circumstances necessitate." I replied that while I appreciated her vote of confidence, I would rather she hold off with any praise until she knew that I actually had done something. As she left the office, I knew I had to do something about Lukno but hadn't a clue what that something was going to be.

Disturbed by the vividness of his recollection, Bernard paused and let out a heavy sigh. His thoughts quickly turned to other scenarios Marie might find helpful.

I'm not sure what gets a hold of parents when they name their children. It seems that some never actually sit down and, with sobriety, consider that the name they choose is for a lifetime. I was struck by that thought right after Richard Hehr (which in the most innocent way could unfortunately be contracted to Dick Hehr), left my office after telling me he had no idea how to handle the bumbling principals in his midst and that they were my "personnel" problems to deal with and solve.

Richard had recently hired a new African refugee assistance program worker, Kiani Okoro, who was assigned to work with at-risk students in an afterschool program at Verdun Middle School and Amiens Collegiate. Ms. Okoro wasn't his first choice, he explained, but his two other choices had declined his generous offer as he said, "for selfish reasons."

One applicant said the schedule conflicted with her need to be home to care for an ailing father, while the other said the late evening hours and minimum-wage salary would just add to an already stressful home life. He declared he had no choice but to hire Okoro or be left without anyone to help these poor, struggling students.

In the six weeks since Okoro had been hired, Richard explained, she had not shown up for work six times. And, on all of those occasions she had still filled out a timecard indicating that she had worked each of those days. He was upset because she had been paid for days she didn't work. "It's impacting my budget!" He declared.

I told him I was a little confused because payroll won't accept a timecard without a supervisor's signature on it. "Did anyone authorize her timecard?" I asked.

"Yes, the two principals both signed it," he replied. "Damn it I don't know what, or if, they were thinking. You'd think they would know better than to allow this to happen," he punctuated.

"Did you know about it?" I pushed a little. "Did you know she was absent and paid for six days she didn't work?"

"Yes, I knew they had done it, after the fact, of course. But, Keith I am not their babysitters. It's their responsibility to verify the time cards. I hired her, but they supervise her. Come on. She's their responsibility!"

"But, you knew that she falsified her timecard for six weeks and claimed hours she didn't work, and you didn't speak to her about it?" I asked just to make sure both Richard and I knew what I was thinking.

"Look Keith, I am too busy to check all of the details. That is not what Chuck wants me focused on. I've got a plan to get the at-risk kids to attend school more regularly, so that they can succeed." He was getting louder and redder in the face.

"Chuck and I have a big presentation that is due after the holiday break for the Ministry of Education folks on our strategies for dealing with this absenteeism problem. They see us as a model for the whole province. As far as I am concerned, this a human resource issue, and you can deal with it. Talk to the principals and they'll tell you about it. She just has to go. She's a poor performer and bad influence on the other staff. I've done all I can be expected to do and now I want her fired." And, with that Dick Hehr walked out of my office.

I could have done nothing in response and passed the problem back to Richard. But I just couldn't stomach the idea. The history of human resources in Arcadia was a gigantic game of pass-the-hot-potato with everyone waiting for the music to stop to see who was left with scalding hands, and an inedible, overcooked potato that no one wanted to touch let alone eat. I just couldn't do that.

Before I began working at Arcadia's central office, they had established an annual tradition for district office staff to sit down for a Christmas luncheon. It was quite popular with superintendents and administrative staff and even the maintenance guys and gals were invited to sit down together, mingle and share good cheer—so long, as Desi had pointed out to me, as the various classes of people sat in the right places at the table.

It had also become part of the tradition to exchange small gifts, inexpensive items wrapped in ribbons and bows. The gift exchange was governed by the rule that when someone's name was drawn he or she could run up to the gift table and choose something. Each subsequent person could choose a gift from the table or steal the gift from a previous contestant. It provided some comic relief to the stuffy, business-like atmosphere that usually dominated the building.

Right after my name was called, I knew that it would be more fun, for me, to steal the gift from Sasha Plaxico, the curriculum specialist. Right after I took her gift with a wry smile and returned to my seat, I heard Chuck bellow, "I can't believe it, the cold-hearted human resources guy is taking a gift from the pregnant lady! Did you see that, he just went over to the lady who is eight months pregnant and snatched away her gift? What a cold heart, ha!" Chuck seemed please to offer his sense of humour as a gift to everyone.

I tried to crack a smile and laugh with the others when he finished, but I also knew that Chuck was taking an opportunity, one that I had given him, to take a cheap-shot at me and my character which would inevitably make him look both funny and somehow give the impression that he was correct and I was wrong in assuming that the state of being pregnant didn't preclude a little party-game fun. Miraculously, or maybe precisely because of his success in painting my image as a cold-hearted human resources bastard, I was able to leave at the end of the day with those very shiny grilling tools.

He gave off an air of wanting, desperately, to be seen as a hip and a with-it kind of guy, a contemporary and emotionally intelligent Renaissance man who had this deep connection to other living things, including pregnant women I suppose. It seemed to work for some people, maybe a lot of people, this public persona of his, as there were many who seemingly hung on almost every word that came out of his mouth.

Truth be told, I don't think it did me any harm, at least professionally, to be thought of as a person who could steal a spatula from a soon-to-be mom or deal in an unemotional manner with employee terminations. I seemed for the most part to be free of the signs of distress and turmoil that often come with the tough decision-making that can profoundly affect people's lives; telling folks that their work-performance is sub-par and they might lose their jobs takes a certain personality, and I guess I possessed that.

The few who really knew me might laugh at that. But Chuck's interpretation of my character, as incomplete or incompatible as it really was, suited me in this particular professional career and allowed me the freedom to act on my ethical beliefs and training, a freedom that was, I suppose, threatening to others now that I look back on it.

I sat down with the large gift bag and rummaged through the tissue paper. Barbecue tools. Not a bad gift, I thought to myself as I watched Duffy, the district's plumber, slowly get up and swagger over to the table. I could feel the swell of excitement just thinking about backyard summertime barbecues with my kids. I felt kind of silly liking that gift so much.

It was four days before the Christmas break when I asked Desi to call in Ms. Okoro for a meeting. I told Desi to let her know beforehand that the meeting was a formal one about terminating her employment contract with the school district.

In the meeting, Okoro shed tears and accused the school district—not me personally, but Richard Hehr and the two principals she worked under—of sheer incompetence.

She cried and dabbed her tears with a tissue as she explained that no one, not a single person, had told her of the job expectations or the absolute requirement for her to accurately record every minute of her whereabouts. As she grabbed more tissues from the box on my desk, I tried to explain that I was not much interested in accounting for her every minute, but rather wanted to know when she actually did or didn't show up for work.

She explained that at her last job, all she had to do was simply fill out her timesheet and kind of account for the hours that she thought she had worked, a rough estimate, she said. Her boss, a trusting fellow, didn't care when or where the work was done, as long as work got done. She thought the district would care more about the successes she was responsible for than where or when the work got done.

The story was painfully reminiscent of the logic Chuck had used to justify Vixie's proclivity to work from home, unbeknownst to anyone but Chuck. As long as the work got done and was a success, why should it matter if people saw Vixie shopping at Costco midweek or midday in her beachwear? It was all about getting the job done, Chuck had said, and Vixie delivered!

Okoro went on to explain that she had made a half dozen phone calls from home on Sunday evening to some of our historically truant students and their parents to get them back into school. She said she never counted the hours or minutes that the calls took out of her family life on a Sunday, which she pointed out was really overtime, double-time she insisted, and was probably eight hours at least.

But it worked, she said, and those kids were back in school on Monday. Did it really matter that she had instead filled in that she had worked on the following Tuesday morning from nine until noon, even if she was really at the doctor with a sick child or maybe in the drive through at Sushi Quick at that moment, she wanted to know? She said she couldn't remember where she was exactly. Maybe she was at the vet's with her sick dog, she wondered out loud.

I calmly told her it did matter what she listed on her timesheet and that I couldn't accept anyone falsifying the district's corporate records. I asked her why she didn't check with either of the principals or Mr. Hehr to see if this was permissible or not?

She had thought about it. She had thought about asking for permission to do it. But, they all seemed too busy. They never had time to answer any of her questions. Why was this such a big issue, she wanted to know? It was just a few weeks before Christmas, and a lot of people skip out from work right before Christmas, she added.

I didn't respond to the last comment but did tell her that on a Friday—two weeks past—she had filled in her time card indicating that she was at the annual district planning meeting with all of the other program assistants who work with at-risk student populations; except she was not there. And, I told her, that it was obvious to everyone in the room that she was not there. Her place at the board table, with her name card, was unoccupied all day long. Mr. Hehr had chaired the meeting, and both of her supervising principals were present. She had indicated on her time sheet that she was really there, at the meeting, when she clearly wasn't. It was indeed a big issue.

Why didn't someone tell her about this back on the day it happened, she stammered out? Had she known that she needed to attend that meeting, she surely would have. She could have gone to the wool shop another day, she disclosed.

I didn't have a reasonable answer to offer.

Four days before the Christmas break, a full week before Christmas day, I handed Ms. Kiani Okoro a letter immediately terminating her employment contract with the school district.

Yes, one week before that day of Christian and secular celebration, I sent a single mother, a member of one of our local marginalized communities, out of my office unemployed and feeling very upset.

It did hurt and, yes, I did lose sleep. Not only because of what I had done to Ms. Okoro, but because of the fact that three men who earned combined salaries in excess of $350,000 were just too gutless to do the right thing and do their jobs. Instead of dealing with an errant employee early in her tenure and trying to solve a small problem before it became an intractable one, they washed their collective hands and walked away from her.

And, I thought that if they had maybe done their jobs and done them well, that Okoro and her kids would be celebrating a happier Christmas than the one I had delivered.

Bernard looked at the people seated in the room and realized they were reading him in multiple ways. From one student came a compassionate nodding of the head, while from another who leaned precariously far back in his chair he got a look of horror. Wilson Lee looked up at the ceiling like a man calculating a big figure, and Ms. Marie was sketching some abstract shape at a high speed in the margin of her notebook, her first unpoised, nervous gesture all day. Then he noticed that even the stenographer had stopped typing and was staring directly at him. Oh if only this story had taken place the week before Groundhog Day or St. George's Day or Victoria Day when people could more clearly see this action for what it was: difficult and just.

Wilson Lee interrupted the awkward silence and said, "This seems like a really good time for a break, Dr. Bernard. We have been over quite a bit of terrain today and you must be tired."

Bernard looked over at Lee and just nodded his head up and down a single time. A break seemed like a very good idea, Bernard thought.

"But, I would like to make it a short one so let's begin right at three o'clock, if that is fine with you Dr. Bernard and you Mr. Lee," Marie said. She seemed impatient to allow for a longer than necessary break. "I'm not rushing anyone but I think we can have it all wrapped up by the end of the business day today."

Bernard, looking tired and a little worn out, realized he had rather counted on another short "lawyer" day. Maybe he did not quite understand lawyers' hours yet. He just said, "Fine."

Marie's poignant "Well then," was both gracious and somehow off-putting, and with that final word from Marie, the timekeeper, people collected some of their electronic and paper belongings, stuffed them into their briefcases, and headed out of the conference room.

TEN

Bernard stared at the framed black and white poster in the reception area of Fowler and Harper enjoying the short break from the deposition. As he looked at the words on the poster, "25th May 1965 Muhammad Ali vs. Sonny Liston First Minute, First Round," and he stared at the impressive Ali towering over the prone Liston, he was surprised to find himself thinking about his father, Bill Bernard.

"Brawlin' Bill Bernard" had deep brown eyes. His pupils were black in a menacing way. His voice was gentle but whenever he was angry it rasped on the ears like the grating of a heavy boot on a sandy floor.

As Bernard gazed at the print, he could remember Bill saying, "That was the best part of my whole life, the fight game. When I was training for a fight, I was in fighting fit shape. I wasn't afraid of any man alive. I had my whole life in front of me and I thought I could do anything. I thought it would never end. I thought it would never end."

Bernard remembered how he used to stare at the old boxing photo of Brawling Bill. His father was in a boxing stance with his left arm thrust forward and his right cocked. He was wearing those black leather shoes with long laces, and white socks rolled down half way to the top of his shoe. His feet were wide apart and he was up on his right toe with his left foot planted. He had on those shiny dark shorts and his gloves looked real thin. He didn't have much hair then either. Bernard remembered how he used stare at that one picture, the only picture from his father's fighting days. It made him feel proud to have a professional boxer as his dad. It made him feel tough.

Bernard's father's story, like so many that shared with him the dream, was borne from desperation. Both Bill's parents died when he was young and Bill would remind his son, he grew up dirt poor. By the time Bill was in grade 7, he had figured out his fists could back up his smart mouth and they were heavier than the enormous chip he carried on his shoulder.

Bernard never became a boxer. He learned pretty early on in life after losing too many schoolyard dust-ups that his hands weren't like his father's, they were neither fast nor heavy. And, in high school Bernard discovered that his mind was swifter and more powerful than his hands. His toughness would not come from being able to physically beat someone into unconsciousness. Bernard had learned that his greatest asset came from keeping his mind sharp and focused.

About three weeks before Bill died, while Bernard and his father were making their weekly trip to the doctor, Bill told him, "When I was at the top of my career, I never thought I'd get old like this. When I was in the gym, training for a fight I thought it would last forever. It seems like only yesterday. But, that's the fight game. You can land on your ass in a minute and no one will remember you. Stay on top of your game, Keith, and don't let someone make you fade away like a memory."

"Dr. Bernard," the receptionist called over to him. "They are ready to get going again."

After the afternoon break, it was apparent that a few more people had been invited to join in for the final session of Bernard's 2-day interrogation. Without trying to show that he was making a precise count, Bernard noted there were five new faces in the room that had not been there earlier.

"I hope you're OK with the fact that we've invited some of our other associates to sit in. I spoke with a few of the firm's other partners and we thought this might be a great opportunity for them to get some more experience in the closing part of discovery deposition. You don't mind, do you?" Ms. Marie asked.

Bernard didn't reply and Marie regarded the lack of protestation as agreement.

"Can we please continue? I would like it if you could pick up where you left off on the whole Bathos Lukno situation," Marie said.

Still fortified by the stale sandwich Bernard had purchased at lunch from "Ayn's Café" in the building's lobby and the recent twenty minutes of peace and quiet, Bernard obliged.

Sometime in mid-January, not long after the one year mark of my taking on the position of Superintendent of Human Resources had come and gone, silently, like all anniversaries of administrative posts, I met with certain administrators who had worked at Daele Middle, separately; I met with the ones who had signed the repugnant card. I asked each one the same rehearsed question, "What the hell were you thinking about when you signed that card?"

Before they could respond, I added, "If I have this correct, after Lukno showed you that card you thought it was a lovely idea to sign it? And, it never crossed your mind that it was a really stupid idea?"

Each said that he felt bad about his error in judgment. But, none admitted that he saw it as a big deal back then or admitted that he had given any thought to it since. Of course, now, with me standing in front of him and making such a fuss about it, each said he could see it in a different light—the distasteful graphics, the inherent violence, the fact that copies of it had circulated like photocopies of Gary Larson's "Far Side" cartoons that seemed to be stapled to the corkboards of the staff rooms throughout the nation - but who could've known that Lukno was so unstable, they asked?

Each of them promised never to do it again. Even with the feeble act of contrition, I wanted to fire them, right then and there. However, this incident had occurred four years ago and no disciplinary action had occurred then. There wasn't so much as a note about it in any of their personnel files. I knew that there was really nothing I could do about them now due to the fact that Frank had not done his job then.

If I attempted to discipline them now, it might be proposed by a labour lawyer that when this whole affair occurred it had obviously not been a serious enough infraction as to warrant a disciplinary charge. Furthermore, as part of a vigourous defense that lawyer could rhetorically ask, "How can it suddenly be such a big deal four years after the fact, now that you are here?

I knew that lawyer would have a decent argument because this unpleasant incident had occurred after April 1999—the infamous month of the fatal school shootings at both Columbine High School in Littleton, Colorado, and W.R. Myers High School in Taber, Alberta. With all of the intense interest in understanding why school shootings happen since 1999, it has been taken for granted that school personnel are more vigilant of the tell tale signs of potential school violence. The labour lawyer might suggest that, obviously, this card was nothing more than an insensitive joke and nothing more ominous, otherwise the people in charge surely would have taken it more seriously.

In my first meeting with Villana DeBoti, she told me she had contacted Frank and told him about the card and her encounters with Lukno. She said that Frank held an emergency staff meeting at Daele Middle and explained to all assembled that, while there had been, perhaps, an error in judgment by the principal and vice-principals, these were three good men and exemplary school leaders who had made honest mistakes and deserved forgiveness. Frank told them that they needed to put the incident behind them and move on. DeBoti said that after the meeting many of the women on staff realized that the meeting exemplified central administration's shameless, guiltless and above reproach mentality that seemed to be focused on protecting the reputations and careers of a few "good men."

I had looked through the various boxes of archived memos and letters written by Frank from the time period, but couldn't find anything about the card or the staff meeting. I asked Desi if she remembered the incident and while I thought her frown answered my question, she said she didn't remember the incident. I thought there must be something somewhere on record about it. Then one afternoon as I was going through a box that was in the basement marked "Frank's miscellaneous - SHRED," I found a copy of the card. I was dumbstruck and sickened by what I saw. It was exactly as DeBoti had described it.

In another meeting, DeBoti told me that she had heard that Lukno was planning to come back to Daele Middle. When I asked who she had heard this from, she told me she was on very good terms with one of the newly elected school trustees and he had told her. "It's still a pretty small town," she added. DeBoti had also heard that Lukno had been sending letters to the school trustees requesting their intervention on his behalf to resolve the predicament he was in. She said she wasn't sure if I had a plan to deal with Lukno or not, but said she was worried for the safety of her female colleagues, her students and herself if he were ever allowed to return to the school. It was obvious to me from her demeanour that she was genuinely frightened by the prospect of Lukno returning to Daele. Now that I had seen the card myself, I thought I had a sense of how she felt.

I knew that there were only so many reassuring words I could offer to her, so I told DeBoti that she might want to contact the local police and file a report about her dealings with Lukno. Then the police could decide if it was something worth pursuing or not. By the end of the meeting, DeBoti told me that was precisely what she planned to do.

I would have a few more meetings with DeBoti because she wanted to know what was happening with Lukno and what was I doing about him. "Can you give me an update?" She would ask. All I ever told her was that I was trying to ensure the safety of the students and staff at Daele. At the end of most of our conversations, DeBoti would say that she trusted me. But I never felt that I had earned her trust because I believed that Frank, who could have addressed the problem in his role as the Superintendent of Human Resources, had let her and her colleagues down. I knew that I had to make sure that Lukno never taught at Daele Middle School or in the district again. I also felt that I had to find a way to not only get him out of Arcadia but also find a way to get him out of teaching altogether. Then perhaps, I thought, there might be a reason to trust the Superintendent of Human Resources.

Bernard glanced over to Marie and said, "Bathos Lukno might have been one of the most mishandled cases of personnel mismanagement in Arcadia, but he certainly wasn't the only individual whose personal life became so inseparable from his professional identity that any imaginary line that is supposed to delineate the two ceases to exist. Did you know that?"

Marie didn't respond, but did seem to be listening.

After almost a full day of this intense across the table process, Bernard felt that he could pick up on the subtle cues that were part of Marie's decorum, like how she lifted her pen about one centimetre off the desk and held it there, as if suspended in air. He took that to mean, "proceed."

Bob Tonney was Arcadia's Manager of Plant Operations and Maintenance and it was his job to ensure that all of the school construction, renovations and regular maintenance were done in a timely, appropriate and cost-effective manner. He was also the person who supervised the schools' custodians. These were the men and women who were in many regards the oddest and quirkiest conglomeration of misfits but who, in many other ways, were among the most honest and genuine individuals employed by Arcadia. One thing this whole group seemed to have in common, I discovered, was a strong mistrust of the central office administrators.

For reasons unbeknownst to me, I have usually been able to connect with the custodians and find them refreshingly honest in their appraisals of how things really are—and how they ought to be. They seem to accept me as one of them, a bit of a misfit. If there were ever a time when two life rafts had to be tossed off a sinking ship, I'd definitely want to be with the custodians rather than spend my days floating adrift with Chuck, Richard and Vixie.

"Hey, Keith," Tonney said as he stood outside my office door in his flannel work shirt and oversized jeans that barely hung on his hips.

"If you're not too busy, do you have a few minutes to talk?" Before I could answer, he said, "If you're busy, I can come back some other time. I know you're busy with something or other. Maybe I should schedule an appointment with Desi?"

As he caught his breath, I replied, "No, come on in Bob. I have time. What's up?"

He asked me if I knew much about Blaine Pict, the division's Head Painter. I said I didn't know much about Pict except that I found it odd that I hadn't met him. I had been at the divisional office for a year and thought that Pict might come by and introduce himself since he was the president of the Painters' union and we were heading into contract negotiations pretty soon.

"I think he's trying to avoid you Keith," Tonney said.

"Why's that?" I asked.

Tonney never answered that question but went on to say that Pict and Frank had an odd relationship. In public they were amicable; however, when they weren't in the same room each spoke very poorly of the other.

I mentioned to Tonney that while the behaviour didn't seem very professional, in my experience it was fairly commonplace—the to-your-face congeniality concealing a behind-your-back acrimony.

Tonney admitted that this kind of two-faced behaviour was common, but added that it was stranger than simply that. He explained that one summer Frank had Pict take a crew of employees out to build a large dock at his cottage. It was a private transaction, Tonney said. Pict didn't do the job at Frank's place during work hours as if to reassure me that it wasn't anything truly improper. But, still Tonney said it did seem to be a highly unusual arrangement. Just plain weird, Tonney said. After that summer, it seemed to Tonney that Frank and Pict had really become quite good friends.

"You know, after that summer I think they started hunting together; they became goose hunting partners. From their stories, it sounded like they'd spend a lot of time buried in the ground at night sharing a bottle of whiskey, telling stories and waiting to open fire on unsuspecting geese at daylight."

I kept on listening to Tonney not sure of where the story was going. Tonney then said that Pict had been issued a company cell phone because his job demanded an immediate response from the chief Painter in case there were any midnight school emergencies.

"Does this have anything to do with the dock Pict built at Frank's cottage or goose hunting?" I asked.

Tonney said "no," and then went on to say that a while back Pict had been caught using his phone to access sex-chat lines. According to Tonney, Liz Clare, a woman I sometimes and warmly referred to as our "pit-bull in a chiffon dress" accounts payable clerk had noticed a whole lot of odd 1-900 phone calls on Pict's cell phone bill.

I wasn't surprised to hear that Clare had carefully read through Pict's cell phone bill because I had learned that Clare was a stickler for details and often took it on herself to know how company property was being used and the public's money was being spent. I also thought that she might have been slightly bored with mind-numbing data entry and decided to fill the void by reading everyone's cell phone bill.

Tonney explained that Clare, a fan of mystery novels, had decided to dial up one of the numbers on Pict' bill to see what the phone calls might be about. She pressed the numbers 1-9-0-0-3-6-7-5-8-7-8.

"Thank you for calling 1-900-FOR-LUST, I'm Candy. What's your name?"

Tonney wasn't sure what happened next but figured there was probably a pause before Clare replied, "Well, this is Liz…hum…no I'm not going to tell you my last name. It's just Liz. Who am I talking to?"

"That's a very sexy name, Liz. I wore something special for you tonight. Can you guess what it is? That's right, I'm wearing a thin white t-shirt and tight cut-off jeans. Gee, Liz I hope you don't mind, but I forgot to wear any panties."

Click! Clare hung up.

Flustered and embarrassed but ever more determined that she needed to know what this was all about, Clare tried another number from Pict's phone bill.

"Thank you for calling 976-SEXY, I'm Jasmine. What's your name? That's a sexy name, Liz. So I guess you like girls? That's perfect because I've got a limo parked right outside my place, and the driver is very discreet."

Click! Clare had solved the whodunit and it was Blaine Pict who had done it and it was not good.

Tonney went on, "I guess Liz told Frank that Pict had racked up almost $1,000 worth of cell phone charges to various 1-900 numbers over three months. At least that's what Frank told me over coffee. And, Frank also said he wasn't looking forward to dealing with Pict."

Not quite sure what to ask next, I stuttered out, "Do you know what Frank did?"

"From what I know, he had a chat with Pict. You know a serious one and he told Pict that he knew what he was up to and that he had better stop doing it."

"He did what?" And, I wondered if any finger wagging might have occurred during the conversation about "it," but couldn't feign enough seriousness to ask it without cracking a sarcastic smile.

Tonney went on, "Pict and his wife were having some issues—you know the marital kind." I was cringing as Tonney spoke, terrified of knowing too much.

"I guess Frank figured that a stern talking to would solve the problem."

I breathed a heavy sigh of relief, "And did it? I mean do you know if Pict stopped calling the sex lines?"

"Not sure about that, to tell you the truth. I know he got to keep his cell phone. Heck we need him to have that puppy. I'm not sure how we could survive if Pict wasn't on call. But to be honest with you, I have another issue with Pict," Tonney said. "Can we talk about that?"

"Does it have anything to do with his cell phone and telephone sex?" I asked.

"No," Tonney looked at me with one of those sad, "try to keep up son," looks. "It has nothing to do with sex. I think Pict has stolen some tools from the shop. We don't usually mind if staff borrows equipment because they need to know how to use stuff and what better way than to try it out at home. But, recently Pict purchased $3,000 worth of air-spraying tools and we can't find any of them in the shop. I'm not sure if they ever made it into the shop. I think they may have just gone straight into Pict's workshop at home. I wouldn't have ever known, but Liz asked me about a whole bunch of purchases that Pict made in the last month on a district purchase card. You know, they are sort of like credit cards. It sure saves a lot of work to not have to get approvals for every little purchase. But, I guess there can be problems with that also?"

I wondered if I had this correct: $1,000 worth of charges on the company cell phone to access sex chat lines that had been dealt with by a stern chat. And, now there was a possible theft of thousands of dollars by the same guy who also happened to be the president of one of the unions. I felt obliged to ask, "Is there anything else I should know?"

"Well maybe you should know that Pict was dating Liz's daughter for a while. Right before all the stuff happened with the sex chats. Guess to some folks it was an affair. I suppose that might be true seeing that Pict was still married and all. And, I guess there was a nasty falling out between Pict and Liz's daughter, downright nasty. Pict told me one morning that he's convinced that Liz is out to get even and ruin his life."

What I had learned five minutes ago about Pict was bad enough, but adding to that this last fact that while he was married he had been romantically involved with the daughter of the district's Accounts Payable Clerk who now might have a vendetta against him, well that sort of took the whole thing over the top and I hoped there was not more to learn from Tonney. Tonney asked if there was anything else I needed him to explain to me.

"Nope, I think I have it now," I said.

As soon as Tonney left my office, I had Desi bring me Pict's personnel file and as expected I didn't find anything on record in his file related to the cell phone abuse. Other than a yellowed and poorly written 16-year-old resume there was nothing in Blaine Pict's personnel file. Against my better judgment, I asked Desi if she knew anything about any of this, and she responded with the words, "I know nothing—NOTHING!" With the poor German accent, I was sure it was said as homage to the inept Sergeant Schultz from the 1960s comedy "Hogan's Heroes." That thought brought me little solace as I remembered that none of the principal TV characters ever escaped from Stalag 13, and I was increasingly feeling more like a prisoner than a guard in this tragedy.

I called upstairs and asked Clare what she could tell me about the phone sex incident involving Pict. She told me that she thought Frank had made Pict pay back the portion of the cell phone bill for the 1-900 calls, but couldn't remember if Pict ever did drop off a cheque. She would have to check the books, she said. But, in the meantime she wanted to know something. "What are you going to do to Pict about the theft of the power tools, Keith?" There was a touch of macabre glee in her tone.

I didn't respond to her but asked, "Does Pict still have a company phone?"

"Yes," she replied, sounding a little disappointed that I wasn't going to divulge any intrepid plan to retrieve the power tools from some unknown shed. "But, don't worry Keith, he knows that I'm keeping an eye on him. He knows I'm watching him."

"Terrific," I thought but I tried not to think about what it would mean to be watched by Clare. I asked her to send the receipts from the power tool purchases downstairs to Desi's office and thanked her for her diligence in her work with the accounts payable.

Nearing the end of the day, I told Tonney to call Pict and let him know that I wanted to see him the next day. I also told Tonney he would need to attend the meeting as Pict's direct supervisor.

"What do you want me to tell him the meeting's about?" Tonney asked.

"Tell him straight up it's about some missing equipment that he purchased with school district funds and then tell him that we can't seem to locate the equipment," I said.

"Do I have a conversation with him about phone sex?" Tonney asked.

There was so much I wanted to say but simply responded, "No, not this time. But, tell him it's serious. Make sure to let him know that he may want to bring a union representative with him." The next day, bright and early Desi came to my office and walked in with a wicked looking smile on her face.

Without even a good morning from her, she handed me a faxed note from Pict's doctor that read, "Due to immense and intolerable workplace stress, Blaine Pict is not fit to work." In the note, the doctor recommended, "A period of not less than 12 weeks of paid medical leave is required for treatment and recovery." The note ended with, "Following that period of treatment Mr. Pict will be re-assessed for possible fitness for return-to-work."

Knowing that we had 90 days of paid sick leave annually for each full-time permanent employee written into the collective agreement, I just accepted the note and then called Tonney into my office. I explained to him that in exactly 60 business days plus one, he needed to set aside a whole morning to attend a meeting with me and Pict.

He asked if I thought Blaine would really show up for the meeting.

Without responding to Tonney's question, I told Tonney that we were planning ahead for a meeting that may or may not happen. "Pencil it in," I told him. "You can always erase the commitment."

"No problem, Keith, " Tonney replied and walked out of my office.

I was tired but content to be done with Blaine Pict and Bob Tonney for the time being. However, a few hours before the end of the workday, the ever-cheery Maggie Antioch, the building custodian, appeared at the very same doorway where Tonney had stood a day earlier. "Hey Keith, do you have some time to talk about something that's bugging me? If you're too busy, I can come back another time. Maybe I should schedule an appointment with Desi?"

Not even thinking about what it might be, I simply smiled and replied, "For you Maggie, I have time. What's up?"

"I don't want to cause a big headache for you Keith," Maggie began, "But, I think Bob Tonney has starting drinking at work—again."

I tried to keep my exacerbated sigh as soft as possible and then just asked Maggie to fill me in.

One of the articling students, who was sporting a wickedly boyish smile asked, "What happened to Blaine Pict? Did you ever confront him about the phone sex and fire him? What about Tonney? Did you fire him?"

Bernard could detect Marie directing an intense glare at the young man.

"I left Arcadia before Pict returned to work from his medical leave. He never came back to work as far as I know," Bernard responded. "We never found out what happened to the tools, and I never pursued the misuse of the cell phone. It was like Lukno's get-well card—just too late to do anything about it now."

Bernard looked toward Marie realizing that she still wanted to run the interrogation and added, "Pict's short-term medical leave just became a long-term disability claim. And, I spoke with Tonney who denied the accusation. However, I did document our conversation and the allegation. It was recorded in Tonney's personnel file."

"Thank you, Dr. Bernard," Ms. Marie replied. "Based on this and your other experiences, how would you characterize the district's approach to dealing with human resources issues? Would you say it was ethical?"

Surprised by the question and tone and wanting to choose his words judiciously, Bernard chose not to reply to the question directly.

"In contemporary philosopher Sam Keen's book 'Inward Bound: Exploring the Geography of Your Emotions' he says there is a promise that is a common theme in world mythology and folklore. We discover beauty only when we confront the beast. Where we stumble and fall, there we find the treasure. Beneath the fault lies the virtue. The stone the builders reject becomes the cornerstone. The treasure is hidden in the trash. Authentic happiness, Keen says, is only possible when we allow ourselves to experience the full range of human emotions, including boredom, fear, grief, anger, and despair. Buddhism has been exploring this philosophy for over a thousand years, of course, but Keen gets to have the book signings and people seem to be willing to part with their money for his pearls of wisdom."

Marie seemed to be annoyed by Bernard's evasive manoeuvre and cut him off. "That's very nice, Dr. Bernard. But, what I want to know is whether or not you felt your central office colleagues were somehow acting unethically in their dealings with staff?"

Bernard realized the junior lawyers and those in-training were staring at him as if he were a deer caught in the headlights of an oncoming car. He decided to change his approach and answer the question.

"One day, while idly thinking about nothing in particular—one of my favourite pastimes while I'm stopped at red lights—it became more clear to me that while Chuck espoused fashionable ideals of distributive or shared leadership, what was really occurring around me was a carefully orchestrated dictatorship fuelled by a thorough campaign of workplace culture indoctrination. Chuck had convinced people that they had some control over the decision outcomes within the school district when they clearly did not. And although they would never experience any control over decision outcomes, they nevertheless believed they had that freedom. Only Chuck, though, was actually in charge, in control.

Chuck portrayed himself as a leader who lovingly planted seeds— seeds of thought that he would water and nurture with words of praise. He provided the seedlings that he felt were worthy with energy to grow by committing money to support their specific initiatives, which inevitably were grown from his particular ideology, so that those initiatives might blossom and bear fruit.

But, like Hegemone, the Greek goddess of plants from which the word "hegemony" comes, it was specifically Chuck's ideology that he wanted to take root, blossom and bear fruit. And, he was equally committed to root out all undesirable species, the weeds, if any of them might be a potential source of discontent that might impede his garden from growing.

Of course, like most leaders in today's world, Chuck would never have admitted to any form of Machiavellian behaviour or thinking and perhaps he didn't even know that he was a walking billboard of Machiavelli's leadership philosophy. The 16th century Italian philosopher had a great deal of insight into the inner workings of leadership and power. In his most renowned work, "The Prince", Machiavelli explained that a prince has to keep control over his territories and people at any cost, by any means, whether through deceit, bribery or any other under-the-table behaviour.

In Machiavelli's view, being a prince—or maybe a Chief Superintendent—requires control over one's subordinates to maintain order in the realm. If there is no formal control in any nation, a rogue nation develops and order gives way to chaos. In fact, Chuck, with the gleeful encouragement of Vixie, once decried a principal for acting like a rogue leader and messing up "his," he quickly corrected himself, "our plans."

Chuck felt his leadership was distinctive and progressive, and he told us that repeatedly. He liked to turn to Jim Collins's books frequently, liberally and gratuitously, and would often tell us that to be a truly great organization, we who worked at Arcadia needed to ensure that we protect the district's core values. Other than these core values, Chuck would state, everything else was subject to change. You can change the strategy or change the people, but never, ever, change the core values, Chuck would pronounce. He never told us specifically what those core values were, but it seemed as if he felt he embodied them and the more we all behaved like him, the better off we would all be.

Consequently, the answer to the question of what bound the employees of Arcadia School District together was a legitimate fear of Chuck's willingness to use the power of his office. There was not a person who doubted that Chuck would do whatever he had to do to get what he wanted—even if it meant ploughing under anything, or anyone, that met his disapproval.

This time it was Marie who seemed to be carefully searching for the right words. She had been busy writing in her notebook but stopped after a little while and asked, "I take it from that example that you had serious issues with Mr. Stihl's leadership, his approach to ethical leadership. Is that a correct conclusion for me to draw?"

"Serious issues? Yes, you could say that, I guess," Bernard replied.

To Bernard it looked like she wrote down a lot more in the notebook than what he had said in response to her question.

"What about Lukno?" she asked. Realizing right away that her question might be misconstrued as a question about Lukno's ethics, she quickly added, "Can you please continue with the issues surrounding Bathos Lukno's employment?"

I arrived at work one Monday morning and found that Nicola, the office receptionist, had placed a fax in my mailbox slot face down. I began to read it as I walked towards my office.

Dear Dr. Bernard,

After speaking with one of Arcadia's trustees, I was told that I should get in touch with you. I was told that you were THE person to speak with about trying to find a resolution to the safety issues that have plagued the scenery shop of the theatre program. And, it is also YOU who can determine any future I might have with the district.

A number of years ago, Mr. Frank Cottingly, your predecessor, invited me to a meeting to "discuss my options." I countered his offer by asking Mr. Cottingly to provide me in writing with a list of what he thought my options might be. Just so you know, I requested that he put the options in writing because I have difficulty managing multiple and complex tasks at the same time. I felt disadvantaged coming to a meeting where the options would be presented orally.

Mr. Cottingly never responded to my request.

Since you are fairly new to the school district, you certainly have benefitted by not being tainted by any misconstrued version of what happened. But, hopefully, you have been provided with copies of the past letters I sent to the trustees.

It seems to me that you are in a most difficult position of trying to get a satisfactory resolution to a number of unresolved issues, with my teaching position in the district being only one of them.

To assist you in addressing my concerns, let me give you the names of two references. I respectfully request that you contact these two men, whom I consider to be of unquestionable character and who know me well. They can give you insight into my character.

Mr. George Frazier, Executive Director of the Encore Community Theatre.
Rev. Joe Foreman, he is the Pastor of the Original Church of God.

If after speaking to the aforementioned gentlemen, you decide that I have something valuable to contribute to the school district, may I suggest that some options - other than teaching in the theatre or in a regular classroom - be considered?

I worked very hard to obtain my professional teaching credentials. It would be unbelievable to have a lawsuit filed by a moronic twit of a student tarnish my unblemished, 10-year teaching record. I have given away a decade of opportunities to pursue my own craft as an actor because of this job and because I felt I had so much to give to my students.

Please inform me of your plans regarding the aforementioned. I am unable to move forward in my life with the issues hanging over my head. And, as you can certainly understand, this has been a tremendous stress to both my professional and personal life.

Respectfully,
Bathos Lukno, B.Ed. T.A.D.

Not long after I read the letter, I left phone messages for the two "gentlemen" asking each to give me a call about a matter involving Bathos Lukno.

I had met George Frazier at a business community luncheon back in the autumn and we had found out that we had some common acquaintances. Over miserably bland sandwiches, we had struck up a bit of a conversation about families and the local performing arts scene. It didn't surprise me when he called me back later that day and just began to talk.

"Hi Keith. It's George, George Frazier. What can I help you with?" I explained that I had received a letter from Bathos Lukno, unsolicited, and in it Lukno had asked me to contact him to get some insight into his character.

"Lukno wants me to tell you about my character?" Frazier replied.

Frazier sounded genuinely confused. "No, Mr. Frazier, Lukno wants you to speak to me about his character," I assured him.

There was short a pause before he spoke. "Based on what he used to tell us during rehearsals, it seems like Bathos had a lot of difficulty with people on staff at the Middle School, especially the women. But, come to think of it he might have been the root of the problem because he had issues with some of the women in our local theatre community. He was just way too abrasive; he rubbed lots of people the wrong way. Don't get me wrong; he was a gifted actor. But, he needed to be listened to. If he thought you weren't listening to him, he could get aggressive, maybe too aggressive, sometimes. Lukno always had a point that he needed to make and he always managed find ways to quote plays he had been in - mostly lines from a protagonist who had to suffer some kind of separation from society - that to him were apropos of the present conversation. And his point was the one that mattered the most in any conversation. He didn't have much tolerance for anyone who did drugs or drank, and in fact, it seemed as if he thought they were the worst kind of pariahs. He also had issues with authority figures that seem to go back, way back." Abruptly he stopped and then asked, "Is that enough?"

"Yes, that's enough. In closing, is there anything else you want to add?" I asked.

"You seem like a decent guy, Keith. I guess you need to know that Lukno is highly intelligent. He's really gifted intellectually and quite the performer, but sometimes his creativity, well it seems as if he is off the scale. Don't cross swords with him, Keith. You never know what he is capable of, and lately he seems a little more unhinged."

I thanked Frazier for the information and assured him I was a pretty clever person myself. But, I did wonder what he meant when he said that Lukno was "off the scale."

A few days later, I spoke with Reverend Foreman from the Original Church of God.

"Yeah I know all about Lukno. It's a sad case, with him being fired and all. And, with his wife leaving him it's downright pathetic."

"Who fired him?" I asked. I had no idea what had happened with his wife, and didn't dare ask.

"Well, he was fired by you guys, of course," Foreman responded seemingly perplexed by my ignorance of the facts.

"He wasn't fired by "us," if you mean the school district. Lukno is still employed by Arcadia. He's just off work right now on an extended disability claim." I replied.

"Oh, he told me he was fired and that he was trying to get back at you guys. I mean get back at the district," Foreman went on.

I explained to Reverend Foreman that Lukno had suggested in a letter that I should contact him as a character reference. "What can you tell me about Lukno's character?" I asked.

"He's a very devote and pious man, but it seems like he's unable to function in social settings. Really, I don't think he can function very well out in public, anymore. I also hear he wants to clear his teaching record so that he can teach somewhere else one day. It's not too much that he wants really. Everyone deserves a chance at redemption, Dr. Bernard. But, you know, I'm not sure he should be around kids anymore. It's not my call, but I'm just not sure he has the patience or the stamina. No, now that I think about it, I'm pretty sure he shouldn't be working with kids at all."

"Why not?" I inquired.

"I think he'll just blow up. He has a lot of anger issues right now. Maybe you could find him a nice easy job there in central office with you?" the pastor added.

I thanked Foreman for sharing some information with me, but didn't respond to his idea that I have an extra desk brought into my office for Lukno to work at. I had done as Lukno requested and contacted his chosen character references. And I can only guess that Lukno anticipated something very different was going to be delivered than what the pair of references actually shared. He skipped a vital step, one I always recommend to job seekers: before you ask and list someone as a reference, you may want to take the time to find out what they are going to say about you when they speak about you in confidence behind your back.

What I took from my two conversations was that Lukno was unstable and ill-prepared to return to work, ever. And, that he might be outright dangerous.

A few days later, I received a telephone call from a police Sergeant named Gibrian who told me he wanted to interview me about Lukno. He initially came to get some more information for the file that had been opened after Villana DeBoti's complaint. It seemed that DeBoti had mentioned to Sergeant Gibrian that I might be able to provide some more background information about Lukno.

Gibrian shared what he had been told by DeBoti and asked if I was aware of her allegations and complaints. Then he asked me if I perceived Lukno to be a threat or danger to DeBoti. I replied that while I thought it was a remote possibility, I didn't believe she was in any imminent peril. Then he asked me if I perceived Lukno to be a threat to my safety.

I was surprised by the question. I hadn't given it much serious thought. Was I in danger? I didn't feel that Lukno was an immediate threat and said so. Gibrian, who told me he was the local police expert in domestic violence but a relative novice in workplace violence, said that while he didn't know if I was in imminent danger or not, he felt it might change quickly depending on what happened to Lukno. He said that based on what he had heard and knew, Lukno seemed very volatile and therefore highly unpredictable.

He asked what we were planning to do about Lukno's employment status. And, I explained that it was my intention to find a way to legally terminate Lukno—as soon as possible. While Gibrian said he understood my reasons, he also told me that I was painting a target on my back when—not "if" but "when"—Lukno came back seeking justice. His point registered with me but I didn't make too much of it at the time.

About a week later, we had another meeting. Gibrian confessed that he had known Lukno, quite well in fact, a number of years back. When they were both in college, Lukno had a reputation for being both a bit peculiar and also a ready source for illicit-drugs. While they didn't travel in the same social circles in college, Gibrian said they occasionally ran into each other at one of the local pubs where they had a beer or three together. Gibrain even would go in the summers to the carnival acts that

Lukno emceed at the local exhibition grounds to hear his amazing crowd-pleasing enticements to come and pay a few dollars to see the world's fattest lady or a dog with two ears on one side of its head or a wine-serving monkey.

He asked if I could keep him in the information loop. Gibrian emphasized that the police department needed to be aware of any changes in Lukno's employment status that might lead Lukno to be on the move and bring him back to town. Things like his firing could make the situation heat up and boil over, Gibrain said. Then he apologized and corrected himself, "All I mean is if Lukno gets terminated he may become agitated."

I knew it before, but had dismissed my thoughts as possibly irrational, until it really struck me fully that day: Bathos Lukno had to be removed from teaching at Arcadia School District. In fact, I knew that I couldn't let Lukno have access to kids. It was obvious to me, moreso than before, that I couldn't let Bathos Lukno return to a classroom to teach, anywhere.

I never mistook my resolve to fire him for some form of foolish bravado or messianic complex. It was simply the only choice I could see in front of me. And as I realized that I had to move to fire Lukno, it was becoming pretty clear that I was the character playing opposite him in some Shakespearean tragedy that culminates in a dual of sorts. However, I have to admit that I had no clear vision of who might triumph. In my resolve to act ethically, I was in danger of making myself the object of Lukno's rage.

Bernard decided it was his turn to ask a question. He scanned the faces of the young associates and articling students and asked if any of them, when they decided to become lawyers, ever considered the rare possibility that they might be killed for doing their jobs.

Everyone seemed genuinely surprised by the question, and remained silent until Peter Hart replied, "No, of course not."

Bernard looked at Hart and said, "Me neither. But, there's always that possibility in your line of work, correct?"

Hart didn't reply. But he, Bernard and the room full of people were aware that it was possible, improbable maybe, but still possible.

After a short period of silence, somberly Hart replied, "Yes, I guess it could happen."

Seeming to be impatient with the pause, Marie said, "Do you have a point, Dr. Bernard? After all, it's just as likely that a person might get killed crossing the street. What does this have to do with Lukno or your work at Arcadia?"

Bernard smiled at Marie. "I'm glad you asked."

"Hi, Keith." I wasn't sure who was on the other end of the telephone. "It's Duval Alexander from Verdun Middle School. We met this past fall at that teacher meet-and-greet event. Well anyway, do you have a few minutes to talk?"

I had a pretty good idea of what Alexander wanted to talk about because the school's lockdown the previous Friday was all anyone was talking about. Four schools with almost 2,000 students between them had been locked down because of a real and perceived threat that someone was coming to school that day with the intent to kill.

The entrance and exit to each of the schools was restricted to the front doors. Out front, on the street—where the four schools' entrances converged—there was a sizeable and obvious police presence in full view. Students had been told in the days leading up to the lockdown that all of their bags and purses would be searched upon entry. And, even after this intrusion into their private space, they would still be required to leave their bags on the floor in the front foyer of their schools. Their belongings, and they, would be under surveillance all day long as they moved between classes.

In the two weeks leading up to the lockdown, tension had been mounting, and student and parent opinions were divided, based on news reports, on what the school district should do. Some people seemed to believe that the schools should just be closed that day. Close them for safety, they said to reporters covering the story to relieve the anxiety and terror of having to attend school that day. But others thought this was a terrible idea because it gave in to the terrorism. For them, closing showed the community would be giving in to an anonymous, cowardly threat scribbled in bathroom graffiti and would have allowed the author to succeed in disrupting the lives of thousands. To them the yielding at the slightest threat was simply not what young people needed to learn. They told reporters that the schools, with heightened security and police presence, should defy the threats of the unimaginable and remain open.

As I listened, intently, to those people who gave those media interviews, I recalled the impact the song "I Don't Like Mondays" had on my psyche. For whatever reason, that song, more than any other I had remembered from my teen years, left an indelible imprint on my psyche. It was back then that I first started to be aware of the randomness and inexplicability of some fatal acts of violence.

I remember hearing that Bob Geldof, of the Boomtown Rats, wrote the song after reading a telex report, while on tour somewhere in the United States, about the shooting spree of 16-year-old Brenda Ann Spencer. Spencer opened fire on children playing in a school playground across the street from her home in San Diego, California. She killed two adults and injured eight children and one police officer on January 29, 1979, in front of Cleveland Elementary School. I remember hearing that during her trial, Spencer showed no remorse for her crime. Her only real explanation for her actions was: "I don't like Mondays; this livens up the day".

I'm not sure there is a teacher working in North America who is not aware of the recent litany of school shootings: the massacre at Columbine High School near Littleton, Colorado, when Eric Harris and Dylan Klebold murdered 13 people on the school campus before they committed suicide galvanized the public's awareness of the possibility of these aberrations in human behaviour. But, there were also the tragedies of Pearl, Mississippi, and West Paducah, Kentucky, and Jonesboro, Arkansas. It's a terrifyingly long list. And, we would be fools to deny that this is an international problem as we witnessed the carnage at Dunblane Primary School in Dunblane Scotland, and at W.R. Myers School in Taber, Alberta, and then again at a school in Vlasenica, Bosnia-Herzegovina.

The fear that our local community seemed to have about the possibility of a school shooting, in my mind, was not out of proportion. It was measured in proportion to the deep sadness over those very young lives that were lost in all of the previous events, not to mention the teachers who had been victims of school violence too.

Bernard looked directly at Kimberley Marie as he spoke.

Mr. Stihl had done an excellent job working with the local police and a threat-assessment expert to try and identify the author of the writing found on the boys' washroom wall that read, "Friday, January 16th, someone is going to die!" From the beginning, Chuck realized this was a credible threat that might be carried out. The manner of the pen strokes, their location in the washroom, the timing of when it was left and other forensic details, suggested to the experts that this was not the idle scribbling of an angst-ridden teen.

Chuck had briefed the school trustees and schools' staffs immediately and then worked with the police to develop not only a plan for securing the schools, but also for presenting an image of calm that might provide comfort and a sense of safety to parents and students.

January 16th came, and while only about a third of the students attended school that day, nothing unusual happened. The schools' communities, which seemed to have been holding their collective breath all day long, all week long, seemed to let out a unified sigh at about five o'clock that afternoon.

"Go ahead Mr. Alexander," I replied. "What do you want to talk about?"

"I want you to know how much I appreciated all that you guys did last week. I think you people did a great job."

"To be honest with you Mr. Alexander," I said, "It was really the Chief Superintendent, Mr. Chuck Stihl, who did most of the work and deserves the credit. He was on top of this from the beginning. If you want I can pass along your comments to him?"

"Sure, okay," he said. Then there was a brief silence, "But, since you are the human resources person, it's you that I really wanted to speak to."

He seemed to speaking painfully slow. "When I became a teacher, really when I was thinking about getting into teaching, I never thought that I might die while I was at work. It just never crossed my mind that by going to work, it might mean that I had to worry about being shot at." He paused again. I think to compose himself, but I don't know for sure. "I guess I thought there might be an off-chance that a student might take a swing at me, or something like that. Hell, there have been days when I have thought I might take a swing at one of them." He paused again, "I probably shouldn't have said that, hey?"

"Don't worry, go on," I let his comment slip away waiting to hear what his point was.

"I wasn't able to sleep at all last week. Each night I kept waking up and wondering, what if a student shows up to school and starts firing, then what do I do? I have two kids at home, and we are expecting a third. I'm not sure I became a teacher to put my family in that position, fatherless. I'm not sure I would step into the line of fire and save someone's life." He stopped and I could hear him breathing heavily. "What if I hadn't shown up for work on Friday? What if I had decided with all of the commotion that it wasn't worth the risk? What would've happened to me? Would I have been fired?"

He caught me off guard. None of us had contemplated that question of: what if some of the teachers don't show up for work? Then what? We had just assumed in our plans that teachers would obviously come to work—just like they did every day—even though that day was clearly not just another day.

It was a damn good, though a damn frustrating question to be asked. I knew that in most jurisdictions, occupational health and safety legislation provides that a worker has the right to refuse work if the worker believes a specific task requested of them is unsafe or hazardous to them or their co-workers. I knew that under the "Canadian Labour Code," an employee couldn't be prevented from leaving work in the event of a bomb threat. I learned that simple fact when I was principal of a school that had a policy directing teachers, in the event of a bomb threat, to vigilantly snoop about their classrooms to try and detect any suspicious packages. Upon discovering any suspicious packages, the policy directed the teacher to bring the potentially explosive device to the principal's office; my office. I'm not sure what I was going to do with the potential bomb when it was dropped off on my desk, the policy never said what to do next.

"I don't know what we would've done, Mr. Alexander. In all honesty, I have no idea what we might have done if you had decided not to come to work." I really didn't know what to say next to Alexander and I didn't want to stammer out something trivial or inane. I thought for a little while and said, "Thank you for showing up to work last week Mr. Alexander." I thought I was ready to end the conversation, but just blurted out, "Thank you for being a teacher and not giving up."

There was a momentary pause on the other end of the phone before Alexander said, "I needed to hear that from someone. I needed to know that our work, our lives as teachers are valued."

No one said a word for a few minutes, and the stenographer stopped typing. As Bernard looked at Marie he said, "Chuck Stihl was a decent man who did care about people. I never doubted that fact. There were distinct times like in moments of crisis or potential crisis when his actions showed me his concern for the wellbeing of others. But this was always done when he knew he was in the public eye and ready to be commended or judged. Where we differed, vastly at times, was how we each enacted a personal ethic of care on a daily basis."

Marie did not write down what Bernard said after: "Chuck Stihl was a decent man who did care about people. I never doubted that fact."

ELEVEN

No one seemed to be in much of a rush to resume the deposition after the impromptu break. The rustle of people shuffling through their notebooks and returning text messages punctuated the hush from time to time.

Bernard sat in silence waiting to see if there was another question to be asked by Ms. Marie. But, sensing that none was forthcoming, he began to talk without the need of a prompt, and his audience quickly settled back into place.

About a week after the school lock down, I arrived at work to find a 24-page fax from Lukno waiting for me on my desk. The style and even most of the contents of the letter were nothing new. It was the same rant that Lukno had previously described about his ongoing victimization by the district. In painstaking detail, he laid out his theory of a conspiracy to blame him—and absolve everyone else—in the electronic cherry-picker lift accident. Lukno wrote of an impending lawsuit and the ineptitude of the lawyers the district had retained to defend its officials and him. He referred to the injured student as "a bastard," "a moron," and "an imbecile." Lukno alleged the high school principal was incompetent and accused him of a dereliction of duty. He suggested his own teachers' union was trying to intimidate him and claimed it was misrepresenting his interests by trying to get him to settle the matter out-of-court and resign his teaching job. And, Lukno demanded to know: Whose career was central office administration protecting?

Lukno ended the letter with his expectation that I would call him in order to determine what "options" he found suitable to contemplate as future action. He also suggested that I keep the day that I chose to phone him free of unnecessary encumbrances, as we would certainly need enough time to have a lengthy conversation.

I waited two days before I called Lukno. I didn't want to give him the impression that he was in control, although I knew that at that moment he was making the demands. After some preliminary small talk, I offered Lukno one month's salary for every year that he had been employed with Arcadia—roughly a year's pay—if he immediately resigned his position with the district and just moved on with his life. I told him if he agreed to leave—right then at that very moment over the phone—that I thought I could probably get my offer committed to paper and make it binding. I extended the offer even though I didn't have permission. But, Lukno didn't know that fact. I took a risk by making Lukno an offer without any certainty that I could deliver. However, I needed to seem like I was in charge and begin the negotiations somewhere and not be seen as a puppet.

Initially, it was hard to tell how Lukno took my proposal. He seemed somewhat composed, and paused rather dramatically. Then he replied that what he really wanted was his teachers' pension plan contributions and health-care contributions to be paid "until the day he retired," and he wanted a large sum of money, "like ten years' worth of salary." And, in what seemed like an afterthought, he said that he wanted to have "glowing letters of reference written" about him. I tried to both sound and remain calm and replied that his request was well beyond what I would recommend to the Board as a severance package.

Lukno quite nonchalantly said that he would be in touch with me, after he gave my initial offer some thought. He ended by thanking me for taking the time to call him. I replied that he was welcome. While it wasn't a lengthy conversation, I did think it was remarkably courteous.

Maybe an hour later, I called up Lukno's teachers' union representative, Christina Urbain, and found out that she and his union had grown tired of working with Lukno because he had been such a frustrating person to deal with. Based on what she knew of him, she wanted him out of teaching. I agreed to keep her informed of any further dealings I had with Lukno, and she agreed to work with me to the best of her ability. When I finished speaking with Urbain, I contacted one of the district's lawyers, Bertram Sinclair, who was an expert in labour law. I knew Chuck used to consult with the district's legal counsel on just about any matter that might have, even remotely, given someone the right to actually sue or even just threaten to sue "his pants off." I asked Sinclair to help me with the legalese that was required in a letter that would recommend to Arcadia's school trustees that they terminate Lukno's contract. Sinclair asked me to send everything I had on file concerning Lukno's employment history with Arcadia. He would, he assured me, begin reviewing the file as soon as the material arrived and start drafting a letter.

In a phone conversation, maybe a week later, Sargent Gibrain recommended that I brief the staff at central office about the possibility that Lukno could show up there unannounced. He also thought I should do the same with the staff at Daele Middle. I distinctly remember during that conversation that Sargent Gibrain first used the uncomfortably euphemistic phrase, "He might go postal."

I knew what that meant. On August 20, 1986, 14 employees were shot and killed and six wounded at the Edmond, Oklahoma, United States Post Office by a postman, David Sherrill, who then committed suicide with a shot to his forehead. The phrase "going postal" has become synonymous with various acts of workplace rage, irrespective of the employer. It's generally used to describe fits of rage—though not necessarily at the level of murder—in or outside the workplace.

Yes, it was quite possible, Sergeant Gibrain elaborated, that given what he knew about Lukno, he might become dangerously volatile, vengeful and violent, if I fired him.

I had the principal at Daele Middle courier over a yearbook photo of Bathos Lukno after realizing that I had no idea what he looked like. It was frightening to think that Lukno could sit down next to me at the local coffee shop and strike up a congenial conversation about the weather and I would have no idea it was he. Or more likely, he could walk up to me on the street, smile and shoot me.

I wanted to meet with the staff at Daele and explain some of what was happening and inform them that they should be careful if they ever saw Lukno near the school. But, Chuck said he was sure Lukno still had friends and supporters on staff at Daele and that a meeting with the staff was not a good idea. Perhaps, he said, I should just ask the current principal and vice-principals—two of three men who had signed that terrible card—to ask their staff to call me if they saw Lukno lurking around. I reluctantly followed Chuck's advice and later found out that none of the administrators ever spoke to the staff at Daele about Lukno.

I met with the district office staff and reviewed the building's lockdown provisions and explained without many details that if Bathos Lukno showed up, they should: "Call the police immediately and quickly try to vacate the building, or lock your office door and get under your desk." I passed around the school yearbook, and as they scanned his photo, I noticed that there were some who looked anxious. I tried to soothe their fears by telling them that in the unlikely event that Lukno showed up, they needn't worry too much because he was really looking for one person—me. They might as well hide or run, I said with a smile. While they were running away I added, I wouldn't mind if they called 911 so that someone would at least try to rescue me. No one laughed at my inept attempt at humour.

On February 1st and then the 14th Lukno sent faxes that gave me what I thought I needed to fire him. These faxes added to both my fear and resolve as it became more evident to me what I had to do, soon.

Nicola, with her typically edgy personality, popped her head through the open door of my office and told me that she had just placed faced-down, of course, a fax in my mail slot. It was from Lukno, she added nonchalantly.

"Hey Nicola," I asked trying to seem as nonchalant as she was, "what's the fax about?"

"Come on Keith, I don't read your confidential faxes," she replied. "Oh, but you're going to enjoy it."

February 1st

Dear Dr. Bernard,

In any negotiations it is always a good idea to allow the other side to take a position that will allow them to save face. This was the tenor of my previous letter. It is also important in negotiations that both parties come out of the process with a sense that their persons have been respected. Your suggested "option" does not meet the minimum requirements of these circumstances.

*I **REQUIRE** certain things from the school district, which I will spell out for you:*

1. My teacher pension is critically important to me so that I do not live in squalor in my children's basement in my golden years.

2. The group insurance and benefits protects my family medical, dental and vision expenses and is something that I considered when I chose to become a teacher. Now, more than ever, I am in need of the support of these benefits as just my prescription medications cost more than $500 per month.

3. The income that I lost due to the negligence of the high school administrators can only be viewed as a result of their sheer incompetence or as a result of a grudge against me personally. There are no other possible words that can explain their behaviours.

As such, the "normal" circumstances of a constructive termination and any subsequent settlement cannot be met in the complete mess surrounding my case. In any normal case, the subject of a dismissal can move forward to another teaching job, somewhere, and most likely earn the same amount of money that he/she had been earning at the end of his/her tenure.

*This is clearly **NOT** the case with **OUR** dilemma. I am left without the necessary skills both mentally and physically to work in any kind of teaching environment.*

182

I had **NO** need for any medication prior to commencing work for *Arcadia School District*.

I was **EASILY ABLE** to pay my personal life insurance policy with the salary I was earning as a teacher and now I will **NEVER** reach that level of income again.

I am the sole guardian for my five adolescent children who will likely stay with me through their post-secondary studies. The level of coverage the group insurance and benefits plan would have provided for my family and I would no longer be available to me by virtue of cost.

My pension, if I were to pay for it out of pocket would be an added expense that I could not afford while raising my children.

My current and immediate past medical conditions, all of which are a result of my mistreatment and abuse while in your employ, were the **DIRECT RESULT OF NEGLIGENCE** on the part of various administrators.

Ultimately I am left with no option but to inform you that a legal remedy will be sought for the impasse we find ourselves in, as I cannot accept one month's pay per year of service as a settlement. It falls gravely short of my **NEEDS** and **DOES NOTHING** to compensate me for the damage that has been done to me. Arcadia has destroyed my career and caused me, and my family, a tremendous amount of unnecessary pain.

I am proposing a full salary, which would provide me with the benefits and protection for my family and the group insurance and benefits paid by the school district.

By supporting me, other than as a result of the moral obligation that the district has to my dependents and me, you will find some pretty good "press." It would make the district look like the "hero," rather than to deny my proposition and fight me in court and lose and look like the "goat." The district is very fortunate that instead of retribution for the obvious incompetence of the administrators, that I am simply seeking reconciliation to find a mutually beneficial solution to this impasse. Considering you are the first person to seek resolution in over three years, and being new to the situation, maybe you should toss this "hot potato" back into the laps of those who gave it to you. They really have no right to embroil **YOU** in the mess **THEY** created.

Yours truly,

Bathos Lukno, B.Ed. T.A.D.

It was interesting to me that Lukno had the self-awareness to use my imagery of the hot-potato problem teacher, and that he recognized that all of the crucial mistakes, in his eyes, had taken place before I arrived at Arcadia. However, it was also obvious, though, from the letter that Lukno was becoming more desperate and hostile. I called Sinclair and told him about the contents of the fax. Sinclair suggested we start working on re-drafting of a termination letter, immediately.

The draft letter informed Lukno of my recommendation to have his employment contract immediately terminated based on a "Frustration of Contract" interpretation. By Lukno's own admission, and as confirmed by the references he had given me permission to contact, he was unable to return to work and fulfill his teaching contract in the foreseeable future. But, I also left open an option—an offer—to explore the specifics of a structured severance agreement that might recognize his years of service to the district. I suggested that we carve out the details of a severance deal by working through his union representative. I was certain that Lukno would never consent to this point but needed to include Urbain as much as possible. Leveraging Lukno out of his job with Arcadia was a challenge that was going to be difficult enough, but something I thought I could succeed at. However, if I were going to get him out of teaching altogether, I would need the teachers' union to find a way to allow me to do it without too much protestation. Urbain, a former high school mathematics teacher, candidly told me she would never want her worst enemy's children to ever be taught by Lukno. I assumed I had an ally in the union, albeit one who, most likely, could only offer support by remaining silent.

Before I could wordsmith and finalize that termination letter, another fax appeared in my mail slot. This one, dated February 14th, looked as if Lukno had copied it and sent it to almost anyone he felt might somehow need to know the depth of his anguish. While it was addressed to me, Lukno indicated that he had sent a copy to Chuck, each of the trustees, four previous school administrators he had suffered under, the district's lawyer, his union representative, the Minster of Education, and oddly, the Minister of Arts and Culture.

The letter read:

February 14th

Dear Dr. Bernard and others,

*The purpose of this letter is to invite each of you to take a good look at your inaction. I have written volumes of letters and corresponded with numerous persons to no avail. With one exception, and you already know who you are, I have had **NO ONE** ready to support me in this dreadful case. Each of you has, in his (or her) own turn, taken the tact that it is not your business. It is either not your place, or you have no authority, or offered some other feeble excuse for passing the buck. You have ignored my cries for help to correct for the situations that led to my disability and have*

184

*denied me any opportunity to move forward in my life by denying me letters of reference, and you have sheltered yourselves by hiding from what many of you have suggested to me in private—that I am **BEING SCREWED**!*

Lukno's letter went on for three or four drawn-out pages as he outlined his version of the truth, the litany of past wrongs that had been perpetrated against him over the past ten years. Nearing the last page Lukno's seemed to go from bad to worse as he wrote:

*Each one of **YOU**, even in the slightest way involved, has run for the tall grasses in order to take cover and hide your involvement. It certainly does not strike me as a moral or ethical way to do things. This is behaviour that I might expect from immoral people rather than what we would all expect from ethical and moral stewards of our future, those charged with caring for a school system and kids. The notion that one can stand idly by and watch as someone's life is destroyed in the name of "furthering the common good," is an amoral, utilitarian principle at best. It is indeed a "sin of omission" and does not fail but to compromise the integrity of the whole school system. The way you have behaved is perhaps in the realm of acting according to legally minimal standards of behaviour. But as you tuck your children into bed, happily knowing that their prescription medications will be paid, their dental work covered, your life insurance intact and paycheques safe and you all with good health— don't you ever wonder how it is that how your lives have all turned out so perfectly? Do you ever wonder if there are some less fortunate who suffered as rungs in the ladder of your career so that you could ascend to such great professional heights?*

*The letters that some of you have received are only the tip of the iceberg. In fact, the only ones who will receive **ALL** of the copious amounts of correspondence will be either the courts or the media. Either option seems reasonable to me now.*

EVERYONE *seems to be stalling, thinking that I won't do anything foolish.* ***HA, HA, HA!***

What is it that you think I have to lose? My health is gone.

I am writing this paragraph at 2:47 a.m. because my abdominal pains will not allow me to fall asleep. I am getting headaches and backs pains regularly as well as dizzy spells, and my mind goes blank in normal conversations. My teaching career is **OVER**, *and I am on the maximum dosage of the painkiller Dilaudid plus heavy-duty anti-depressants! If I get to sleep, there is a certain chance of having nightmares, horrible bone-chilling ones, during the night.*

NONE *of my conditions existed prior to the accident. It is due to your abuse that I am in the state that I find myself now. I have no better luck with my own teachers' union, which has been useless in helping me find a resolution that would allow the truth to come out.*

I understand there is a provincial election looming this spring. What a wonderful time for me to wade into the political fray.

"STUDENTS' LIVES PUT AT RISK DUE TO SUPERINTENDENT'S INCOMPETENCE!"

Or, how about:

"DRUGS IN THE SCHOOL AND THE TRUSTEES COULD CARE LESS!"

Don't they each make a nice sound bite?

How fast can you come up with a reasonable offer? I can release all of this information that I have in a matter of minutes with the push of a button.

YOU think you can hold my professional credential hostage? What use do I have of them anymore? They are totally useless to me; so don't even think about trying to have them revoked.

YOU HAVEN'T SEEN ANYTHING YET!

YOU think you can put my children's welfare at risk? Don't underestimate how hard, or nasty, I would fight for them.

DON'T PICK A FIGHT WITH ME. YOU WILL LOSE!

ARE THERE ANY GOOD REASONS I SHOULD NOT GO PUBLIC WITH THESE ISSUES?

How about you make me a real offer?

MY EXPECTATIONS FOR A SETTLEMENT WILL BE CONFINED TO THE OFFICE AND EYES OF DR. BERNARD. THESE EXPECTATIONS ARE NOT NEGOTIABLE!

I expect an answer in writing within ten (10) days. This all the rest of you need to know.

ACT NOW OR RISK THE CONSEQUENCES OF YOUR INACTION.

And, as usual it was signed,

Bathos Lukno, B.Ed. T.A.D.

I wasn't trembling as I finished reading, but I probably should have been because when I re-read it about a month later I understood just how erratic Lukno had become and how menacing his words were. The references to his physical pain and psychic anguish, his allegations of being both abused and ignored all hauntingly read like a manifesto for retribution. His unshakable belief that he was now in a predicament like an animal that had been backed into a narrow corner and had no escape and thus, in self-defense, had to go on the attack was abundantly clear. Lukno had become volatile and unstable, a toxic mix.

186

More than ever before it was apparent that Lukno's convoluted rants had escalated to full-blown threats and extortion. His demands, in an attachment meant just for me, read as follows:

MY NON-NEGOTIABLE EXPECTATIONS:

1. Full teaching salary until age 65.

2. The extended health-care and dental-care insurance premiums for my family and me to be paid for by the district, for my entire life,

3. The district pays all pension contributions until my retirement.

4. A cash settlement, to return the 30% salary lost by virtue of having to be on long-term disability, placed in trust accounts for my children.

5. Raving letters of reference and recommendation written about me; whether the authors of the letters are sincere or not doesn't much matter, the letters just had to be stellar.

6. Full tuition paid, if I ever decide to pursue post-graduate studies in the performing arts.

7. To be left alone by the school district and to not be bothered by it or any of its employees or contracted personnel unless I need something—I will let you know if I need something.

8. All of the costs for a lawyer, of my choice of course, covered by the district to represent me in any lawsuit brought against the district or me by the injured student's parents.

9. To have all of this committed in writing, legally and binding, within fifteen (15) days.

Although it was part of my job, I never bothered to cost out his idea of a reasonable settlement, as it was pure fantasy. I told Chuck about Lukno's demands and requested that the whole matter be left with me, for the time being, as I worked with the district's lawyer and the teachers' union representative to try and find a solution: a resolution, I told Chuck, that would not further bankrupt us fiscally or morally. Chuck unenthusiastically agreed to leave the matter in my hands but expected daily updates. In the days that followed I could rarely find Chuck to offer any. Seems his backyard deck had sank in one particularly swampy corner of his steeply inclined lot and was pulling dangerously on the wall of his house.

I sent Lukno's latest letter to both Sinclair and Urbain to review and they agreed that Lukno's instability was so obvious and pronounced that it was clear that I was dealing with someone who was potentially a danger to himself and possibly others. Based on the contents of his last two letters, I felt confident that I could terminate him without ever having to verify the truthfulness of the past events—the horrible card and terrible accident—that seemed to have pushed Lukno to the brink of madness.

I set about drafting a different letter recommending to the Board of Trustees that Mr. Bathos Lukno, B.Ed. T.A.D., be immediately terminated with cause, without notice and without further compensation based on his admission of being incapable of returning to teaching, together with his threats and attempts to extort money.

I recognized in drafting the letter that under the principles of fairness and natural justice that Lukno had to be offered the right to appeal my recommendation. This meant that Lukno would be offered a time-limited opportunity to appeal my recommendation for immediate termination.

Part of my letter read:

In the event that you wish to appeal this recommendation for termination, the Chief Superintendent of Schools, Mr. Chuck Stihl, will hear such an appeal. Any decision to appeal the recommendation for termination must be made in writing within seven (7) business days of the receipt of this letter. In the event of an appeal and pending the outcome, Mr. Stihl's decision shall be considered final. Arcadia Consolidated School District No. 66 will grant no further appeal regarding this recommendation for termination.

I informed Chuck that he would have to hear the appeal and watched his face turn very pale as he realized that he might have to actually sit down and face Lukno. He alone would be the final arbitrator in the event that Lukno appealed my recommendation.

Chuck looked ill with the prospect.

Chuck wanted to know if the police would provide us with an extra protection, specifically for him on the day of the appeal. After all, he said, Lukno might try something stupid. I reassured Chuck that I had already contacted the police, and they were apprised of the situation. It didn't seem to lessen his anxiety. Finally, I told Chuck not to worry because I was pretty sure I knew who the real target might be and it wouldn't be him, but rather me. Chuck's narcissism was so perfect that he didn't offer a single word of concern for me or anyone else. My reassurances seemed to calm him down a little. I had an idea that I knew what I was doing in writing this termination letter. I was making myself the sole person who Lukno could point at and say, "That bastard had me fired!"

While Sinclair worked on the legal finesse of the letter, I made sure to contact Sargent Gibrain who came by the office one afternoon. We sat with coffee cups on the table and spoke candidly about Lukno coming to town for his appeal hearing. Gibrain said that it wasn't out of the realm of possibility that Lukno might turn up sooner, rather than at his appeal date, and be looking for me. He said it wasn't unfathomable that Lukno might even show up at my home. And then Gibrain jolted me into the immediate gravity of the situation by asking if I wished to have my family put under unofficial police surveillance, just for my peace of mind, he added.

It was only after that meeting that I told my wife, Susan, just how much the Lukno case had escalated. I chose to forego most of the specific details, as I thought it was too convoluted to explain to anyone. Susan didn't panic when I told her that the police thought there was a slight chance that I might be in some kind of danger. I never mentioned Gibrain's offer to provide a watchful police eye over the family. But, maybe half an hour after we finished talking, I overheard her on the phone with her parents discussing the possibility that she and the kids might fly out for a visit, and that maybe they might stay over for a week or two.

After hearing her, I started to realize just how dangerous this situation was, not just for me, but also for others that I loved. And for the first time, I understood why Frank had done nothing about Lukno. I winced a little when I thought back and remembered how many times I heard people say what a great guy Frank was. Frank always took care of people and made sure they weren't left out in the cold, people would say. However, at that moment as I thought about Frank, I was feeling down right frozen in my place.

After numerous drafts and a few second thoughts, I signed a final copy of the undated termination letter. On the day before I was to send the letter to Lukno, I received a phone call from a Mr. Xavier St. Louis, who said he was a representative from the teachers' union. He said he had taken over the Lukno file from Christina Urbain. I didn't bother to ask why and decided not to try and figure it out.

St. Louis said he had spoken to Lukno a few minutes before and Lukno was now a changed man, a contrite man who wanted to be cooperative with everyone. Lukno, according to St. Louis, had realized that he had succumbed to the immense stress of a situation that he had mostly brought upon himself. The cocktail of prescription medications he had been taking for years had clouded Lukno's thinking. Lukno was now repentant and hoping for some sympathy.

St. Louis explained that the previous night, Lukno suffered from some kind of a psychotic breakdown and wanted, desperately, to work all of this out—this unfortunate mess—through his union. Lukno felt that Urbain might not be the best person to deal with, as he knew he had damaged the working relationship irreparably. Lukno just needed a little time to pull himself back together and get his life in order before we began any formal discussions about his future status with Arcadia, St. Louis said.

Then St. Louis asked if I could I please consider not sending my letter recommending Lukno's termination for a week or so, maybe not until the middle of the next month. Urbain had informed St. Louis that I was on the cusp of sending a termination letter to Lukno. Could I please find it in myself, St. Louis seemed to be asking, to be compassionate and cut Lukno some much undeserved slack?

I wasn't sure what to make of the request, or the conversation. I had no idea if Lukno was sincere, or if I was being played for a fool. I told St. Louis I would get back to him later that day. I spoke with Sinclair and relayed the details of the conversation I had with St. Louis. Sinclair thought for a while and said it might be wise to be seen as being a sympathetic employer in dealing with Lukno, given his current state of mind. Sinclair said it wasn't prudent to be seen as pushing Lukno over the edge and provoking him. I reluctantly told Chuck about my conversations with St. Louis and Sinclair, and Chuck said he liked the lawyer's advice—it seemed sensible to back off Lukno at this time.

Reticently, I agreed that the termination letter, the final undated one with my signature on the bottom, should be not sent and rather filed away for the time being.

I got back to the other personnel issues that were still ever present.

A few days after my conversation with St. Louis I received another fax from Lukno.

February 28th
Dear Dr. Bernard,
I would like to sincerely apologize for the last few letters that I sent to you. It was unprofessional of me to assume such an aggressive approach and to be disrespectful to you both personally and professionally. I have no "reasonable" excuses or explanation for my temper tantrums and outbursts. Perhaps, I succumbed to my penchant for the theatrical.

Please forgive me for my blunders, and I hope that at some point we can resume exploring a structured settlement severance package agreement as you indicated we might in conversation.

At the moment, I am seeking psychological counseling and have scheduled a series of appointments to get the help I need.

My situation is not good, as my current partner and I are in the process of separating. My children and I are actively looking for someplace to hang our hats and that alone is a daunting task.

It is not my wish to hinder the process of negotiating a severance package agreement. Nor do I wish to stall it, but with everything that is going on right now, I am somewhat overwhelmed and exhausted. I cannot, at this time, sort things out so as to do the right thing for everyone concerned. I even question my own ability to make basic reasoned choices.

Thank you for your patience and tolerance. I will be in contact with you in the near future.

Sincerely yours,

Bathos Lukno, B.Ed. T.A.D.

P.S. Please, please extend my sincere apologies to Mr. Chuck Stihl.

I never heard from Bathos Lukno again. In the middle of March, St. Louis phoned and said Lukno was not returning his phone calls. All of his emails to Lukno bounced back as undeliverable. St. Louis said that Lukno had closed his email account and seemingly had vanished. From that moment, Bathos Lukno should have ceased to exist in my world.

The noblest question in the world, observed Benjamin Franklin in "Poor Richard's Almanack" is: "What good may I do in it?" I had hoped that by leading or prodding others or by contributing in the thick of things that somehow I could be working for good in the world. Instead, I would abandon all that I had invested in getting Lukno fired. It was a hard pill to swallow. But, both Sinclair and Chuck told me that my desire to fix things and leave them better than I had found them could easily be misunderstood as a course of action that took advantage of Lukno at his weakest moment. I might be seen as capitalizing on his weaknesses at an obvious time of incapacitation and diminished mental capacity. In early April, when I spoke with Chuck about severing the employment relationship — once and for all — he suggested that demonstrating compassion and leaving Lukno alone was a more appropriate strategy, given the current circumstances.

As unsettling as it was for me, I left Lukno the way I found him when I walked into that job. I simply left Lukno hanging around for the next Superintendent of Human Resources to stumble across; a problem for the new guy to deal with if he wanted and was permitted. I also realized at that point that I needed to terminate an employment contract–to terminate someone - and accepted wholeheartedly that the contract to terminate was mine. I resolved to step down from the reified perch of central office administration.

Bernard paused and looked directly at Lee when he spoke next.

Philosopher David Hume argues that the seeds of compassion are sown in our very nature as human beings. But compassion, a virtue that takes seriously other peoples' reality, their inner lives, their emotions, as well as their external circumstances, is greatly diminished by procrastination. Margaret E. Sangster, the 20th century American poet and author, vividly captured the brunt force of procrastination in her poem, "The Sin Of Omission." Two verses have always stood out for me:

"...It isn't the thing you do, dear;
It's the thing you leave undone;
That gives you a bit of heartache
At setting of the sun...

...For life is all too short, dear,
And sorrow is all too great;
To suffer our slow compassion
That tarries until too late..."

Because Bathos Lukno had on some level suffered from the procrastination of others, by letting Lukno be and leaving things undone, I wondered if what I was doing, not pursuing him and the termination, was an attempt to not "tarry until too late with a too slow compassion." The unsent letter sitting in its own unmarked folder in my desk drawer- the letter I had been willing to write and send and take the consequences of - not sending it felt like some kind of sin of omission alright, but also an act of compassion that gave me no choice but to deeply reconsider everything I believed in regarding improving schools.

Bernard scanned the room with his eyes, avoiding Lee as he said, "I was reminded then, at the beginning of April, what it meant to be and become human again. The Canadian philosopher Jean Vanier claims that people must open themselves up to those who are hurting or have been hurt to discover the deep compassion that comes from understanding another person. The process of becoming human is found through experiencing people whose lives are punctuated by loneliness, despair, a lack of belonging and the kind of inner pain that springs from rejection. By becoming part of their story—whether they are weak or hurt or marginalized—we enter into a relationship with that person and thereby discover him or her as a human being, and in turn, we discover ourselves as human beings.

I wouldn't suggest that any of the oddballs employed by Arcadia School District made me more fully human. To do so would be narcissistic and gratuitous. Yet, each painful interaction challenged me to find a sense of decency in personnel management and some of my beliefs about leadership. Each one forced me to push aside any preconceived notions that leadership was more science and less art. And in the end, my work could not be enacted without human emotion. Attempting to take an objective approach to personnel management, sorry it's called human resources management these days, that's devoid of human values may allow some to survive the pain of making difficult choices in the moment. But, that type of clinical approach would have deadened me from the sensations, the highs and lows, of what the work entails. For me, the pain I felt as I dealt with the "Staffing Hotspots" named Easton McCoy, Tony Daniel, Noelle Chabanel, and Bathos Lukno made it clear to me that I was human."

Wilson Lee looked directly at Bernard, and Lee nodded in what Bernard desperately hoped was gesture of understanding.

Abruptly, Lee asked, "Are you saying you never sent a termination letter to Bathos Lukno?"

"That's correct, Mr. Lee. I never had it mailed."

Lee averted his gaze from Bernard and refocused on Kimberley Marie. He wanted to ask: Who sent the letter to Lukno then? But, he knew better from Ms. Marie's return expression that he had already mistakenly asked an off-script question.

TWELVE

One of the articling students raised her hand and left it raised, desperately trying to make eye contact with Ms. Marie. When she did, Marie nodded, signaling that she had given permission and the young woman said, "Is it okay if I ask you a question, Dr. Bernard?"

Bernard felt obliged to look over at Marie who nodded to him as if she thought he also required her permission. Bernard replied that he was fine with questions.

"Your experiences, if you don't mind me saying, seem rather melancholy. They are utterly depressing, really. Wasn't there anything that brought you some happiness while you were at Arcadia? Or was it all just that miserable and sad?" she asked.

Bernard thought for a little while and smiled. "No, the work wasn't all bad. In fact, I didn't mind the work. I worked with some fantastic people like Desi, who was witty and made me smile. There were others who understood that while the work we did was terribly important, to survive the work we shouldn't take ourselves too seriously. I derived joy from doing my work and doing it well.

But, I have to admit that there was a fair amount of suffering. There was an uneasiness that I felt from working alongside people who were desperate to be leaders. People who were so busy looking ahead, so myopically focused on a single vision and self-absorbed in being a leader that they never bothered to ask if anyone was willingly following them or rather if they were just trudging behind out of fear.

The good news is that suffering isn't all bad. The chorus in "Agamemnon," the first play of the great tragic trilogy believed to be written around 458 B.C. by Aeschylus, recites: 'Zeus, whose will has marked for man the sole way where wisdom lies, ordered one eternal plan: Man must suffer to be wise.' Indeed, there is a lot to learn through suffering.

Bernard looked directly at the young woman who had asked the question and said, "In response to your original question, I tried to find some humour in the bizarre professional life I was living. Some days it was easier than others. However, quite early on, I knew that it wasn't going to work out—the working relationships with my central office colleagues—and something had to change.

I didn't want to become someone who abused the power of his office. I didn't want to be socialized to regard others as the objects of my manipulation who required retooling so that they could see the world the way I wanted them to see it. I didn't think it was my destiny to transform other people. And I didn't want to be yet another administrator who had read all of the leadership texts, especially the ones about ethical and moral leadership, but who lacked the very wisdom to realize that reading about a subject and living it were dramatically different undertakings.

What I realized from my time at Arcadia School District was what I didn't want to be and couldn't stomach being—a leader who disregarded the impact of my actions on the very real lives of people, in favour of the district's well-being, as if any of our schools existed without the people who gave them life.

Over time it became clearer to me that there was a seductive allure to the pretentiousness, pomposity and social hypocrisy of claiming to be a servant-leader, because in that simple invocation, your motives can't be challenged. In serving the best interests of children, no one can possibly suggest your motives are anything but honourable. I couldn't do it; couldn't find it in myself to say those words. I knew I couldn't be one of them and had to leave."

"So, was that it? Was that the end?" asked Peter Hart, who immediately seemed aware that he hadn't looked to Marie for permission to speak.

Recognizing the look of displeasure in Marie's eyes and not wanting to embarrass Hart, Bernard replied, "That was almost it, but not quite. A lot of times when you are dealing with people, they surprise you. That's one of the things that made working with people interesting and drew me to it in the first place. I tried to help people in their professional lives, and tried to do it with a sense of humanity. But no matter how well we think we know human beings and their actions they almost always find ways to defy conventional wisdom. No, Mr. Hart that wasn't it. And, even in my last few weeks there were still a few surprises."

Not a single person who attended the administrators' emergency meeting was looking forward to the unenviable task I had set for that late-May day. Arcadia was faced with having to make deep staffing cuts, the scale of which had never occurred before. There was no other choice but to cut teaching positions and reduce the size of the workforce. It was the final executive decision-making processes that I would be involved in before I relinquished my role as Superintendent of Human Resources and moved on with my life.

Throughout the day, it was difficult to sit, listen and watch as principal after principal tried to save their staff members' jobs. Each would take a turn explaining how any reduction in teaching staff hurt kids. Students, they would tell me, not only paid the price in their learning when we cut good teachers, but they also lost out in developing stable and lasting relationships with adults in the schools. They pleaded that while they understood the bleak financial reality the district was facing, they weren't the architects of the disaster. Those responsible for getting us into the mess, they argued, should be held to account.

In response to the pleas, all I could offer was the fact that there was not enough money in the system. Something had to give, and I had tried everything else to avoid this. What I didn't tell them was that the root of the problem was the total district staffing, not just the number of teachers, which had been allowed to bloat over years of inattention to become financially unsustainable. The bottom line: there were too many people on payroll, collecting paycheques that the district couldn't afford to issue any longer.

And, I didn't tell them that what really needed to happen was for the district to fire some of the overpaid, overfed and overstuffed superintendent-types who were still running around spending too much money, money the district didn't have. I didn't tell them this, as much as I wanted.

But, I did tell Chuck. Chuck had heard me say this once, and it was clear that he had no patience to listen to it again. He showed me - after I told him we had too many people on the payroll, especially in central office - the shiny plaques at the board office given by the Ministry of Education to recognize the excellent work done in the district. He said these commendations were a testimony to the value that central office personnel made in directly supporting student learning. No, Chuck insisted, every dollar spent on district office staff was an investment in meeting students' educational outcomes.

I couldn't admit to the principals in a public forum that I agreed with them. They were correct that most of the blame for overspending was a result of poor decision-making and weak financial oversight by Chuck. And, as Chuck was conspicuously absent from the meeting, I listened, remained sympathetic to their needs to vent and accepted some of the central office blame, even if I deserved none of it.

However, I steadfastly maintained that the staffing cuts had to be made, and I needed their professional advice on how best to proceed. When the day was done and the dust had settled I assured them they needn't worry because it would be my name and not their names that would appear at the bottom of each termination letter.

We started with teachers on term-limited and interim contracts. This part was relatively easy, as their existing contracts were about to expire. But still, it was difficult to do as each teacher had a story, and each principal needed to tell it.

There was Marion the newly graduated term teacher at Cambrai who had recently left an abusive relationship. She was a single mother of three and had been so happy to have landed a term job working with special needs students. Her principal told us that Marion and her students were accomplishing great things.

And, what about Ian? The male Middle-Years Language Arts teacher who had, miraculously, managed to get boys to read novels and not just magazines. Certainly he had to be offered another contract somewhere in the district, his principal argued. We couldn't afford to lose him. Twelve and 13-year-old boys were going to the library and taking out books, classics! "Do you know how impressive that is?" I was asked.

There were at least as many stories that had to be listened to and honoured, as there were positions that had to be cut. But, by the end of the morning, we had cut and reduced staffing by 17 teachers and the district's payroll by about $900,000.

Next we had to decide which of the teachers on probationary contracts—teachers who had been hired initially believing that if they did a good enough job they might get continuous contracts—we could keep. There were a few who would be offered continuous contracts out of necessity because core educational programs would collapse without them. But, what we didn't discuss was the obvious fact that these new teachers—the few fortunate ones who were offered continuing contracts—might still lose their jobs in a year or two if the district was not be able to afford them because the recurring budget deficit was still unresolved.

After lunch we continued the back and forth discussion, which at times was punctuated by loud debate and pleas for mercy, but we cut another 9 positions. It was all we could do. They had done their part to address the deficit. It was clear to me that any further staffing losses would lead to a sense of desolation among the principals. I looked over at the Director of Finance and signaled that we were done cutting positions. She looked relieved to see that sign.

We weren't completely done for the day though. We had to deal with transferring some of the existing staff between schools to fill up vacancies that were created as a result of the cuts. Before we began, I said that nobody was allowed to place a lemon-of-a-teacher on the table and then try to convince, or hoodwink, an unsuspecting colleague into taking Monsieur or Madame Citron. A couple tried to do it early on in the process. Someone said something like, "He really is pretty good." Another tried, "I just think he needs a new start or a change of scenery or someone else needs to mentor him." However, quite quickly the ones who tried that slight of hand knew that their colleagues just wouldn't tolerate it. They stopped trying to trade-in their clunker of a teacher for a newer model.

By the end of the day, an exhausting day, we had made the necessary adjustments so that schools were staffed to minimum specifications and the district had realized a reduction in the upcoming year's operating budget by about $1.3 million. And this was accomplished by telling a bunch of teachers—a group of human beings who desperately wanted to teach and believed they had a calling to teach—that they and their services were no longer needed.

Surprisingly, by the end of the day, Tony Daniel was transferred to a school where the principal felt Daniel might possibly be successful. Somehow Daniel, the forgotten man, the last of Frank's "Staffing Hotspots," who had been left to simmer for the past year and a half, was not lost in the shuffle. He had benefitted from that day, and that was enough for me to conclude that the day had been a story of one human's success.

That joy was short-lived because at the end-of-the-year principals' barbecue, Daniel's receiving principal confided to me—after her third margarita—that she didn't think that he would ever be happy teaching, anywhere. She said he was a wimp and a whiner who she had dated once upon a time. He really wasn't any good at anything, she said.

I didn't dare ask what "anything" might mean. I just hoped it was the tequila talking and made sure someone called her a cab at the end of the night.

About three weeks after the budget cutting session, having never asked how the day went, Chuck stopped by my office to say he had heard good things about the process. He was glad to hear that the principals, finally, had been held to account and forced to reduce the staffing in their overstuffed schools. Deadpan, he asked if, now that we had made such deep cuts, there was $100,000 in next year's budget so he could hire someone for a central office project of vital importance.

"What's the position, Chuck?"

"It's for a Director of Budget Compliance," he replied and added, "I haven't scoped out the position exactly, but you know I wouldn't ask you if I didn't really think the district needed to fill this void. I need to stop those principals from spending so much money!"

Trying not to vomit on his expensively tailored suit and fine Italian shoes, I told Chuck he would have to wait to ask the next Superintendent of Human Resources, as it wasn't really my responsibility to oversee next year's budget, which I reminded him was still showing a projected $100,000 deficit.

He ignored my comment and smiled as he walked out the door dusting off some lint that had migrated onto his suit while he stood in my office. I laughed to myself because by that time, I had resigned, literally, to having done all that I could or would do to help Chuck out anymore.

It's odd that after an intense stint as the guy who was in charge of people at Arcadia, I was the one who needed to leave, to be fired, in essence, and move on in his life. Working at Arcadia had given me insight into the kind of personality, the kind of character that seemed to be valued in successful school leaders. According to the public accounts of the elected trustees, Chuck, Richard and Vixie were the epitome of the selfless leaders that kids deserved to have shepherding the system. And I was a useful contributor to the organization, but someone who was destined to work somewhere else.

Destiny; go figure.

Shortly after I left, I heard from Desi that while the Director of Finances struggled to address an increasingly large projected annual budget shortfall, Chuck, Richard and Vixie received generous pay raises for jobs well done. Arcadia, in a short span of six years—the exact length of Chuck 's tenure as Chief Superintendent—had gone from a modest operating surplus of $850,000 to drowning in an accumulated multi-million dollar debt.

Inexplicably, the trustees decided that the district should inflate the leaders' six-figure salaries. It reminded me of the bank executives who got hefty bonuses after the financial meltdown of 2009. Arcadia's trustees, like the boards of directors at bankrupt financial institutions, seemed worried that they might lose their brilliant leaders to some other district that could offer fancier offices and fatter paycheques.

Marie pulled some pages from the file folder on the table in front of her, and glanced at them as she asked, "Don't you think it was highly unethical of you to speak negatively, caustically about Mr. Stihl behind his back without any opportunity for him to defend himself?"

Bernard was caught off guard, again.

Marie thumbed through the few pages in her hand, and said, "Come on, Dr. Bernard; don't you think these allegations you've made in this 'Exit Interview' could easily be construed as malicious and vexatious?"

Bernard chose not to reply. The only copy of the 'Exit Interview' was sent to the Chair of Arcadia's School Board. "How did Kimberley Marie get a copy," he wondered?

"You must have known it would cause Mr. Stihl some problems and might even erode the confidence that the Trustees had in him. After all, Dr. Bernard, you have presented yourself here as a rather calculated risk taker. You obviously knew what you were doing, didn't you?"

Bernard was about to reply, but Marie interrupted him before he was able to utter a word in his defense.

"Anyway, I'm not sure if what happened after you left Arcadia matters much in this deposition, but you seem rather bitter or maybe envious of Mr. Stihl's position, or at least his good fortune."

Before Bernard could respond, she added, "Let me make sure I have this clear. Number one, you do not have a recognized certificate or diploma in human resources management? "

Bernard, who seemed a little puzzled by the various accusations followed by what had become rhetorical questions, replied, "I wasn't envious of Mr. Stihl, if that's what you alleging. And, yes, that's correct. I don't have a human resources certificate."

Ms. Marie continued, "Number two, you do not have a recognized accounting designation, like a CGA or CA or CMA. While you might know a thing or two about budgets, you are certainly not an authority on finances, correct?"

"That's correct," replied Bernard still unsure of the direction things had taken.

"Thirdly, you have never been a chief superintendent of schools and never been fully or solely responsible for a school district's operations, right?" Marie asked.

"True," responded Bernard.

After taking a deep breath and leaning back slightly in her chair, Marie said, "Don't you think it might be a little more reasonable, actually

200

more fastidious, to hold your personal opinions in check until you've earned some expertise or authority on which to draw your wisdom from before you start offering opinions and giving lectures?"

Rather defensively, Bernard replied, "I never claimed to be an expert at anything. I never said I had some special wisdom to share. You asked me to come here to answer some questions and ..."

Before he could finish his sentence Marie, dressed in a stiff, brilliantly white blouse under her tailored black suit jacket, cut him off. "Thank you Dr. Bernard. I think we've covered enough material. I think we know what you think about a great deal of things. This is a great place to end the deposition."

"But," Bernard tried to add, "all I was going to say was ..."

"That's fine, Dr. Bernard. We have enough." Marie turned away from Bernard and nodded to the stenographer to stop recording. She turned back to Bernard and in a patronizing tone said, "You did a great job. Thanks for showing up."

At thirty-five minutes after five, Bernard looked up at the wall clock and stopped talking. No one said a word to him, and everyone, including the stenographer, knew that the interrogation was over.

Ms. Marie turned to the students and associates and reminded them of the rest of the week's busy schedule. It was an awkward moment for Bernard who was the only person in the room left out of the conversation.

Realizing that Bernard was just sitting there, Lee stood up without permission and quietly thanked the stenographer. He turned to Bernard and asked, "How about I walk you out to the reception area, Dr. Bernard?"

"It's not necessary, really, but I suppose that would be nice," Bernard replied as he finished gathering up his papers and carefully placed them into his briefcase looking over to see if Ms. Marie might say goodbye. She neither looked at him nor said goodbye.

Lee and Bernard arrived in front of the stainless steel elevator doors near the reception area and stood side-by-side in silence. As Bernard pushed the down button, Lee was compelled to ask a question he had wanted to ask for the past two days. Outside of the formality of the deposition, Lee felt more comfortable broaching the subject.

"Dr. Bernard, do you know whose termination is being arbitrated in this case?" he said. "I mean do you know who was fired and is suing the school district?"

Bernard looked over to Lee and replied, "No," as the elevator bell rang and the doors opened.

Before Bernard stepped into the elevator, Lee asked, "Aren't you curious, at least a little, who brought this wrongful dismissal claim against the district, and why are here?"

Bernard breathed out a deeply relaxing breath, one that allowed the prominent vein in his forehead—the one that had been bulging during the inquisition—to recede and his shoulders to relax.

"Mr. Lee I don't have a clue who brought the lawsuit forward, and I couldn't care less who was fired." As Bernard stepped through the open doors he said, "In the grand scheme of things, I'm not sure it matters. There were many people who lost jobs, and others who should have lost them but didn't. What matters to me is whether those who lost jobs were treated properly, with dignity and humanity. I just want to know that I did the right thing by people."

Just as the doors began to close, cutting the two men off, Bernard asked Lee, "Isn't that really what should matter? I realize that acknowledging responsibility for one's choices is a risky way to make a living, but I have a feeling that isn't what I was brought here to determine, was it? I was brought here so someone can be blamed and held responsible. When that happens, when you find someone to blame, you get to shift the responsibility for the outcome off of someone else."

The elevator doors closed in front of Bernard, and Lee stood in the reception area for a moment by himself wondering if Bernard was correct. Maybe it didn't matter who was fired. Perhaps what mattered was that there was a person, one individual, who accepted responsibility for doing the right thing even if it made someone's life difficult. And, at the end of the day, he didn't try to shirk that responsibility.

Lee, the Junior Associate, noticed that Marie was standing in the reception area not far from him admiring the ficus. "Too much discretion and sentimentality, Mr. Lee," she said

"Pardon me?" Lee replied.

"Too much subjective judgment and personal discretion," said Marie. "People stray from the organization's goals and then their ideals get in the way of doing the work. They stop acting rationally and in the company's best interests and think their values should matter. That is where the problem begins, Wilson. Don't worry though; you'll get used to putting your own feelings away, and it'll eventually become easier to succeed here at Harper and Fowler, or any corporate structure. You just can't let your emotions get in the way of doing your job. You have to watch out for that naïve idealism," she waved her hand in the direction of the deposition room, as if what Keith Bernard stood for was still lingering, like a scent in the air, and might be inhaled by this young and impressionable lawyer. "It gets you nowhere, Mr. Lee."

She pointed at him and smiled, but it was done as a gesture of ownership, and Lee felt it so much that he became a little nauseous. He suddenly realized that maybe he had his own Chuck Stihl to deal with in this mentor figure of Ms. Marie. "You can learn from me," she commanded.

Ms. Marie began to walk down the hallway toward her office and as she did she said over her shoulder, "The facts of this case will speak for themselves and the truth will be told. You did a great job, Mr. Lee. I'll make sure the Partners know that you were responsible for this successful deposition." Then she disappeared into her office.

By then Lee had had time to take a long deep inhale, the kind that travels up and down your spine, during which he noted the smell of the moist soil of the office's potted plants. He suddenly knew that Ms. Marie would benefit from the "successful deposition" even as she offered graciously to give him credit. As that thought and feeling evaporated from his consciousness, he just hoped that he might be the kind of guy who would suffer in his day-to-day work, as a Partner someday, because he would be alive, not dead.

Lee glanced at his cell phone and decided to give himself a fifteen-minute break before he needed to head out to grab some dinner. He sat down in one of the soft, oversized leather chairs in the reception area, looked at his distorted reflection in the elevator doors and waited for his partner, Mr. Hart.